Hearts & Flours
COOKBOOK

A Sampler of Recipes from the Heart of Texas

Published by JLW Publications
The Junior League of Waco, Texas
6801 Sanger, Suite 160B, Waco, Texas 76710

The Junior League of Waco is an organization of women committed to promoting voluntarism and improving the community through the effective action and leadership of trained volunteers. Its purpose is exclusively educational and charitable.

ISBN   0-9620531-0-4
The Junior League of Waco, Texas, Inc.
Library of Congress Card Catalog 88-080735

Copies of HEARTS AND FLOURS may be obtained from
The Junior League of Waco, Texas, Inc.
6801 Sanger, Suite 160B
Waco, Texas 76710
(817) 776-2665

Artwork—DeWall Burks Pollei Advertising
Needlepoint Design—Susan Bates
Holly Hill Designs Stitching—Johanna Nystrom

First Printing, October 1988, 10,000 copies

WIMMER BROTHERS
Memphis   Dallas

HEARTS AND FLOURS
COOKBOOK

*"Preserving American regional traditions
and improving the quality of life."*

Dear Friends,

Thank you for purchasing our cookbook.
Your generosity allows The Junior League of
Waco the opportunity to improve the quality
of life in our little slice of America. The
monetary gifts which you have made possible
through your purchase will ultimately benefit
us all.

It is our feeling that the recipes in *HEARTS
AND FLOURS* will give you an idea of Waco's
unique traditions and provide a glimpse into
the lifestyles of our Central Texas community.

We offer to you a sampling of our hearts, our
dreams, our individual lifestyles, our Texas
pride, our traditions, and our tastes. Most
importantly we offer you our thanks by giving
you this sampler from the HEART OF TEXAS.

Enjoy!
The Cookbook Committee

❤ COORDINATORS ❤

Development Committee
Sharron Cutbirth, Chairman
Kim Doss
Mary Martha Dossett
Fran Farmer
Mary Helen George
Beth Mayfield
Kathy Myatt
Debbe Trippet
Caroline Wylie

Testing Committee
Caroline Wylie, Chairman
Kim Doss
Fran Farmer
Dorothy Jones
Kathy Myatt
Debbe Trippet

Testers

Jeanne Becker
Trisha Brindley
Barbara Clifton
Jan Copeland
Jan Crawford
Susan Duncan
Mary Helen George

Edi Gibney
Sharon Fielder
Lynette Holder
Carol Horner
Jean McKinney
Ruth Miller
Ellie Morrison

Kris Olson
Karen Pyland
Carmen Rolf
Sarah Sheppard
Suzanne Starr
Katy Walters
Mary Wentworth

Sustainers

A. J. Cole, Chairman
Pinkie Bostwick
Rosalie Davis
Jean Darden
Mary Katherine Dietz
Mary Ruth Duncan

Drane Haw
Linda Hicks
Liz McGlasson
Beverly Mayfield
Mary Stringer
Jane Winchell

Production Committee
Kathy Myatt, Chairman
Mary Byrd
Betty Gandy
Susan Mathis
Diane Schlecte
Caroline Wylie

Marketing Committee
Diane Schlecte, Chairman
Susan Cleveland
Jan Crawford
Carol Horner
Missy Lowder
Elaine Restivo

Steering Committee

Jan Crawford
Sharron Cutbirth
Sharon Fielder
Lucy Latham
Beverly Mayfield

Kathy Myatt
Sharon Robertson
Diane Schlecte
Caroline Wylie

❤ CONTRIBUTORS ❤

Bobbie Affleck
Joan Alexander
Marsha Alvarado
Carolyn Anderson
Rebecca Bailey
Sallye Bales
LaWanda Ball
LaVonia Barnes
Anne Barrett
Kay Barrett
Jill Barrow
Alyce Beard
Beth Beard
Janna Beatty
Danna Beaty
Jeanne Becker
Melissa Bennett
Nancylu Bennett
Kay Bond
Linda Bostwick
Pinkie Bostwick
Betsy Bracken
Sally Brashier
Christi Breeding
Trisha Brindley
Cindy Britt
Carolyn Brooks
Carolyn Brophy
Crissy Browder
LuAnn Browder
Golda Brown
Margaret Brown
Nan Brown
Julie Buchanan
Carolyn Burleson
Debra Burleson
Mary Byrd
Nancy Callan
Sandra Callan
Paula Campbell
Catherine Cantwell
Jean Cartwright
Adrienne Cash
Ellender Chase
Mary Lacy Chase
Carol Clark

Susan Cleveland
Barbara Clifton
Laura Clifton
Pat Clifton
Trudy Cohen
A. J. Cole
Julia Colgin
Karen Conine
Jewel Copeland
Kay Corwin
Jane Cox
Jan Crawford
Keren Crawford
Jole Cromwell
Agnes Crow
Pam Crow
Edana Croyle
Sharron Cutbirth
Janice Davis
Rosalie Davis
Tommye Lou Davis
Jeannie Dickson
Susan Diebolt
Mary Dietz
Kim Doss
Mary Martha Dossett
Gail Dow
Sylvia DuBois
Jane Dudgeon
Ann Duncan
Mary Ruth Duncan
Susan Duncan
Jean Epperson
Rosalis Estes
Lillian Fadal
Laura Fair
Fran Farmer
Lisa Feather
Nan Felton
Betty Ferguson
Susan Ferguson
Sharon Fielder
Judy Filer
Debbie Fillip
Sally Firmin
Carol Fischer

Vivian Fisher
Ricki Florsheim
Sharon Fontaine
Sharon Fowler
Rosanne Fuller
Geneva Gamble
Betty Gandy
Mary Helen George
Joan Gervig
Debbie Getterman
Sue Getterman
Edith Gibney
Susan Gibson
Wanda Giotes
Linda Goble
Karen Goss
Judy Graves
Julia Graves
Cindy Gregg
Betty Haas
Judy Haller
Debbie Haltom
Sara Harrison
Alice Harwell
Linda Hatchell
Drane Haw
JoAnn Hawkins
Kay Hawkins
Tracie Hermann
Davina Hicks
Janelle Hicks
Leslie Hicks
Linda Hicks
Mary Frances Hicks
Kathy Hillman
Mary Hooker
Ann Marie Howard
Martha Howe
Peggy Hudson
Pam Hughes
Vicky Hunt
Hyden Hunter
Judy Hurst
Loeen Irons
Janice Jackson
Camille Johnson

5

Contributors (continued)

Deanie Johnson
Paige Johnston
Claudia Jones
Dana Jones
Dorothy Jones
Diane Jordan
Carolyn Kallus
Collette Karr
Marylin Kelly
Suzanne Kelly
Dorothy Kendrick
Lyn Kent
Laura Lee Kilgore
Betty Ruth Killion
Trudy Kizer
Luanne Klaras
Lynn Klatt
Debbie Kondrach
Marjorie Lacy
Carol Lane
Lucy Latham
Nancy Latham
Sara Lee
Virginia Lewis
Missy Lowder
Debbie Luce
Bonnie Luft
Cindy Mabry
Nancy Maness
Tricia Mankin
Marilu Mann
Jean Manske
Barbara Martin
Brenda Marwitz
Norma Jo Marwitz
Carolyn Matteson
Beth Mayfield
Beverly Mayfield
Debbie McCall
Jill McCall
Melody McDermitt
Carol McIntosh
Margaret Megarity
Kay Merritt
Anne Meyer
Deborah Meyer
Sue Milam
Jana Millar

Nell Miller
Pat Miller
Ruth Miller
Suzanne Miller
Pati Milligan
Raye Lynn Morris
Ellie Morrison
Nan Mosley
Betty Myatt
Kathy Myatt
Jane Nash
Pat Nielson
Trish Nunley
Betsy Oates
Alice Ogden
Kris Olson
Kathy Orr
Robin Owens
Ada Patton
Mary Payne
Sharon Perry
Janie Peterson
Diane Pittman
Cathy Plietz
Dinka Poehl
Cheryl Potts
Helen Price
Gail Pryor
Karen Pyland
Debbie Quebe
Millie Read
Edith Reitmeier
Nelwyn Regan
Elaine Restivo
Elaine Reynolds
Clara May Richards
Susan Richards
Sara Richie
Linda Rinehart
Sharon Robertson
Melanie Rogers
Carmen Rolf
Darla Rominger
Frances Rountree
Jeanne Rutherford
Krista Salome
Elizabeth Sanger
Jeanne Sartain

Jane Saxton
Diane Schlecte
Jane Scruggs
Carol Sedberry
DeeDee Shrum
Ann Sims
Cindy Smith
Ida Lou Smith
Debbie Speckmiear
Cynthia Squires
Rebecca Stèm
Janice Stewart
Ginger Strickland
Mary Stringer
Frances Sturgis
Fay Swann
Cynthia Swift
Edye Tarbox
Brooke Taylor
Lucy Taylor
Donell Teaff
Bea Terry
Linda Totten
Debbe Trippet
Linda Tubbs
Dorothy Veiluva
Jean Wagnon
Margaret Walding
Katy Walters
Billye Warner
Teemus Warner
Kay Watson
Nancy Welch
Lucy Westbrook
Nannette Wheelis
Ellen White
Elizabeth Wicklund
Peggy Wieser
Barby Williams
Marguerite Williams
Shirley Williams
Jane Winchell
Karen Wolfe
Caroline Wylie

❤ *TABLE OF CONTENTS* ❤

Appetizers and Beverages

Thank you for your financial support
of the following Junior League of Waco project:

The Heart of Texas Family Outreach

A community based volunteer counseling program working
toward the prevention of child abuse and neglect through
aid to families experiencing child-related problems.

CHEESE PUFF SURPRISES

A delightful surprise when you bite into the pastry. These are perfect for a make ahead and freeze appetizer.

2 cups sharp Cheddar
  cheese, shredded
1 stick margarine, softened
1 cup flour

½ teaspoon salt
1 teaspoon paprika
48 green olives, well-drained

Preheat oven to 400°. In a medium mixing bowl, blend cheese with margarine. Stir in flour, salt, and paprika; mix well. Wrap a teaspoon of mixture around each olive. Bake on cookie sheet for 15 minutes.

*Note: These can also be made by using chunks of ham or spam instead of olives.

Yield: 48 pastries

FESTIVE APPETIZER PIZZA

1 sheet puff pastry
12 ounces cream cheese,
  softened
½ cup mayonnaise
2 ounces bleu cheese,
  crumbled

Cherry tomatoes, sliced
Fresh parsley, chopped
Fresh mushrooms, sliced
Yolk of 1 hard boiled egg,
  grated
Ripe olives, chopped

Preheat oven to 400°. Thaw pastry sheet 20 minutes. Roll out on lightly floured surface. Using a dinner plate, cut a large circle. Place on a cookie sheet. Crimp edges with your fingers and prick all over with tines of a fork. Bake for 10 to 12 minutes or until lightly brown. Cool. In a mixing bowl thoroughly blend cream cheese, mayonnaise, and bleu cheese. Spread over cooled pastry sheet. In circular form starting with the outside edge, and working towards the center, garnish with cherry tomatoes, parsley, mushrooms, and grated egg yolk. Finish with the ripe olives. Chill 2 hours and slice into wedges to serve.

Yield: approximately 15 servings

SAUSAGE PINWHEELS

Children love these for breakfast and they are so easy to prepare.

2 cups flour	5 tablespoons shortening
½ teaspoon salt	⅔ cup milk
3 teaspoons baking powder	1 pound bulk sausage

In mixing bowl, blend first four ingredients. Add milk and stir until well blended. Divide dough into two parts. Roll dough on a floured surface into a rectangle. Crumble sausage and spread ½ on rectangle. Roll up like a jelly roll, starting with long end. Repeat with second half of dough. Freeze.

To serve, remove from the freezer and allow to set for a few minutes. Slice very thin and bake on a cookie sheet at 400° for 15 to 20 minutes.

Yield: approximately 3-4 dozen

GODFATHER'S SAUSAGE CHEESE LOAF

These are a great pick-up food for a brunch or a coffee.

2 1-pound frozen bread loaves	½ cup mozzarella cheese, shredded
1 pound bulk sausage, crumbled	1 4½-ounce can sliced mushrooms
½ cup Cheddar cheese, shredded	1 2¼-ounce can sliced ripe olives
½ cup Monterey Jack cheese, shredded	1 bunch green onions, chopped

Defrost bread according to package directions. Preheat oven to 350°. Brown sausage in skillet and drain well. Add remaining ingredients to sausage. Simmer 15 to 20 minutes.

Roll out each loaf of bread in long narrow strips. Cut the dough in half, if desired. Spread sausage mixture down the center of each strip of dough. Roll up in jelly roll fashion. Seal tightly by pinching dough together. Place seam side down on cookie sheet. Bake for 30 minutes or until golden brown.

*Note: To freeze, reduce cooking time 5-10 minutes. Wrap in foil.

Yield: 2-4 loaves

BACON WRAPPED CHICKEN BITES

3 medium chicken breasts
¼ cup soy sauce
2 tablespoons dry sherry
1 tablespoon sugar
1 tablespoon white vinegar
¼ teaspoon ginger
1 cup salad oil

½ cup lemon juice
½ cup Worcestershire sauce
¼ cup prepared mustard
1 tablespoon cracked pepper
2 cloves garlic
6 pieces of bacon, cut into
   2-inch strips

Cut chicken breasts into bite size pieces. Combine remaining ingredients except bacon. Wrap chicken with bacon strips and marinate
in sauce for 1 hour. Remove from marinade and bake in oven at 375°
for 10 to 15 minutes or until bacon is done.

Yield: 24-30 bite size pieces

CHINESE EGG ROLLS

*Serve these egg rolls with Chinese mustard or Sweet and Sour Sauce.
They can be cooked ahead and reheated in the oven. Stretch them to
serve a larger group by increasing the amount of cabbage and bean
sprouts.*

¾ cup ground pork
½ cup celery, minced
2 tablespoons oil
½ cup bamboo shoots,
   minced
3 tablespoons soy sauce

2 tablespoons green onions,
   minced
1 16-ounce can bean sprouts
2 cups cabbage, shredded
Wonton wrappers
Oil

Lightly brown pork in skillet. Add next seven ingredients. Stir fry until
cabbage is limp. Drain very well. Place about ¼ cup mixture on
wonton wrapper with one corner facing you. Pull corner towards
center and roll, pulling side corners into center while rolling. Top
corner will be on outside and can be held down by dampening with a
small amount of water. Deep fry in oil until golden brown. Be sure to
use enough oil to completely cover.

Yield: approximately 2 dozen egg rolls

SWEET AND SOUR SAUCE

½ cup brown sugar
¼ cup catsup
½ cup pineapple juice,
  reserved from pineapple
  chunks
⅓ cup white vinegar

½ teaspoon garlic powder
2 tablespoons cornstarch
⅓ cup cold water
1 14-ounce can pineapple
  chunks, drained

In medium saucepan, bring first five ingredients to a boil. Mix cornstarch and water together; add to liquid. Cook slowly until mixture thickens. Remove from heat. Add pineapple chunks. Cool to room temperature.

Yield: 2½ cups

BLACK-EYED PEAWHEELS

Serve these on New Year's Day for good luck.

1 15-ounce can black-eyed
  peas, drained
½ stick butter or margarine,
  melted
Dash of garlic powder
Cayenne pepper to taste
¼ teaspoon seasoned salt

2 3-ounce packages cream
  cheese, softened
2 4-ounce packages sliced
  imported ham; rectangular
  slices
8 green onions

In heavy sauce pan heat peas in butter and seasonings. Simmer 15 minutes. Cool. Process black-eyed peas and cream cheese together in a food processor until creamy and well blended. Spread mixture in a thin even layer to edges of each slice of ham. Place green onion lengthwise at edge of each ham slice. Roll slice tightly around onion and secure with plastic wrap. Chill. Cut into ½ inch slices. Serve appetizers with toothpicks.

Yield: approximately six dozen

MUSHROOMS ELEGANTE

This is superb poured over boneless chicken breasts as an entree. Bake at 300° for 1½ hours.

1½ pounds fresh
   mushrooms, sliced
4 tablespoons butter
½ teaspoon pepper
½ teaspoon salt

½ teaspoon oregano
⅛ teaspoon nutmeg
Juice of ¼ lemon
½ cup dry white wine
1 pint sour cream

In a large skillet saute mushrooms in butter. Add remaining ingredients except sour cream. Heat to boiling. Boil for 10 minutes, to absorb liquid. Add sour cream and heat thoroughly. Serve in chafing dish with toast points.

Yield: 8 to 10 servings

CRISPY CHEESE WAFERS

Serve these wafers with Hearty Cheese Soup.

2 cups sharp Cheddar
   cheese, shredded
2 sticks butter, softened
2 cups flour

¼ teaspoon salt
½ teaspoon Tabasco sauce or
   red pepper
2 cups Rice Krispies

Preheat oven to 350°. In medium mixing bowl, cream together cheese and butter; add flour, salt, and Tabasco sauce. Mix in Rice Krispies. Roll into small balls and press flat onto cookie sheet. Bake for 15 to 20 minutes.

Yield: 6 dozen

OYSTER CRACKERS

These are so good, they are habit forming.

2 tablespoons dillweed
1 teaspoon lemon pepper
1 package buttermilk salad
   dressing mix

¼ teaspoon garlic powder
1½ cups cooking oil
2 12 ounce packages oyster
   crackers

Preheat oven to 200°. Mix first five ingredients together in small mixing bowl. Spread crackers out on a cookie sheet and pour mixture over crackers. Bake for 30 minutes, stirring every 10 minutes.

Yield: approximately 3-4 cups

OYSTERS ROCKEFELLER

3 tablespoons butter
½ 10-ounce package frozen
  chopped spinach, slightly
  thawed
1 tablespoon instant minced
  onion
1 tablespoon parsley,
  chopped
1 bay leaf, finely crumbled
½ teaspoon salt

¼ teaspoon cayenne pepper
¼ cup dried breadcrumbs or
  ¼ cup Pepperidge Farm
  dressing mix
18 large or 24 small oysters
  on the half shell
2 bacon slices, diced
Grated Parmesan cheese
Lemon wedges for garnish

Preheat oven to 425°. Melt butter in 1 quart saucepan over medium heat. Add next six ingredients. Cook until spinach is heated thoroughly, stirring occasionally. Toss in bread crumbs. Set aside. Place oysters in a baking pan. Spoon 2 tablespoons of spinach mixture on the top of each oyster. Sprinkle with bacon and cheese. Bake at 425° for 10 minutes or until bacon is crisp. Garnish with lemon wedges.

Yield: 18 servings

SHRIMP CERVICHE

It is best to choose a firm fish when preparing this recipe.

1 pound fish
Juice of 2 lemons and 2
  limes
1 onion, thinly sliced
1 tomato, peeled and diced
2-4 chili peppers or
  jalapenos, chopped

4 tablespoons oil
1 tablespoon vinegar
½ teaspoon oregano
Salt and pepper to taste
½ pound shrimp, shelled
  and cooked about 2
  minutes

Skin fish and cut into small squares. Place fish in a glass bowl with enough lemon and lime juice to cover. Allow to stand 3 hours, turning occasionally. Add remaining ingredients and chill well. Serve with crackers.

Yield: 8 servings

AVOCADO DIP EXCELLANTE

1 medium tomato, chopped
1 medium jalapeno pepper, chopped
1 teaspoon fresh lemon juice

1½ teaspoons picante sauce
2 teaspoons onions, chopped
Salt to taste
1 avocado, chopped

Mix all the ingredients except the avocado together in mixing bowl. Toss in avocado after ingredients are well blended.

Yield: approximately 1 cup

HOT AND SPICY BEAN DIP

This is also good as a base for layered dip: Bean dip on bottom, sour cream, guacamole, and shredded cheese.

1 15-ounce can ranch style beans, drained and mashed
1 stick butter
½ pound Cheddar cheese, shredded

2 jalapeno peppers, finely chopped
½ onion, minced
1 clove garlic, crushed
Jalapeno juice to taste

Combine beans, butter, and cheese in the top of a double boiler and heat slowly until the cheese is melted. Add remaining ingredients and mix well.

Yield: 2 cups

GREEN CHILI AND BACON DIP

2 8-ounce packages cream cheese, softened
½ cup mayonnaise
1 tablespoon lemon juice
1 small clove garlic, crushed
½ large onion, minced

½ large bell pepper, minced
8 strips of bacon, fried crisp and crumbled
1 4-ounce can chopped green chilies

Mix first three ingredients together in a food processor until smooth. Put mixture in a mixing bowl and add remaining ingredients. Chill 3 to 4 hours before serving. Serve with melba toast or corn chips.

Yield: approximately 3 cups

MILD AT HEART QUESO

Unless you like a real spicy dip, do not add the entire can of green chilies.

1 stick butter
1 white onion, chopped
2 tomatoes, peeled and
  chopped
1 7-ounce can chopped
  green chilies

1 8-ounce package cream
  cheese
¾ cup whipping cream or
  Half and Half

Melt butter and saute vegetables in skillet until onions are translucent. Turn heat off. Add cream cheese and stir until melted. Turn heat on low and add whipping cream. Serve in chafing dish with tortilla chips.

Yield: 8 servings

SOMBRERO DIP

2 tablespoons margarine
1 medium onion, chopped
1 green bell pepper, chopped
Jalapeno peppers to taste,
  chopped
1 tablespoon chili powder
1 tablespoon cumin
1 tablespoon oregano
1 teaspoon black pepper

1 teaspoon minced garlic
½ teaspoon salt
2 pounds ground beef
1 12-ounce bottle hot catsup
1 16-ounce can kidney
  beans, undrained
1 cup Cheddar cheese,
  shredded

In a large skillet saute the first ten ingredients. Add beef and simmer until brown, about 10 minutes. Drain and return to skillet. Stir in catsup and beans; simmer for about 5 minutes. Pour into chafing dish and top with cheese. Serve with tortilla chips.

Yield: 12 servings

PICO DE GALLO

For best results, do not add tomatoes more than 2-3 hours before you are going to serve. This sauce is delicious with chips and a must for fajitas.

4 large tomatoes, very ripe;
   skinned, seeded, and
   chopped
1 large onion, chopped
3 fresh jalapeno peppers,
   seeded and finely chopped
2 cloves garlic, minced

¼ cup freshly squeezed lime
   juice
½ cup fresh cilantro, finely
   chopped
1 teaspoon oregano
Salt and pepper to taste

Combine all ingredients in a medium mixing bowl and cover. Chill until ready to serve.

Yield: approximately 2 to 3 cups

BLACK-EYED PEA DIP

A Texas tradition on New Year's. If you prefer you may use sharp Cheddar cheese instead of Old English.

4 cups black-eyed peas,
   drained
Jalapeno peppers to taste,
   chopped
1 medium onion, chopped
1-2 cloves garlic, minced

1 4-ounce can chopped
   green chilies
½ pound Old English
   process cheese, shredded
2 sticks butter

Mix peas with next four ingredients in blender. Process till smooth. Heat cheese and butter in double boiler until cheese melts. Add black-eyed pea mixture and heat thoroughly. Serve with tortilla chips.

Yield: approximately 6 cups

CRUNCHY CHEESE DIP

2 5⅓-ounce cans evaporated
milk
1 pound Velveeta cheese,
cubed
1 medium onion, finely
chopped

1 cup pecans, finely chopped
1 cup green olives, sliced
1 cup mayonnaise

Heat milk in saucepan over low heat; add cheese. Cook and stir until smooth. Cool to room temperature. Stir in remaining ingredients. To serve heat and pour in chafing dish. Use corn chips for dipping.

Yield: 4 cups

RED, WHITE, AND GREEN DIP

Pour this over your next salad and try a new kind of dressing.

¾ cup sour cream
¾ cup mayonnaise
½ cup green bell pepper,
chopped
¼ cup pimentos, chopped

½ cup onion, chopped
1 teaspoon salt
½ teaspoon black pepper
¼ teaspoon garlic powder
¼ teaspoon Tabasco

Mix all ingredients together in a medium mixing bowl. Chill for 2 to 3 hours. Serve with raw vegetables.

Yield: approximately 2 cups

CLAM DIP

1 8-ounce package cream
cheese, softened
1 tablespoon mayonnaise
1 teaspoon onion, grated
1 tablespoon lemon juice
½ teaspoon garlic salt

½ teaspoon Worcestershire
sauce
Dash of Tabasco sauce
1 7½-ounce can minced
clams, drained (reserve
juice)

Mix all ingredients except clams in mixing bowl and blend thoroughly. Add clams and mix well. Use clam juice to achieve desired consistency. Serve with chips.

Yield: 12 servings

FABULOUS CRAB DIP

This is best with fresh crab but frozen or canned can also be used.

2 pounds crabmeat
3 8-ounce packages cream
  cheese, softened
½ cup white wine
⅓ cup mayonnaise

1 tablespoon dry mustard
1 tablespoon confectioners
  sugar
Seasoned salt to taste
Tabasco sauce to taste

Check crabmeat carefully for shells and remove. Mix all ingredients together in a mixing bowl. Heat in a double boiler or in the oven at 350° until warm. May be served hot or cold with crackers or melba toast.

Yield: 30 servings

SMOKED OYSTER DIP

You may want to add a little chopped green onion and Tabasco sauce for a slightly different taste.

1 8-ounce package cream
  cheese, softened
1 7½-ounce can smoked
  oysters, chopped

Garlic salt to taste
½ cup ripe olives, minced
Mayonnaise

Mix cream cheese to a smooth consistency in a medium mixing bowl. Add oysters, garlic salt, and olives. Add enough mayonnaise to reach desired consistency for dipping. Serve with chips.

Yield: approximately 2 cups

SHRIMPLY DELICIOUS

2 4½-ounce cans minced clams
1 4½-ounce can cocktail shrimp
3 8-ounce packages cream cheese, softened
1 tablespoon lemon juice

1 tablespoon parsley, chopped
Garlic powder to taste
Salt to taste
1 loaf Shepards bread or wide loaf French bread
1 egg, slightly beaten

Preheat oven to 250°. Drain clams and shrimp reserving ½ of the liquid. Mix all the ingredients except bread together in a large mixing bowl with reserved juices. Cut the top off the bread and remove the inside of the bread by pulling out bite size chunks. Reserve these for dipping. Pour ingredients into bread shell, replace the top of the bread, and cover with heavy aluminum foil. Bake for 3 hours. Remove bread from oven, open foil, and brush top of bread with egg. Place back in oven and bake an additional 10 minutes.

Yield: 24 servings

H.O.T. SHRIMP DIP

2 8-ounce packages cream cheese
½ cup mayonnaise
1 clove garlic, minced
2 teaspoons onion, grated
2 teaspoons prepared mustard

2 teaspoons sugar
½ teaspoon seasoned salt
1 pound fresh shrimp; cooked, peeled, deveined, and chopped
6 tablespoons dry white wine

In medium saucepan, melt cream cheese over low heat. Stir in remaining ingredients and heat through. Serve warm in chafing dish with crackers.

Yield: 8-10 servings

CHUTNEY CHEESE BALL

This makes an attractive appetizer.

1 8-ounce package cream cheese, softened	1 teaspoon curry
1 8-ounce package sharp Cheddar cheese, shredded	2 tablespoons dry sherry
	1 8-ounce bottle chutney
	1 cup green onions, chopped

Blend first four ingredients together in medium mixing bowl. Mold into ball and chill. Mixture may also be put in a quiche dish. To serve, spread cheese ball with chutney. Sprinkle with green onions.

Yield: 8-10 servings

OLIVE CHEESE BALL

1 pound cream cheese, softened	1 cup Muenster cheese or Monterey Jack cheese, shredded
½ teaspoon Worcestershire sauce	1 4½-ounce can chopped black olives
¼ teaspoon dry mustard	Garnish: Fresh parsley, chopped
Dash of red pepper	
2 cups Cheddar cheese, shredded	

Combine first four ingredients in mixing bowl. Stir in both cheeses and olives. Chill until mixture is firm enough to hold its shape. Form into a large ball and chill. Just before serving, garnish lower half of ball with chopped parsley. Serve with crisp crackers.

Yield: approximately 20 servings

OLIVE SPREAD

2 8-ounce packages cream cheese, softened	1 bunch green onions with tops, finely chopped
1 cup mayonnaise	
2 4½-ounce cans chopped ripe olives	

Mix together, by hand in a mixing bowl, cream cheese and mayonnaise. Combine with olives and onions. Serve as a spread with assorted crackers.

Yield: 12 servings

BRIE AND EASY

Round of Brie cheese
½ cup walnuts, chopped

¼ cup raisins
½ cup green onions, chopped

Thinly slice off the top of the Brie. Place in Pyrex dish. Decorate the top with remaining ingredients. Heat at 350° about 15 minutes until Brie begins to soften. Do not overheat or it will become runny. Serve warm with thinly sliced tart green apples or crackers.

Yield: 12 servings

BAKED BRIE AMARETTO

Toasting the almonds to put on top of this Brie makes it very appealing.

Syrup:
½ cup sugar
¾ cup water
Wedge of Brie cheese cut from a big wheel

2 sheets Filo dough
½ stick butter, melted
2 tablespoons amaretto
½ cup almonds, sliced

Slowly boil sugar and water together in saucepan. Using a candy thermometer, remove from heat when the temperature reaches between 200° and 210°.

Preheat oven to 400°. Set out the wedge of Brie. Spread out each piece of Filo dough, one at a time, and brush with melted butter. Stack the sheets of dough and wrap it up and around the Brie as you would a package, making sure to use all of the dough. Pinch the edges to seal. Bake for 15 to 20 minutes. The cheese should melt slightly, and the dough should brown slightly.

Warm the sugar syrup and add the amaretto. Place the cheese on a serving dish and pour the syrup over the cheese. Sprinkle with almonds. Serve with crackers.

Yield: 8 servings

SWISS CHEESE SPREAD

Spread leftover cheese mixture on bread and toast. Serve with soup.

1 pound Swiss cheese,
  shredded
1 bunch green onions,
  minced

1 cup mayonnaise

Mix all ingredients together in medium mixing bowl. Allow mixture to reach room temperature. Serve with crackers.

Yield: approximately 3 cups

A BETTER CHEDDAR SPREAD

Garnish with parsley to make an attractive appetizer at a Christmas party.

1 pound sharp Cheddar
  cheese, shredded
1 cup pecans, chopped
¾ cup mayonnaise
1 medium onion, grated

1 clove garlic, pressed
½ teaspoon Tabasco sauce
½ cup parsley, chopped
1 cup strawberry preserves

Mix all ingredients together in mixing bowl, except preserves and ½ cup pecans. Grease 3-cup ring mold and sprinkle reserved pecans in bottom. Pack cheese mixture into mold and chill. Unmold and fill center with preserves. Serve with crackers.

Yield: 20 servings

DILLY ARTICHOKE CHEESE SPREAD

1 6-ounce jar marinated
  artichoke hearts, drained
1 cup Parmesan cheese,
  grated
1 8-ounce cream cheese,
  softened

½ cup mayonnaise
½ teaspoon dillweed
2 cloves garlic, crushed

Chop artichokes. Blend in remaining ingredients. Bake in 375° oven for 15 minutes. Serve hot with crackers.

Yield: 6-8 servings

RED SALMON ROLL

1 15-ounce can red salmon; deveined, deboned, and crumbled
1 tablespoon horseradish
2 tablespoons lemon juice
1 8-ounce package cream cheese, softened

1 tablespoon liquid smoke
1 cup pecans, chopped
1 bunch green onions with tops, chopped

Mix all ingredients, except pecans and green onions together and chill several hours or overnight. Divide mixture into two parts. Roll out mixture between two sheets of wax paper in a rectangular shape. On another sheet of wax paper, sprinkle pecans and green onions, the same size as the salmon rectangle. Place salmon on the wax paper with the nuts and onions and roll up like a jelly roll. Repeat the process. Wrap and chill until ready to serve.

Yield: 2 rolls

VEGETABLE SPINACH SPREAD

One important hint when making this is to be sure you thoroughly squeeze the water out of the spinach. To vary this recipe add chopped dried beef.

1 8-ounce package cream cheese, softened
1 cup sour cream
1 tablespoon lemon juice
1 package Knorr's vegetable soup mix

2 10-ounce packages frozen chopped spinach, thawed and drained
4 green onions, chopped
1 8-ounce can sliced water chestnuts

Blend together in a medium mixing bowl the first four ingredients and allow to set all day or overnight.

About an hour before serving, add remaining ingredients to cream cheese. Mix well. Serve with your favorite chips or crackers.

Yield: approximately 3 cups

LAYERED AVOCADO CAVIAR MOLD

This attractive appetizer can be made up to two days ahead. Simply wait to add the caviar just before serving.

1 envelope gelatin	¼ cup water

Avocado Layer:

1 medium avocado, diced	½ teaspoon salt
1 large shallot, minced	Dash freshly ground pepper
2 tablespoons fresh lemon juice	Generous dash Tabasco sauce
2 tablespoons mayonnaise	

Egg Layer:

4 hard boiled eggs, finely chopped	¼ cup parsley, minced
½ cup mayonnaise	½ teaspoon salt
1 large green onion, minced	Dash pepper
	Generous dash Tabasco sauce

Sour Cream Layer:

1 cup sour cream	¼ cup onion, minced

Caviar Layer:

1 3-ounce jar red caviar	1 3-ounce jar golden caviar
1 3-ounce jar black caviar	

Combine gelatin and water in 1 cup Pyrex measuring cup. Allow to stand 5 minutes. Set cup in 1 inch boiling water and heat until gelatin is dissolved. Combine avocado, with next six ingredients. Stir in 2 tablespoons dissolved gelatin. Spoon in 7x3 inch spring form pan, spreading evenly to edges. Chill for 30 minutes. Combine egg with next six ingredients. Add 1 tablespoon and 1 teaspoon dissolved gelatin. Spoon onto avocado layer, spreading evenly to cover. Chill for 30 minutes. Combine sour cream, ¼ cup onion, and remaining gelatin. Spoon over egg layer. Cover and chill at least 8 hours until set.

To serve, remove sides of pan and garnish with caviar in a bull's eye design; black on the outside, yellow next, and red in the center. Serve with crackers or pumpernickle bread.

*Note: If gelatin begins to congeal when preparing the different layers, simply return it to the water and heat.

Yield: approximately 36 servings

CRAB SPREAD

1 8-ounce package cream
  cheese, softened
1 3-ounce package cream
  cheese softened
1 small onion, finely
  chopped
1 tablespoon Worcestershire
  sauce
2 tablespoons lemon juice

2 tablespoons mayonnaise
¼ teaspoon garlic powder
¼ teaspoon salt
1 12-ounce bottle chili sauce
12 ounces lump crabmeat,
  canned or fresh
Prepared horseradish
Parsley, chopped

Mix together cream cheese and onion. Add next five ingredients and blend well. Spread cream cheese mixture in bottom of quiche dish or pie plate. Spread ¾ bottle chili sauce on top. Add crabmeat and sprinkle with parsley. Place mound of horseradish in middle. Sprinkle with paprika. Chill. Serve with crackers.

Yield: 15 servings

CHAMPAGNE AND CITRUS

This makes a good punch for school parties when you substitute the wine and champagne with 1½ quarts ginger ale, and use frozen fruit juices.

2 cups sugar
4 cups water
½ cup lemon juice
½ cup lime juice
4½ cups orange juice
2 cups grapefruit juice

2 cups Rhine wine
1 bottle champagne
Lemon, lime, and orange
  slices (optional)
Ice ring (optional)

Combine sugar, 2 cups water, and lemon juice in saucepan. Boil one minute or until sugar is dissolved, stirring constantly. Add 2 cups cold water and let cool. Combine with remaining juices and chill. Just before serving, pour into punch bowl. Add wine and champagne. Add sliced fruit and ice ring.

Yield: approximately 20 servings

CHAMPAGNE AND FRAMBOISE

1 16-ounce can whole
   raspberries in syrup

8 ounces framboise
   (raspberry liqueur)
1 bottle champagne, chilled

Divide raspberries and syrup among ice cube trays and freeze. To serve, place one cube of raspberries in a champagne glass. Add 2 tablespoons framboise and fill glass with chilled champagne.

Yield: 8 servings

VELVET HAMMER

½ ounce brandy
1 ounce triple sec
½ ounce creme de cacao

½ ounce milk or cream
Vanilla ice cream

Place liqueurs in a blender. Fill blender with ice cream and process until smooth.

Yield: 4 servings

SANTA'S FAVORITE EGGNOG

Four ounces of Tia Maria added to this eggnog gives it a delightful and slightly different flavor.

1 dozen eggs, separated
1½ cups sugar
½ cup rum
½ cup brandy
1 quart Bourbon

1½ quarts milk
1 pint whipping cream
Nutmeg
Cinnamon

Beat egg yolks until pale yellow. Add sugar; beat mixture until fluffy. Add rum, brandy, Bourbon, and milk. Chill at least 2 hours. Just before serving, whip egg whites until stiff and fold into mixture. Beat cream and fold into mixture. Sprinkle with nutmeg and cinnamon.

Yield: approximately 24 servings

IRISH CREAMY NOG

An excellent alternative for the more traditional eggnog.

6 eggs
½ cup sugar
3 cups milk
1½ cups Irish cream liqueur

½ teaspoon ground nutmeg
½ cup whipping cream,
   whipped
Ground nutmeg

Beat eggs with an electric mixer on medium speed until foamy. Gradually add sugar, beating 5 minutes or until thick and lemon colored. Reduce speed to low. Slowly add milk, liqueur and ½ teaspoon nutmeg. Mix well and chill thoroughly. To serve, stir in whipped cream and sprinkle with nutmeg.

Yield: 8 cups

FREEZER MILK PUNCH A LA PAULA

1 fifth Bourbon
3 quarts milk
1 tablespoon vanilla
1 cup sugar

½ cup water
½ gallon vanilla ice cream,
   softened

Mix Bourbon, milk, and vanilla in a large plastic container. In saucepan boil the sugar and water, stirring constantly. Cool and add to the Bourbon mixture. Place in freezer overnight.

Remove from freezer one hour prior to serving. Place in a large punch bowl and add ice cream. Mix and chop with a wooden spoon. Sprinkle with nutmeg.

Yield: approximately 24 servings

HOITY TODDY

This is attractive served in a punch bowl with an ice ring and fresh flowers. It is also delicious frozen and served as a slush.

1 cup lime juice
4 cups orange juice
1 cup orgeat syrup

1 cup brandy
1 cup gin
2 cups white rum

Add one ingredient at a time in a punch bowl and stir well. Serve over ice. Garnish with fresh citrus slices and mint leaves.

Yield: 12 servings

COUNTRY INN PEACH FREEZE

This tastes just like a fresh peach.

2 ounces peach schnapps
2 ounces Half and Half

2 cups ice

Place all ingredients in a blender and process until slushy.

Yield: 2 servings

SECRETARY'S PUNCH

Add red food coloring for extra holiday appeal. Serve with caution.

2 liters vodka
2 liters champagne
4 liters ginger ale

2 12-ounce cans frozen pink
lemonade, thawed
Crushed Ice

Chill all ingredients. Mix together in a large punch bowl with ice.

Yield: 2½ gallons

AMARETTO FREEZE

1 ounce amaretto
¼ ounce cognac

¼ ounce creme de cacao
1 pint vanilla ice cream

Pour liqueurs in a blender. Add ice cream and process until smooth.

Yield: 2 servings

BANANA BANA PUNCH

Left-over frozen punch makes great popsicle treats.

8 cups water
4 cups sugar
2 quarts pineapple juice
4 6-ounce cans frozen
  orange juice, diluted

½ cup lemon juice
5 large bananas
2 quarts ginger ale

Combine water and sugar in a large saucepan and bring to boil. Boil 15 minutes. Allow to cool. Mix with fruit juices. Puree bananas in a blender with a small amount of juice. Mix bananas with remaining fruit juice. Freeze. Thaw 2 hours before serving. Add ginger ale.

Yield: 50 servings

SPARKLING RED PUNCH

A tart flavor.

3 12-ounce cans frozen
  lemonade, thawed
1 12-ounce can frozen
  5-Alive fruit juice, thawed

2 quarts cranberry juice
  cocktail
12 12-ounce cans water
Sprite to taste
Red food coloring

Combine juices, water, and Sprite. Add a few drops of red food coloring.

Yield: approximately 40 servings

FRUIT AND FROSTIE

Garnish with a sprig of mint or slice of fruit. Children love this for an afternoon snack.

½ cup sugar
½ cup milk
⅓ cup powdered milk
1 teaspoon vanilla

1 6-ounce can frozen fruit juice (pineapple, orange, or lemonade)
1 cup water
Ice cubes

Place all ingredients in a blender. Process until smooth. Serve immediately.

Yield: 4 servings

HEART STOPPER PUNCH

A little Kahlua adds an interesting flavor.

1 quart coffee, cooled
1 cup sugar
1 tablespoon vanilla extract
¼ teaspoon orange extract, optional
½ teaspoon cinnamon

¼ teaspoon ground cloves, optional
1 gallon milk
½ gallon vanilla ice cream, softened
1 quart chocolate ice cream, softened

Mix coffee, sugar, extracts and spices together in a large mixing bowl. Add milk and blend well. Chill. Before serving, place ice cream in a punch bowl and break into chunks. Pour coffee mixture over ice cream and stir well.

Yield: approximately 30 cups

ALMOND TEA

If you prefer hot tea, simply add all of the water before steeping the tea bags.

2 cups water
3 tea bags
1 cup sugar
1 teaspoon vanilla extract
1½ teaspoons almond extract

Juice of 3 lemons or 6
 tablespoons Real Lemon
 Juice
6 cups of water

In a saucepan, bring 2 cups water to a boil. Reduce heat to a simmer and steep tea bags for 5 minutes. Add sugar, extracts, and lemon juice. Simmer and stir until sugar is dissolved. Add water and chill. Serve over ice.

Yield: ½ gallon

HEART WARMING WASSAIL

Rum may be added to this if one prefers.

2 cups orange juice
2 cups cranberry juice
2 quarts apple juice
¾ cup sugar

1 teaspoon whole cloves
1 teaspoon whole allspice
2 cinnamon sticks

Combine juices and sugar in percolator. If frozen juices are used, be sure they are diluted according to the directions on the container. Place spices in top of percolator and perk.

*Note: This may also be prepared on the top of the stove in a saucepan. Wrap the spices in a cheesecloth, and add the juice. Bring to a boil and let simmer for 10 minutes.

Yield: ¾ gallon

ARTICHOKE SHRIMP SOUP

This soup is wonderful with or without shrimp.

1 14-ounce can artichokes, sliced
1 10¾-ounce can cream of celery soup
1 10¾-ounce can cream of mushroom soup
3¼ cups Half and Half
½ teaspoon each curry, onion powder, and Accent
Dash of Tabasco, pepper, and allspice
1 6-ounce can shrimp or 8 ounces of frozen shrimp, cooked and deveined

Mix all ingredients except shrimp together in a large saucepan and cook over medium heat for approximately 15 minutes. Add shrimp about 15 to 20 minutes before serving. Serve hot in soup cups.

Yield: approximately 8 servings

OAXACA BLACK BEAN SOUP

Looking for something to do with last night's leftover corn? Add it or any green or yellow vegetable to this soup.

2 cups black beans
Enough water to cover beans
2-5 ribs celery with some leaves, chopped
2 tablespoons parsley
1 onion, chopped
5 cloves
½ teaspoon thyme
1 bay leaf
Dash of rosemary and Tabasco sauce
Salt to taste
1 cup ham, chopped
Garnish: Chopped onion, lime slices, shredded cheese, chopped egg yolk, sour cream, yogurt, or corn

Bring all ingredients to a boil in a large covered pot. Remove from heat and allow to stand 1 hour. Return to heat and cook 2-3 hours or 40 minutes in a pressure cooker. Serve with your choice of garnish.

Yield: 8 servings

BEEF AND VEGGIE SOUP

Serve with NEVER FAIL TEXAS CORNBREAD for a quick and easy meal. For a heartier tomato taste, add an 8-ounce can of tomato sauce. You may also like to cook your meat with soup bones and chopped onion.

1 pound stew meat	2-3 ribs celery, sliced ¼ inch
1 tablespoon oil	thick
1 teaspoon salt	3-4 carrots sliced ¼ inch thick
¼ teaspoon ground pepper	1 16-ounce can green beans,
¼ teaspoon garlic salt	drained
1 teaspoon Cavender's Greek	1 large potato, cubed
seasoning	1 14½-ounce can stewed
1 tablespoon sugar	tomatoes, chopped
1 onion, chopped	3-4 cans water

Remove all fat from meat. Cut into bite size pieces. Heat oil in a large pot. Add meat, seasonings, sugar, onion, and celery. Cook over medium heat until meat is browned. Add remaining ingredients. Cover and cook over low heat for 3 hours, stirring occasionally.

Yield: 6 servings

VELVETY BRIE SOUP

Simply delicious. Serve with French bread and a bottle of red wine.

6 ounces Brie cheese	1 bay leaf
2 ribs celery, finely chopped	1 teaspoon thyme
2 carrots, finely chopped	½ cup whipping cream
½ onion, finely chopped	Garnish: Seasoned croutons,
8 tablespoons butter	chopped pimento, or
8 tablespoons flour	chopped parsley
2 cans chicken broth, heated	

Cut away the rind from the Brie and discard. Cut cheese into cubes and set aside. Saute vegetables in butter in a skillet over medium heat. Add flour and blend, making a roux. When butter is absorbed and the mixture is thick, add the broth and stir until thickened again. Add the bay leaf and thyme. Slowly add the cheese, stirring until melted. Add cream and heat thoroughly. Serve with your choice of garnish.

Yield: 4-6 servings

CURRIED CREAM OF BROCCOLI SOUP

1 tablespoon oil
1 small onion, chopped
4 cups broccoli, chopped
2 ribs celery, diced
2 15-ounce cans chicken stock
1 cup ricotta cheese

1 cup lowfat milk
2 tablespoons Half and Half
½ teaspoon curry
1 teaspoon salt
½ teaspoon pepper

Heat oil in a 4-quart saucepan and saute onion. Add broccoli, celery, and chicken stock; bring to a boil. Simmer 10 to 15 minutes. Cool slightly. Combine ricotta and milk in a blender and process until smooth. Pour into a separate saucepan. Slowly stir in Half and Half, and seasonings; add to broccoli mixture. Heat for a few minutes. Remove from heat and puree in batches in a blender. Return to saucepan and heat. Do not boil.

Yield: 6 servings

HEARTY CHEESE SOUP

Sure to become a family favorite.

4 tablespoons butter
3 green onions, chopped
2 carrots, grated
3 ribs celery, finely chopped
1 10½-ounce can chicken
    broth
3 10¾-ounce cans cream of
    potato soup

8 ounces medium or sharp
    Cheddar cheese, shredded
8 ounces sour cream
Salt and pepper to taste
Milk

Melt butter in a 3 quart saucepan or Dutch oven. Saute onions, carrots, and celery in butter. Add broth and simmer covered about 20 minutes. Add soup, cheese, and sour cream, stirring well. Cook over low heat until cheese is melted. Season to taste. Dilute with milk if a thinner soup is desired.

Yield: 6 servings

CREAM OF CORN SOUP

If you prefer a thicker soup, add an extra tablespoon of cornstarch.

1 onion, chopped
4 strips bacon, cooked and
  crumbled, reserve
  drippings
4 10-ounce packages frozen
  cream style corn, thawed

4 quarts chicken broth,
  reserve 1 cup
4 tablespoons cornstarch
2 pints Half and Half
Salt and pepper to taste

In a large pot saute onions in bacon drippings until tender. Add corn and chicken broth. Cook over medium heat for 40 to 45 minutes. Combine 1 cup chicken broth with cornstarch and add to broth mixture. Stir in Half and Half until mixture is hot. Make sure it does not boil. Add seasonings and serve immediately. Garnish with bacon.

Yield: approximately 12 servings

DILLY GAZPACHO

What to do with leftover salad? Add it to gazpacho.

1 clove garlic
2 ribs celery
1 cucumber, peeled
1 green bell pepper, seeded
4 green onions
½ bunch parsley
3 stalks fresh dill
4 tomatoes or a 16-ounce can
  of tomatoes

1 13-ounce bottle Clamato
  juice
1 13-ounce can V-8 juice
1 teaspoon French dressing
Worcestershire sauce to taste
Juice of 1 lemon and 1 lime
Salt and pepper to taste

Chop first eight ingredients in a food processor. Add the juices and seasonings and blend until just mixed, making sure ingredients are chunky. Do not puree mixture. Chill thoroughly before serving. Will keep several days in refrigerator.

Yield: approximately 4 servings

GREAT GUMBO

To make seafood gumbo, omit chicken and use 1½ pounds fresh fish in its place. If you like add raw oysters 5 minutes before serving.

1 fryer chicken
4 ribs celery
1 onion, chopped
3 pounds shrimp, shelled
   and deveined
1 tablespoon Crab Boil
1 stick butter
½ cup flour
4 bunches green onions,
   chopped
3 cloves garlic, minced

1 green bell pepper, chopped
¼ cup parsley, chopped
2 10-ounce cans Rotel
   tomatoes, chopped
1 20-ounce bag frozen sliced
   okra
½ teaspoon thyme
Salt and pepper to taste
Worcestershire sauce to taste
4 tablespoons Gumbo File

In a large pot, cook chicken with celery and onion, in enough water to cover chicken. When tender cool, debone and cut chicken into bite size pieces. Strain broth and reserve.

Place shrimp in a large pot, cover with water and add Crab Boil. Bring to boil and cook for 3 to 4 minutes. Drain and cool. Set meats aside. Make a Roux by melting butter in a skillet over medium heat, add flour and stir constantly until it turns a dark brown. This will take about 15-20 minutes. Add green onions, garlic, and bell pepper; cook until onions are browned. Combine the chicken stock and the roux mixture in a large deep pot. Add water if needed to fill the pot. Add parsley, tomatoes, okra, thyme, salt, pepper, and chicken. Simmer for three hours.

A few minutes before serving, chop 1 pound of the shrimp; add chopped and whole shrimp to gumbo. Add Worcestershire sauce and Gumbo File. Serve over rice in soup bowls and sprinkle with additional Gumbo File.

Yield: approximately 12 servings

HAMBURGER SOUP

For a different flavor, substitute macaroni noodles in place of potatoes and add canned corn.

1 pound ground beef
1 onion, chopped
1 14½-ounce can tomatoes, chopped
2 10½-ounce cans beef bouillon

2 large potatoes, chopped
6 carrots, chopped
Salt and pepper to taste

Brown beef and onion in skillet over medium heat. Drain well. Combine all ingredients in a large pot. Heat thoroughly. Dilute with water if desired.

Yield: 6 servings

LEEK AND WATERCRESS SOUP

Delicious served with Crispy Cheese Wafers.

1½ cups leeks, washed well and minced
1 cup onion, minced
1 clove garlic, minced
½ stick butter or margarine, melted
2 medium potatoes, peeled and thinly sliced

1¾ bunches watercress, coarsley chopped
3 cups chicken broth
1 cup milk
1 cup Half and Half
Salt and pepper to taste

Place leeks, onion, garlic, and butter in a large saucepan. Cover vegetables with a round of buttered waxed paper and place lid on saucepan. Cook for 20 minutes or until vegetables are very soft. Remove waxed paper and add potatoes, watercress, and chicken broth. Simmer for 25 minutes.

Transfer mixture to a blender and puree. Return to saucepan; add milk and Half and Half. Simmer and season to taste. Serve immediately. Garnish with watercress leaves.

Yield: 6 servings

SOUPER SPLIT PEA SOUP

1 leek with tops, chopped
1 large onion, chopped
4 ribs celery, chopped
2 heaping teaspoons bacon
  drippings
2 tablespoons fresh parsley,
  chopped
2 cloves garlic, minced
1 carrot, chopped
⅛ teaspoon cayenne pepper
1 teaspoon salt

1 teaspoon pepper
4 ham hocks or 1 ham bone
1 cup ham, diced
1 16-ounce package split peas
1½ quarts water
1 teaspoon Tabasco sauce
1 teaspoon Worcestershire
  sauce
1 10½-ounce can chicken
  broth

Place all ingredients in a large soup pot and bring to boil. Reduce to simmer; cover and cook for 2 hours, stirring occasionally. Allow to cool and remove bone or ham hocks. Puree soup in blender. Place in quart jars. When ready to serve, heat in saucepan and thin with milk.

Yield: 6 quarts

VALENTINE SOUP

1 16-ounce can sliced beets,
  drained
1 10½-ounce can chicken
  broth

1 cup sour cream
Tabasco sauce to taste
Seasoned salt to taste
Creole seasoning to taste

Blend beets and chicken broth in blender until beets are thoroughly pureed. Stir in sour cream until mixture is smooth. Add seasonings. Chill. Stir chilled soup before serving.

Yield: 4 servings

PORTUGUESE SOUP

Serve in big bowls with a knife, fork, spoon, and lots of cornbread.

2 cups onion, chopped
4 tablespoons oil
1 pound garlic-smoked
  sausage, sliced
2 teaspoons garlic powder
1 teaspoon salt
1 teaspoon pepper
3 quarts beef stock

1 16-ounce bottle catsup
2 cups canned kidney beans
1 head green cabbage, cored
  and chopped
6 medium boiling potatoes,
  cubed
½ cup vinegar

Saute onions in oil in a large stew pot. Add sausage and cook for 3 to 4 minutes over low heat. While stirring add seasonings. Add remaining ingredients except vinegar. Bring to a boil and continue stirring. Reduce heat to simmer. Add vinegar and cook until cabbage and potatoes are cooked, about 30 to 40 minutes.

Yield: approximately 12 servings

CHEESY POTATO SOUP

6 medium potatoes
1 medium onion
1 quart water
4 teaspoons seasoned salt
½ teaspoon pepper
1 stick butter
2 tablespoons flour

3 cups milk
1 pint Half and Half
½ pound Velveeta cheese,
  cubed
2 tablespoons parsley,
  chopped

Chop four of the potatoes and the onion in the food processor with the metal blade. Dice the remaining potatoes in small pieces. Place in a 4-quart Dutch oven with water. Add salt and pepper; simmer until thick, about 20 minutes. Melt butter in a 2 quart saucepan. Add flour and stir until smooth. Add milk and Half and Half. Cook over low heat until thickened and smooth for about 20 minutes. Stir the Velveeta into the milk mixture until melted; add parsley and combine with the potato mixture.

Yield: 3 quarts

PENNY'S HAM AND POTATO SOUP

1 large onion, chopped	1 cup celery, diced
3 tablespoons butter	¾ cup carrots, diced
7 large potatoes, cubed	1½ cups ham, diced
1 quart chicken broth	1 quart Half and Half
1 tablespoon salt	

Saute onions in butter in a large pot. Add five potatoes, chicken broth, and salt. Bring to a boil and cook 30 to 40 minutes, until potatoes are tender. In a separate pan, cook the remaining potatoes, celery, carrots, and ham in enough water to cover. Cook over medium heat until vegetables are tender. Drain and add to the potato mixture. Add Half and Half and heat slowly; do not boil.

Yield: 6 servings

ROQUEFORT VICHYSSOISE

Crumbled bacon also makes a delicious garnish for this soup.

2 cups onion, finely chopped	⅛ teaspoon white pepper
⅓ cup butter	9 ounces Roquefort cheese
4 cups chicken broth	½ cup Chablis
3½ cups potatoes, peeled and diced	2½ cups buttermilk
¼ teaspoon salt	3 tablespoons dried chives

Saute onion in butter in a 6-quart pan until tender and slightly golden. Stir in chicken broth, diced potatoes, salt and pepper. Bring to a boil, reduce heat, and simmer uncovered for 20 minutes or until tender. Process mixture ⅓ at a time in a blender until smooth. Return to pan. Crumble 6 ounces of cheese and add with wine to the potato mixture. Cook over low heat, stirring constantly for 5 minutes or until cheese melts. Allow to cool. Cover and place in refrigerator for 4 hours until thoroughly chilled. Stir in buttermilk. Spoon into chilled bowls. Garnish with remaining cheese and chives.

Yield: approximately 8 servings

SAVORY SENEGELESE SOUP

1 large chicken
6 chicken thighs
1 large onion, chopped
2 leeks with tops, chopped
3 ribs celery, chopped
3 carrots, chopped
2 cloves garlic, chopped
Salt and pepper to taste
Water
½ cup green bell pepper, chopped
½ 4-ounce jar chopped pimento
2½ teaspoons garlic salt

1 tablespoon dried parsley flakes
1½ tablespoons seasoned salt
1½ teaspoons seasoned pepper
1½ tablespoons Accent
5½ tablespoons cornstarch, diluted in ¼ cup cold water
3 teaspoons curry powder, diluted in 2 tablespoons cold water
4 tablespoons Spice Island Chicken Stock Base
3 cups milk

Place chicken in pot. Add next six ingredients. Cover with water and simmer for 1 hour until chicken is tender. Remove chicken and reserve for another use. Add 1 quart water to stock and vegetables. Puree in blender. Place pureed mixture in a heavy pan and add next 7 ingredients. Simmer for a few minutes. Add cornstarch and stir until slightly thickened like heavy cream. Add curry powder and simmer about 5 minutes. Stir in chicken stock base. To serve, add 1 cup milk for each 1 quart soup and heat thoroughly.

Yield: 3 quarts

WAYNE'S ZUCCHINI SOUP

Substitute zucchini with 1 pound yellow squash, if you prefer.

4 zucchini, unpeeled and sliced
2 cups chicken broth
5 green onions, sliced
¼ teaspoon dill weed
1 teaspoon salt

1 8-ounce package cream cheese
½ cup sour cream
Garnish: chopped chives, chopped parsley, or paprika

Combine zucchini, broth, green onions, dill, and salt in a large pot. Cook over medium heat for 15 minutes. Remove from heat. Place in blender with cream cheese and blend until pureed. Add sour cream and mix until smooth. Serve chilled or warm with your choice of garnish.

Yield: approximately 6 servings

DORIS' BROCCOLI SOUP

If you like spicy, hot food, you will love this easy to prepare soup.

2 10-ounce packages frozen
chopped broccoli
3 10¾-ounce cans cream of
mushroom soup
2 6-ounce rolls jalapeno
cheese, cubed

3 soup cans water
1 teaspoon Accent
Croutons

Combine all ingredients in a saucepan except croutons. Cook over low heat for 1 hour. Garnish with croutons.

Yield: 6 servings

CREAMY CLAM CHOWDER

This is simple to put together and tastes like you have been in the kitchen all day.

3 10¾-ounce cans New
England clam chowder
3 10¾-ounce cans cream of
potato soup
1 10¾-ounce can cream of
celery soup
2 7½-ounce cans clams with
juice

1½ pints whipping cream
½ teaspoon Tabasco
Dash cayenne pepper
Seasoned salt to taste
Pepper to taste

Combine all ingredients in a large heavy pot. Cook over low heat, stirring occasionally until hot.

Yield: 10 servings

TASTY TOMATO BISQUE

Garnish with parsley or crumbled bacon.

3 sticks butter
4 large onions, minced
1 large green bell pepper, minced
1 cup Wondra flour
6 cups milk
4 28-ounce cans whole tomatoes

2 14½-ounce cans stewed tomatoes
Salt, seasoned pepper, and Accent to taste
¼ teaspoon thyme
¼ teaspoon basil
3 drops red food coloring

Melt butter in Dutch oven or large soup pot. Add onions and green pepper; saute until tender. Sprinkle with flour and gradually add milk, stirring often. Cut tomatoes into small pieces or chop in blender. Add tomatoes, seasonings, and food coloring. Simmer 20 minutes.

Yield: approximately 16 servings

BROILED AVOCADO

1 cup macaroni
4 avocados
3-4 drops Tabasco sauce
1 5-ounce package stick pepperoni, chopped
½ cup mozzarella cheese, shredded

¼ cup carrots, grated
1 tablespoon onion, minced
¼ cup mayonnaise
¼ cup dry breadcrumbs
1 tablespoon butter, melted

Cook macaroni according to package directions, drain well, and set aside. Slice avocados in half and scoop out insides and mash with Tabasco. Spread avocado mixture in bottom and around sides of avocado shells. Combine macaroni with pepperoni, cheese, carrots, onion, and mayonnaise. Spoon mixture into avocado shells. Sprinkle with breadcrumbs and drizzle butter on top. Place in baking dish and broil 3 to 5 minutes.

Yield: 8 servings

TOSSED CLUB SALAD

For a light meal serve with fresh fruit and bread.

½ pound bacon
1 cup French bread, cubed
3 cups chicken, cooked and diced
2 tomatoes, sliced and quartered or cherry tomatoes, halved
¾ cup mayonnaise

1 tablespoon Worcestershire Sauce
1 tablespoon parsley, minced
1 tablespoon green onion, chopped
1 tablespoon capers
1 teaspoon salt
¼ teaspoon pepper

Cut bacon slices into quarters and fry until crisp. Drain and crumble. Reserve 2 tablespoons bacon grease. Add bread to reserved grease in pan and toast until brown. Remove and drain bread on paper towels. Just before serving, combine the chicken, bacon, tomatoes, and bread cubes in a bowl. Blend remaining ingredients and pour over chicken mixture. Toss lightly until well coated. Serve on lettuce cups.

Yield: 4 servings

MIDSUMMER NIGHT'S DREAM CHICKEN SALAD

This is attractive molded in a ring mold with fresh strawberries in the center.

4 cups chicken, cooked and diced
½ cup celery, chopped
½ cup apple, chopped
½ cup seedless grapes, sliced
1 banana, sliced

2 cups mayonnaise
1 teaspoon curry powder
¼ cup whipping cream, whipped
Salt to taste

Blend all ingredients in a mixing bowl. Chill overnight before serving.

Yield: 10 servings

FRUIT 'N CHICKEN SALAD

A salad with an Oriental flair.

5 cups chicken, cooked and diced
1 16-ounce can pineapple tidbits, drained
1 11-ounce can Mandarin orange sections, drained
1¼ cup celery, chopped
⅔ cup green bell pepper, chopped

½ cup medium pitted ripe olives, sliced
2 tablespoons onion, grated
1 cup mayonnaise
1 tablespoon prepared mustard
1 5-ounce can chow mein noodles
Lettuce leaves

Combine first seven ingredients in a large mixing bowl. Blend mayonnaise and mustard; toss gently with chicken mixture. Cover and chill several hours. Before serving, mix in chow mein noodles and turn salad into a lettuce-lined bowl or spoon individual servings on lettuce leaves.

Yield: 8 servings

CHICKEN AND WILD RICE SALAD

1 6½-ounce package long grain and wild rice
2 cups chicken, cooked and cubed (cooled in broth)
¼ cup green bell pepper, chopped
3 tablespoons pimento, chopped

½ cup mayonnaise
2-3 tablespoons Russian salad dressing
1 tablespoon lemon juice
¼ teaspoon salt
2-3 avocados, sliced

Cook rice and cool. Add next three ingredients. Combine mayonnaise with remaining ingredients except avocados. Toss dressing into rice mixture. Chill. To serve, garnish with avocado slices.

Yield: 4-6 servings.

GOBBLIN UP SALAD

Although it is always nice to have a recipe to use leftover holiday turkey, this is wonderful year round. It is especially good in the summer, in place of chicken salad.

2 cups turkey, cooked and diced
1½ cups celery, diced
½ cup onion, grated
1 tablespoon lemon juice
1 teaspoon garlic salt

2 tablespoons mango chutney
½ teaspoon white pepper
1 teaspoon red pepper
¾ cup mayonnaise
½ cup yellow raisins

Mix all ingredients together in a large mixing bowl. To serve hot, top with ¾ cup shredded Cheddar cheese and bake at 375° for 25 minutes or until cheese bubbles. To serve cold, spoon into scooped out tomato halves or on a bed of lettuce. Sprinkle with Hungarian paprika.

Yield: approximately 6 servings

ARTICHOKE, SHRIMP, AND RICE SALAD

1 6½-ounce box chicken flavored rice or 1 cup rice cooked in chicken broth
¼ cup green onion, chopped
¼ cup green bell pepper, chopped
¼ cup pimento stuffed green olives, sliced
1 6-ounce jar marinated artichoke hearts, drained and quartered
½ cup mayonnaise

¼ cup sour cream
½ teaspoon dried dillweed or ½ teaspoon curry
½ teaspoon salt
⅛ teaspoon pepper
1 pound shrimp; cooked, peeled, deveined and chopped
Lettuce leaves
Garnish: Pimento stuffed green olives
Paprika

Cook rice according to package directions. Stir in next ten ingredients. Chill. Spoon salad into lettuce lined bowl; garnish with olives and sprinkle with paprika.

Yield: approximately 4 servings

SOUR CREAM POTATO SALAD
Great with hamburgers or fried chicken.

11 California white potatoes
6-8 sweet pickles, grated
2 tablespoons celery seed
4 hard-boiled eggs, chopped
1 onion, partly chopped and
   partly grated
2-3 tablespoons parsley,
   finely chopped

½ cup mayonnaise
1 pint sour cream
3-4 tablespoons sugar
3-4 teaspoons cider vinegar
2½ teaspoons salt
¼ teaspoon red pepper
½ teaspoon black pepper
Paprika to garnish

Peel and boil potatoes in water until tender. Drain, cool, and chunk potatoes. Toss thoroughly with remaining ingredients except paprika. Garnish and refrigerate.

Yield: 10-12 servings

NEW POTATO SALAD

5-6 large new potatoes
   (5 cups)
1 large onion, chopped
1 bunch green onions,
   chopped
2 4-ounce jars chopped
   pimento

6 hard-boiled eggs, chopped
4 avocados, chopped
1 cup mayonnaise
¼ cup lime juice
Salt and pepper to taste
1 pound bacon, cooked and
   crumbled

Place potatoes in a large pan with enough water to cover and bring to a boil. Boil until tender; drain and allow to cool. Slice potatoes with the skins on. Combine potatoes and remaining ingredients together in a large bowl; serve immediately.

Yield: 10 servings

PERFECT POTATO SALAD

Try adding a half-pound cooked and crumbled bacon, three grated sweet pickles, and one half cup chopped celery as a variation.

⅓ cup Italian salad dressing
5 medium potatoes, boiled
   in skins, peeled, and cubed
1 cup celery, finely chopped
¾ cup green onion, chopped
4 hard boiled eggs, chopped

1 cup mayonnaise
2 heaping teaspoons Dijon
   mustard
1½ teaspoons salt
1 teaspoon white pepper
Celery seed to taste

Pour dressing over potatoes and chill 2 hours. Add celery, onions and eggs. Mix mayonnaise with mustard and fold into salad. Add salt, pepper, and celery seed. Chill 2 hours.

Yield: 8 servings

CURRY RICE SALAD

This salad is better the second day.

1 tablespoon vinegar
2 tablespoons corn oil
¾ cup Hellmann's mayonnaise
1 teaspoon salt
1 teaspoon curry powder
1 cup rice

¼ cup onion, finely chopped
1 cup celery, chopped
1 10-ounce package frozen
   green peas, cooked
   slightly

Mix first five ingredients in a large bowl. Cook rice according to package directions. Add hot rice and onions to curry mixture. Allow to cool; add celery and peas; toss until well blended.

Yield: 8 servings

VERMICELLI SALAD SUPREME

Plan to begin preparing this a day ahead.

1 16-ounce package
  Vermicelli noodles
1 tablespoon seasoned salt
3 tablespoons lemon juice
4 tablespoons cooking oil
1 4-ounce jar diced pimento

¾ cup green onion, chopped
1 4-ounce jar ripe olives,
  chopped
2 cups celery, diced
1½ cups Hellmann's
  mayonnaise

The day before serving, cook, rinse, and drain noodles. Marinate overnight in seasoned salt, lemon juice, and oil. The next day, add remaining ingredients and mix together in a large bowl. Chill several hours
before serving. This is especially good chilled overnight.

Yield: 10 servings

SULTRY SUMMER SALAD

This salad keeps well in the refrigerator.

½ cup cooking oil
¾ cup vinegar
¾ cup sugar
1 teaspoon salt
1 teaspoon pepper
1 17-ounce can seasoned
  green beans, drained
1 17-ounce can green peas,
  drained

1 17-ounce can shoepeg
  corn, drained
1 cup celery, chopped
1 bunch green onions,
  chopped
1 green bell pepper, chopped
1 4-ounce jar pimento, diced
  and drained
1 6-ounce can sliced water
  chestnuts, drained

Combine first five ingredients in a medium saucepan and bring to a
boil. Allow mixture to cool and pour over vegetables in a large salad
bowl. Chill before serving.

Yield: approximately 16 servings

MARINATED GREEN BEAN SALAD

Keeps for several weeks in your refrigerator.

1 large purple Italian onion, sliced and separated into rings
1 6-ounce can sliced water chestnuts, drained
2 17-ounce cans green beans, drained
1 17-ounce can green peas, drained
1 cup celery, chopped
½ cup green stuffed olives, sliced
1 4½-ounce package slivered almonds, toasted
Juice of 1½ lemons and 1½ oranges
2 cloves garlic, crushed
1 cup salad oil
1 teaspoon Worcestershire sauce
¾ teaspoon pepper
1 teaspoon salt
¾ cup confectioners sugar
1 teaspoon mustard
½ cup vinegar

Combine first seven ingredients in a large bowl. Combine remaining ingredients for marinade and pour over vegetables. Marinate 24 hours in refrigerator.

Yield: 8 servings

MARINATED MUSHROOM AND ARTICHOKE SALAD

This salad adds a lot of color to a plate and is delicious.

½ pound fresh mushrooms, simmered in water until barely tender
1 8½-ounce can artichoke hearts, drained and halved
1 4-ounce can ripe olives, drained
½ cup cherry tomatoes, cut in halves
½ medium onion, chopped or sliced
¼ cup fresh parsley, chopped
Marinade dressing:
⅓ cup French olive oil
2 tablespoons salad vinegar
1½ cloves garlic, minced
1 teaspoon oregano
½ teaspoon fine herbs

Combine first six ingredients in a medium bowl. Combine dressing ingredients and pour over salad. Cover and chill.

Yield: approximately 6 servings

AVOCADO ASPIC MOLD

The green and red color make this perfect for a holiday buffet.

3 large avocados
1 8-ounce package cream
  cheese, softened
½ cup mayonnaise
1 cup onion, chopped

1 cup celery, chopped
1 6-ounce package lime jello
1 cup hot water
1½ recipes Tomato Aspic
  (recipe follows)

Cream avocado with cream cheese in a medium mixing bowl. Add mayonnaise, onion, celery and blend. Dissolve jello in 1 cup hot water. Fold into avocado. Chill in a one quart mold or a 9x13 greased Pyrex in two layers. Layer bottom with tomato aspic and top with avocado mixture.

Yield: 12 servings

TOMATO ASPIC

1 6-ounce package lemon
  jello
2 cups tomato juice, boiling
1½ cups tomato juice, cold
½ teaspoon salt
2 tablespoons horseradish
1 tablespoon onion, grated
⅛ teaspoon Tabasco sauce
1 tablespoon cider vinegar

½ teaspoon Worcestershire
  sauce
Optional:
1 cup celery, chopped
1 6-ounce jar artichoke
  hearts, chopped
1 10½-ounce can asparagus,
  chopped

Dissolve jello in boiling tomato juice in a medium saucepan. Combine dissolved jello and remaining ingredients in a mixing bowl. Congeal.

Yield: 12 servings

EB'S BLUEBERRY SALAD

For a different flavor, add two mashed bananas to jello.

1 6-ounce package
  blackberry jello
2 cups boiling water
1 15-ounce can blueberries,
  drained, reserving juice
1 8-ounce can crushed
  pineapple, drained,
  reserving juice

1 8-ounce package cream
  cheese, softened
½ cup sugar
1 cup sour cream
½ teaspoon vanilla
½ cup pecans, chopped

Dissolve gelatin in boiling water. Add enough water to reserved fruit juices to make 1½ cups and mix with gelatin. Stir in blueberries and pineapple. Pour into a two quart Pyrex dish and chill until firm. Blend cream cheese, sugar, sour cream, and vanilla in a medium mixing bowl. Spread over the congealed blueberry salad. Sprinkle with pecans.

Yield: approximately 8 servings

THREE DAY CRANBERRY SALAD

1 16-ounce package fresh
  cranberries
2 cups sugar
1 16-ounce carton sour
  cream

1 10-ounce package
  mini-marshmallows
1 20-ounce can crushed
  pineapple, drained
1 cup pecans, chopped

First day: Wash and stem cranberries and finely chop in a blender. Add sugar; cover and chill overnight.

Second day: Add sour cream and marshmallows to cranberries. Stir and cover; chill overnight.

Third day: Add pineapple and pecans and allow to sit several hours or overnight before serving.

Yield: 16 servings

MANGO TANGO SALAD

3 3-ounce packages lemon
  jello
3 cups boiling water
1 21-ounce can mangos,
  reserve juice

1 8-ounce package cream
  cheese, softened
1 8-ounce carton sour cream
1 tablespoon confectioners
  sugar

Dissolve jello in boiling water. Add enough cold water to reserved mango juice to measure 1 cup. Cream together cream cheese, mangos, and mango juice in a blender. Stir in jello and pour into a mold. Chill until set. Mix sour cream and confectioners sugar together; spread on top.

Yield: approximately 12 servings

FINISH YOUR SPINACH SALAD

Cherry tomatoes added to the center of the mold are very attractive.

2 1-ounce envelopes
  unflavored gelatin
1 10½ ounce can condensed
  beef broth
¼ cup water
½ teaspoon salt
2 tablespoons lemon juice
1 cup mayonnaise

1 10-ounce package frozen
  chopped spinach, thawed
¼ cup green onion, chopped
4 hard boiled eggs, chopped
½ pound bacon, cooked and
  crumbled
Pimento strips for garnish

Soften gelatin in beef broth; stir over low heat until dissolved. Stir in water, salt, and lemon juice. Gradually add gelatin to mayonnaise, mixing until well blended. Chill until slightly thickened; fold in spinach, onion, eggs, and bacon. Pour into 1½-quart ring mold. Chill until firm. Garnish with pimento strips.

Yield: approximately 12 servings

FABULOUS FROZEN FRUIT SALAD

Good enough for a dessert. Freeze in individual muffin tins.

1 8-ounce cream cheese,
  softened
2 cups sour cream
4 tablespoons lemon juice
1 cup sugar
¼ teaspoon salt

2 bananas, mashed
1 20-ounce can crushed
  pineapple, drained
¼ cup maraschino cherries,
  chopped
½ cup pecans, chopped

Beat cream cheese with mixer in a medium bowl. Add sour cream and blend. Add lemon juice, sugar, and salt. Blend well. Stir in bananas, then pineapple. Follow with cherries and nuts. Add 2 to 3 tablespoons cherry juice for color. Pour mixture into mold or Pyrex dish. Freeze. Cut into squares and serve on crisp lettuce leaves.

Yield: approximately 10 servings

FROZEN WALDORF SALAD

1 8-ounce can crushed
  pineapple, drain and reserve juice
2 eggs, slightly beaten
¼ cup lemon juice
⅛ teaspoon salt
½ cup sugar
¼ cup mayonnaise
1 cup whipping cream,
  whipped

1½ cups apples, unpeeled
  and diced
¾ cup celery, diced
1 cup maraschino cherries
½ cup pecans, coarsely
  chopped
1 cup miniature
  marshmallows

Combine reserved pineapple juice with eggs, lemon juice, and salt. Add sugar. Place in saucepan and cook over medium heat until thickened, stirring often. Cool. Fold in mayonnaise and whipped cream. In a separate bowl, combine pineapple with remaining ingredients. Pour sauce over fruit and toss lightly. Freeze in 8 cup mold until very firm, approximately 3-4 hours.

Yield: 8-10 servings

GRAMMA DOXIE'S FROZEN CRANBERRY SALAD

1 12-ounce carton Cool Whip
1 16-ounce can whole
  cranberry sauce
1 8-ounce can crushed
  pineapple, drained

1 8-ounce package cream
  cheese, softened
1 teaspoon almond extract
½ cup sugar
1 cup pecans, chopped

Blend ingredients thoroughly. Pour in 9x11 inch cake pan. Freeze.

Yield: 12 servings

CAESAR PLEASER SALAD

Coddle eggs by submerging the whole egg in boiling water.

1 clove garlic
½ cup olive oil
½ teaspoon salt
Pepper to taste
Juice of 1 lemon
2 teaspoons dry mustard
¼ teaspoon Worcestershire
  sauce
1-2 drops Tabasco sauce

2 eggs, coddled 1 minute
1 2-ounce can anchovy
  fillets, mashed (optional)
3 heads romaine lettuce, torn
  in pieces
¾ cup fresh Parmesan
  cheese, grated
2 cups onion garlic croutons
  or 2 cups bagel chips

Marinate garlic in olive oil several hours. Combine salt, pepper, lemon juice, mustard, Worcestershire, and Tabasco in a large salad bowl. Allow olive oil to drip into mixture while whipping to slightly thicken. When oil begins to turn cloudy, break the eggs into oil mixture and beat well. Beat in mashed anchovy until well blended. Toss in lettuce until well coated. Add cheese and croutons; serve immediately.

Yield: 8 servings

ROMAINE AND STRAWBERRY SALAD

Substitute 3 pounds of spinach in place of romaine for a different flavor.

6 heads romaine lettuce, torn
   into bite-size pieces
3 bunches watercress, torn
   into bite-size pieces
2 pints fresh strawberries,
   washed and hulled
2 medium red onions, thinly
   sliced

1 cup olive oil
⅓ cup wine vinegar
2 tablespoons sugar
Juice of 2 small lemons
½ teaspoon salt
¼ teaspoon black pepper

Combine first four ingredients in a large salad bowl. Process the remaining ingredients in a blender. Pour over lettuce and toss well.

Yield: 25 servings

ROSIE'S GREAT SALAD

Try this salad with our own Special Italian Dressing.

1 head romaine lettuce, torn
   into bite-size pieces
1 head red tip lettuce, torn
   into bite-size pieces
1 head lettuce, your choice,
   torn into bite-size pieces
1 11-ounce can Mandarin
   oranges, cut each section
   in half

1 8½-ounce can artichoke
   hearts, drained and
   chopped
2 avocados, peeled and sliced
2 green onions, chopped
Garlic salt
Italian dressing

Combine lettuce, oranges, artichoke hearts, avocados, and onions in a large salad bowl. Sprinkle with garlic salt and toss with Italian dressing.

Yield: approximately 16 servings

WILTED LETTUCE SALAD

½ pound bacon, cooked and
  diced
Red wine vinegar
1½ teaspoons sugar
1 small head lettuce, torn
  into bite-size pieces
1 package fresh spinach,
  torn into bite-size pieces

Pepper to taste
Optional:
1 cup fresh mushrooms,
  sliced
⅓ cup green onions,
  chopped
2 hard boiled eggs

Fry bacon over low heat in a skillet until well browned; remove and drain on paper towels. Measure drippings and return to skillet, adding an equal quantity of vinegar. Stir in sugar and heat thoroughly. Place salad greens in a large salad bowl and pour hot dressing over greens. Season with pepper and sprinkle with bacon bits. Add optional ingredients.

Yield: 6 servings

BEST EVER SPINACH SALAD

1 package fresh spinach,
  torn into bite-size pieces
1 16-ounce can bean sprouts,
  drained
6-8 strips bacon, cooked and
  crumbled
3 hard boiled eggs, chopped
½ cup cooking oil
10 tablespoons sugar

6 tablespoons bottled chili
  sauce
5 tablespoons vinegar
½ teaspoon salt
1 tablespoon onion flakes
½ teaspoon Worcestershire
  sauce
Sliced fresh mushrooms and
  croutons, optional

Combine first four ingredients in a salad bowl. Mix remaining ingredients in a small bowl and pour over salad. Add optional ingredients.

Yield: 8 servings

LOVER'S DELIGHT STRAWBERRY CREAM SAUCE

Place this in a bowl and surround with strawberries or put strawberries in individual parfaits and pour sauce over them.

1 8-ounce package cream
   cheese, softened
1⅓ cups confectioners sugar,
   sifted

⅓ cup whipping cream
Pinch of salt
¼ teaspoon vanilla
¼ cup sherry

Combine ingredients in a mixing bowl and beat with a mixer at moderate speed. Chill in refrigerator overnight.

Yield: approximately 1½ cups sauce

WONDERFUL FRUIT SALAD DRESSING

A fruit salad's delight.

1 8-ounce package cream
   cheese, softened
⅓ cup orange juice
2-3 tablespoons sugar

½ teaspoon confectioners
   sugar or ½ teaspoon fresh
   ginger, grated

Process ingredients in a food processor until well blended. This will keep in the refrigerator for several days.

Yield: 1½ cups dressing

ROSEMARY'S POPPY SEED DRESSING

¾ cup sugar
1 teaspoon dry mustard
1 teaspoon salt
⅓ cup vinegar

1½ teaspoons onion juice
1 cup oil
1½ tablespoons poppy seed

Place first five ingredients in blender. Process. Slowly add oil while blending. Blend until thick. Stir in poppy seeds. Serve over fresh fruit.

Yield: 2 cups

SPECIAL ITALIAN DRESSING

A great spread for submarine sandwiches.

1⅓ cups oil
⅓ cup tarragon vinegar
2 tablespoons garlic, minced
1 teaspoon salt
2 teaspoons fresh ground
  pepper
3 tablespoons fresh parsley,
  chopped
1 teaspoon oregano

1 teaspoon basil
⅓ cup pimento stuffed olives
¼ cup Parmesan cheese,
  grated
1 tablespoon plus 1 teaspoon
  lemon juice
2 teaspoons sugar
4 green onions with tops,
  coarsely chopped

Combine all ingredients in a blender and process. Chill.

Yield: 2½ cups dressing

DUNCAN VINAGRETTE DRESSING

3 heaping teaspoons Dijon
  mustard
1 teaspoon salt
1 teaspoon sugar
¼ teaspoon black pepper,
  coarsely ground

1 cup olive oil
½ cup garlic flavored red
  wine vinegar

Add first four ingredients to olive oil in a mixing bowl, blending well.
Slowly add vinegar and mix well.

Yield: approximately 2 cups dressing

MARILYN'S TARRAGON GREEN SALAD DRESSING

½ cup tarragon vinegar
1 cup oil
1 teaspoon dry mustard
½ teaspoon Worcestershire
  sauce

½ teaspoon each salt and
  pepper
¼ teaspoon celery seed
Powdered dillweed to taste

Combine all ingredients except dillweed in a jar or bottle. Allow to
chill for several hours. Sprinkle salad with dillweed, add dressing, and
toss.

Yield: 1½ cups

TOASTED CHEESE SANDWICHES

Serve with Beef and Veggie Soup.

½ pound box Old English
   cheese, softened
2 sticks butter, softened

⅛ teaspoon red pepper
9 slices extra thin sliced day
   old bread, crust trimmed

Preheat oven to 350°. Mix cheese and butter in a mixing bowl. Add red pepper. Take three slices of bread; spread cheese mixture on first slice, top with second piece of bread, then spread the top of that slice with cheese mixture, then finally top with last slice to make a three layered sandwich. Cut into quarters and spread mixture on all sides like an icing. Repeat with remaining bread. Bake 10 minutes.

Yield: 12 squares

BEST PIMENTO CHEESE SPREAD

This pimento spread will keep for three weeks in the refrigerator.

2 pounds sharp Cheddar
   cheese, shredded
3 hard boiled eggs, grated
1 large onion, grated
2 7-ounce cans whole
   pimentos, chopped, with
   juice
1 pint mayonnaise

3 tablespoons prepared
   mustard
3 tablespoons Worcestershire
   sauce
1½ teaspoons salt
½ teaspoon each pepper,
   onion salt, garlic salt, and
   celery salt

Stir all ingredients in a large mixing bowl until well blended. Mixture should be coarse and loose; it will firm when chilled.

Yield: 8 cups

CHICKEN SALAD SANDWICH SUPREME

To cut down on calories, serve on a lettuce leaf and garnish as desired. You may also use light mayonnaise.

2 cups chicken, cooked and diced
2 tablespoons green olives, chopped
¾ cup celery, chopped
¼ cup sliced almonds, toasted
2 tablespoons ripe olives, sliced
1 tablespoon sweet pickle relish
1 tablespoon dill pickle relish
2 hard boiled eggs, chopped
½ cup mayonnaise
1 teaspoon lemon juice

Combine all ingredients in a large mixing bowl. Chill until ready to serve. Serve on croissants.

Yield: 4 servings

PARSLEY AND BACON SANDWICHES

1 bunch parsley, chopped
½-¾ cup mayonnaise
1 8-ounce cream cheese, softened
2 pounds bacon, fried and crumbled
½ teaspoon garlic powder
1 stick butter, softened
2 loaves bread

Mix first four ingredients together. Combine garlic powder and butter. Spread one side of bread with parsley mixture and one side with butter mixture. Cut off crusts and slice into thirds.

Yield: approximately 2 dozen

STUFFED HAM SANDWICHES

Great for a pregame tailgate picnic.

1 loaf French or Italian bread, unsliced	2 tablespoons onion, finely chopped
¼ cup mayonnaise	¼ teaspoon salt
⅓ cup parsley, chopped	2 packages boiled ham, sliced
1 8-ounce package cream cheese, softened	2 dill pickles, sliced lengthwise into quarters
½ cup Cheddar cheese, shredded	

Split bread lengthwise and hollow out each half, leaving about one-quarter inch bread around each cavity. Spread mayonnaise over bread halves. Sprinkle parsley over mayonnaise. Blend cream cheese, Cheddar cheese, onion, and salt together in a small mixing bowl. Spoon into bread halves and spread. Roll each pickle slice inside two slices of ham. Place ham and pickle rolls end-to-end in scooped out section of bread half. Place the other half of bread on top to complete sandwich. Wrap tightly in plastic wrap and chill for several hours. Slice to serve.

Yield: approximately 6 servings

ASPARAGUS SANDWICHES

Pretty at a ladies' luncheon and wonderful with Hearty Cheese Soup.

1½ cups mayonnaise	2 loaves thin sliced sandwich bread
½ teaspoon lemon juice	
Dash of salt and paprika	2 10½-ounce cans asparagus spears, drained
½ teaspoon seasoned salt	

Combine first five ingredients. Trim crust off bread and roll flat. Spread each slice of bread with mayonnaise mixture. Place one asparagus spear on each slice of bread and roll up tightly. Place sandwiches, seam side down, in a container lined with moistened paper towels. Repeat until bread has all been used. Cover sandwiches with a moistened paper towel and chill overnight in a sealed container.

Yield: 48 sandwiches

PICANTE PIMENTO CHEESE SPREAD

This is great served with corn chips as well as a sandwich spread.

1½ pounds sharp Cheddar
  cheese, shredded
1 3-ounce package cream
  cheese, softened
1 tablespoon onion, finely
  minced

1 4-ounce jar chopped
  pimentos, undrained
½ cup mayonnaise
Freshly cracked black pepper
1 8-ounce jar hot picante
  sauce

Stir all ingredients together thoroughly. Chill.

Yield: 4 cups

MUSTARD SAUCE

Wonderful spread for ham sandwiches.

3 ounces dry mustard
1 cup white vinegar
1 cup sugar

1 teaspoon tumeric
¼ teaspoon salt
2 eggs, well beaten

Mix mustard and vinegar together in a small mixing bowl and allow to stand overnight. Add remaining ingredients. Place in the top of a double boiler and cook over medium heat, stirring occasionally until thick.

Yield: 1 cup

HOMEMADE MAYONNAISE

Be sure to add the oil slowly or the mayonnaise will not thicken.

2 egg yolks
1 teaspoon salt
1 teaspoon sugar
1 teaspoon dry mustard

½ teaspoon paprika
½ teaspoon red pepper
3 tablespoons lemon juice
2 cups light cooking oil

Combine all ingredients except oil together in a mixing bowl and blend with a mixer. Gradually add oil while mixing bowl is turning.

Yield: 2 cups

Breads, Eggs, and Cheese

Thank you for your financial support
of the following Junior League of Waco project:

The Children's Performing Arts Series

Four performances per year in the disciplines
of music and theater, targeted at 4 to 12 year-olds.

BISHOP'S BREAD

The legend accompanying this recipe states that this bread was made in olden times for the Bishop's house-to-house visits. The bread tastes like chocolate fruit cake.

3 eggs
1 cup sugar
1½ cups flour
1½ teaspoons baking powder
¼ teaspoon salt
1 cup dates, coarsely
   chopped
1 8-ounce package candied
   pineapple, chopped

1 cup maraschino cherries,
   reserve juice
1 cup pecans, coarsely
   chopped
1 6-ounce package
   semi-sweet chocolate chips

Preheat oven to 325°. Grease 9x5 inch loaf pan. Line bottom with greased waxed paper. Beat eggs and add sugar in a large mixing bowl. Sift dry ingredients together. Mix fruit and pecans with dry ingredients. Add chocolate chips. Mix into egg and sugar mixture; beat until stiff. Press batter into loaf pans. Bake 1 hour and 25 minutes. Remove loaf from pan when cool. Pour reserved cherry juice over loaf and wrap in foil. Let mellow for a day or so. Slice thin to serve.

Yield: 1 loaf

GREAT PUMPKIN BREAD

This is delicious thinly sliced and spread with a mixture of cream cheese and orange or pineapple marmalade.

1 cup plus 2 tablespoons oil
3 cups sugar
3 eggs
1 tablespoon vanilla
3 cups flour
1½ teaspoons cinnamon
1 teaspoon each cloves,
   ginger, and nutmeg

1 teaspoon salt
1 teaspoon baking powder
½ teaspoon baking soda
1 16-ounce can pumpkin
1 cup pecans, chopped

Preheat oven to 325°. Grease and flour a 9x5 inch loaf pan. Blend together oil, sugar, eggs, and vanilla. Set aside. Mix dry ingredients together and add to mixture. Add pumpkin and pecans and mix well. Bake for approximately 1 hour.

Yield: 1 loaf

BREAKFAST TEA RING

At Christmas, decorate this bread with green and red cherries. Sprinkle with colored sugar to give a wreath effect. This freezes well.

Dough:

3 egg yolks, beaten
2 sticks butter, softened
1 cup milk
4 cups flour

1 teaspoon salt
¼ cup sugar
1 tablespoon dry yeast
¼ cup water

Filling:

½ stick butter, melted
¼ cup sugar

1 tablespoon cinnamon
½ cup pecans, chopped

Frosting:

2 tablespoons butter, softened
1½ cups confectioners sugar

2 tablespoons hot water
1½ teaspoons vanilla

Preheat oven to 375°. Grease 9 inch cake pan. Set eggs and butter out for 30 minutes to reach room temperature. Heat milk to scalding. Remove from heat and cool. Combine dry ingredients. Cut in butter until mixture resembles meal. Dissolve yeast in warm water and set three minutes. Add yeast and egg yolks to dry ingredients. Add milk. Beat well by hand until completely mixed. Cover and chill overnight.

Combine sugar, cinnamon, and pecans for filling. Roll ½ of dough into a 9x12 inch rectangle and brush with melted butter. Sprinkle with ½ of the filling. Roll up in jelly roll form, starting with the shorter end. Place in pan. Moisten fingers and connect ends. Cut the dough with scissors partially through at 3 inch intervals. Arrange so that the cinnamon mixture is visable. Repeat with the other half of dough and filling. Cover and let rise for one hour.

While dough is rising, prepare frosting. Beat butter, confectioners sugar, and water in mixer. Stir in vanilla. Bake dough 20 minutes. Allow to cool and frost.

Yield: 2 rings

BLACKBERRY JAM BREAD

After bread comes out of the oven, punch small holes in it and ice with additional blackberry jam.

2 sticks butter, softened
2 cups sugar
4 eggs, separated
3 cups flour
2 teaspoons cinnamon
1 teaspoon each nutmeg,
   cloves and allspice

1 cup buttermilk
1 teaspoon baking soda
1 teaspoon vanilla
1 cup blackberry jam

Preheat oven to 300°. Grease and flour two 9x5 inch loaf pans or seven 6x3 inch loaf pans. Cream butter and sugar together. Beat the egg yolks and add to butter and sugar. Sift dry ingredients together (except for soda). Add soda to buttermilk in a separate measuring cup. Add dry ingredients to egg and butter mixture alternately with buttermilk. Mix together well. Add vanilla and blackberry jam.

Beat the four egg whites until fluffy. Fold into batter. Pour into pans. Bake at 300° for 15 minutes; turn up oven to 350° and bake for 15 additional minutes; turn up oven to 360° and bake for 30 final minutes.

Yield: 2 9x5 inch loaves or 7 6x3 inch loaves

MOM'S STRAWBERRY NUT BREAD

This bread is easy to make and is really moist. Makes great Christmas gifts for friends and neighbors.

3 cups flour
1 teaspoon soda
1 teaspoon salt
1 tablespoon cinnamon
2 cups sugar

4 eggs, beaten
2 cups frozen sliced
   strawberries, thawed
1¼ cups vegetable oil
1¼ cups nuts, chopped

Preheat oven to 350°. Grease six 6x3 inch or two 9x5 inch loaf pans. Sift dry ingredients together into a large mixing bowl. In another mixing bowl, combine eggs, strawberries, oil, and nuts. Make a well in the center of the dry ingredients. Add liquid mixture, stirring just enough to moisten the dry ingredients. Pour into pans and bake 40 minutes for small pans and 60 for large. Allow to cool 10 to 15 minutes and remove from pans.

Yield: 6 mini or 2 large loaves

ELIZA JANE'S GINGERBREAD

Mother's Lemon Cake Sauce also tastes delicious on top of this gingerbread.

1 cup shortening	⅛ teaspoon salt
1 cup sugar	2 cups flour
4 eggs	1 teaspoon soda
1 cup cane syrup	1 cup buttermilk
1 tablespoon ginger	1 teaspoon vanilla
2 tablespoons pumpkin pie	Juice of one orange
spice	1 cup brown sugar

Preheat oven to 350°. Grease 11x13 inch pan. Cream shortening and sugar in a large mixing bowl. Beat in eggs, one at a time. Slowly beat in syrup. Sift together dry ingredients and add alternately with buttermilk. Add vanilla. Bake for 55 to 60 minutes. Blend orange juice with brown sugar and spread on gingerbread while still warm.

Yield: approximately 10 servings

BETTY'S WHIPPED CREAM SAUCE

Also delicious served on warm gingerbread.

½ pint whipping cream	½ teaspoon cinnamon
2 tablespoons honey or 3	
tablespoons confectioners	
sugar	

Beat cream well in a mixing bowl until just before it holds a peak. Add honey and cinnamon and complete beating until it forms a peak. Chill.

Yield: 1 cup

FRESH CRANBERRY TEA BREAD

Wrap bread in red cellophane and tie with a festive bow to give out at the holiday season.

3 cups flour
3 teaspoons baking powder
1½ teaspoons salt
¾ teaspoon soda
1 stick butter or ½ cup
  shortening, melted
1½ cups sugar
2 eggs

¾ cup fresh squeezed
  orange juice
1¼ tablespoons orange rind,
  grated
¾ cup pecans, chopped
2¼ cups fresh cranberries,
  coarsely chopped
1 cup raisins (optional)

Preheat oven to 350°. Grease 9x5 inch loaf pan. Sift first three ingredients together and set aside. In a large mixing bowl, mix soda and melted butter; gradually stir in sugar. Beat in eggs one at a time. Add flour alternately with orange juice. Stir orange rind, nuts, cranberries, and raisins into batter. Bake for 1½ hours. Remove from pan to cool.

Yield: 1 loaf

BANANA DATE BREAD

Save your leftover coffee cans to bake this bread in. Store the bread in the cans and save kitchen clean up time. Slice baked bread into thin rounds and spread with cream cheese mixed with pineapple preserves. Top with another bread slice and serve as a finger sandwich.

4 cups sugar
4 cups banana, mashed
1 cup oil
5¼ cups flour
1 teaspoon salt
1 teaspoon cinnamon

½ teaspoon nutmeg
4 teaspoons baking soda
2 cups pecans, chopped
18 dates, finely chopped
2 teaspoons vanilla

Grease and flour five one-pound coffee cans. Preheat oven to 350°. In a large bowl of electric mixer beat sugar with bananas. Add oil and blend well. Sift dry ingredients together reserving 1 cup for later use. Add flour mixture to bananas on low speed. Combine reserved flour with dates and nuts; blend with batter. Add vanilla and pour into cans. Bake 1 hour and 15 minutes. Remove from oven and invert cans on cake racks to cool. Remove cans when cool. This bread freezes well. Just leave in cans, cover with lid, and store in freezer.

Yield: 5 loaves

BRENDA'S BLUEBERRY COFFEE CAKE

Try this with Betty's Whipped Cream Sauce.

1 18¾-ounce package
  Pillsbury Plus Lemon Cake
  mix
1 stick butter or margarine,
  softened

⅔ cup milk
2 eggs
1 16-ounce can blueberries,
  drained

Icing:
½ cup confectioners sugar
1 teaspoon butter, softened

2½ teaspoons milk

Preheat oven to 350°. Grease and flour a 9x13 inch pan. Combine cake mix and butter in a large bowl until crumbly. Reserve 1¼ cups of the mixture for topping. Add milk and eggs to the remaining crumb mixture and beat two minutes at the highest mixer speed. Pour into pan. Arrange blueberries evenly over batter. Sprinkle with reserved crumbs. Bake for 30 to 45 minutes or until toothpick inserted in center comes out clean. Cool completely. Mix confectioners sugar with butter and milk; drizzle on top of cake. Refrigerate leftovers.

Yield: 12 servings

CRANBERRY COFFEE CAKE

To enjoy this year round, be sure to buy extra cranberries during the holiday season and freeze.

2 cups cranberries
½ cup nuts, chopped
1½ cups sugar

2 eggs, beaten
1 cup flour
1½ sticks butter, melted

Preheat oven to 325°. Sprinkle cranberries in a 9x9 inch foil pan. Sprinkle nuts and ½ cup sugar over cranberries. Add remaining sugar to eggs in a mixing bowl and blend. Add flour and butter, mixing well. Pour over cranberries. Bake 1 hour.

Yield: approximately 8 servings

BUTTERY SOUR CREAM COFFEE CAKE

1 stick butter or margarine,
  softened
1 cup sugar
2 eggs
1 cup sour cream

1 teaspoon vanilla
2 cups flour
1 teaspoon baking powder
½ teaspoon salt

Topping:
⅓ cup brown sugar, firmly
  packed
¼ cup sugar
1 teaspoon ground
  cinnamon

¾ cup pecans, chopped
1 stick butter or margarine

Preheat oven to 325°. Grease one 11x7 inch pan. Cream butter and sugar in a mixing bowl until light and fluffy. Add eggs and mix well. Stir in sour cream and vanilla. Add flour, baking powder, and salt; mix well. Combine topping ingredients except butter in a small mixing bowl until well blended. Pour batter into baking pan and sprinkle with topping. Slice ½ stick of butter and dot over batter. Cut through batter using a knife to give it a marbled effect. Bake for 35 minutes or until lightly browned. Spread remaining ½ stick butter over warm cake immediately until melted.

Yield: 10 servings

STRAWBERRY COFFEE CAKE

Serve this on Christmas morning!

1 8-ounce package cream
  cheese, softened
1 stick butter, softened
¾ cup sugar
¼ cup milk
2 eggs
1 teaspoon vanilla
2 cups flour

1 teaspoon baking powder
½ teaspoon baking soda
1 18-ounce jar strawberry
  preserves
¼ cup brown sugar, packed
½ cup pecans, chopped
½ stick butter, melted

Grease a 9x13 inch pan. Preheat oven to 350°. Cream together cream cheese and 1 stick butter. Add next three ingredients, beating well. Add vanilla. Combine flour, baking powder, and soda; blend with cream cheese mixture. Beat well. Batter will be stiff. Spread ½ batter into pan. Ice evenly with preserves and dot with remaining batter. Mix brown sugar and pecans to sprinkle over top. Drizzle with melted butter. Bake for 40 minutes.

Yield: 8-10 servings

CELEBRATION COFFEE CAKE

1 18¾-ounce box yellow
  cake mix
1½ cups sour cream
4 eggs

2 9.9-ounce boxes coconut-
  pecan frosting mix
1 stick butter or margarine,
  cubed

Grease and flour a 9x13 inch pan. Preheat oven to 350°. Blend cake mix with sour cream and eggs. Pour ½ of the batter into pan. Sprinkle with one box dried frosting mix. Repeat layers. Dot top with butter. Bake 35-40 minutes. Serve warm.

Yield: 8-10 servings

SANDRA'S PUMPKIN ROLL

You may roll this starting with the long end; slice and serve as a pick up food. Try adding a bit of orange marmalade and chopped pecan to the filling.

3 eggs
1 cup sugar
⅔ cup canned pumpkin,
  mashed
1 teaspoon lemon juice
¾ cup flour
1 teaspoon baking powder

2 teaspoons cinnamon
1 teaspoon ginger
1 teaspoon nutmeg
½ teaspoon salt
¼ cup confectioners
  sugar

Filling:
1 cup confectioners sugar
1 8-ounce package cream
  cheese, softened

1 3-ounce package cream
  cheese, softened
½ stick butter, softened
½ teaspoon vanilla

Preheat oven to 375°. Grease and flour a jelly roll pan. Beat eggs for 5 minutes in large bowl on high speed of mixer. Gradually stir in sugar and beat well. Add pumpkin and lemon juice. Sift flour with baking powder and spices. Add to pumpkin batter, blending well. Spread batter in pan and bake for 15 minutes. Turn out of pan immediately onto a towel sprinkled with ¼ cup confectioners sugar. Starting at narrow end, roll towel and cake together in jelly roll form. Cool and unroll. Combine ingredients for filling, beating until smooth. Spread filling on top of cake; re-roll. Cover and chill with seam side down. Sprinkle with confectioners sugar before slicing. Slice and serve.

Yield: 12 servings

SPICY BRAN MUFFINS

4 cups Kellogg's All Bran
   cereal
2 cups Nabisco 100% Bran
   cereal
2 teaspoons salt
2 cups boiling water

1 quart buttermilk
1 cup shortening
3 cups sugar
4 eggs
5 cups flour
5 teaspoons baking soda

Mix cereals in a large bowl. Add salt, water, and buttermilk. Cream shortening and sugar; add eggs one at a time, beating well after each addition. Cream with cereal mixture. Blend in flour and soda. Mix well. Store covered in refrigerator. Will keep for several weeks. To cook, grease miniature muffin tins; fill 2/3 full, and bake for 15 minutes at 350°.

Yield: 3-4 quarts or 18 dozen miniature muffins

CINNAMON MUFFINS

⅓ cup margarine, softened
½ cup sugar
1 egg
1½ cups flour
1 teaspoon baking powder
1 teaspoon salt

¼ teaspoon nutmeg
½ cup milk
1 teaspoon vanilla
6 tablespoons butter, melted
½ cup sugar
2 teaspoons cinnamon

Preheat oven to 350°. Grease and flour small muffin tins. Mix first three ingredients together in a medium mixing bowl. Sift together flour, baking powder, salt, and nutmeg. Add flour mixture and milk alternately to above egg mixture and blend well. Add vanilla. Fill muffin tins ⅔ full and bake for 15 minutes. Remove immediately. Mix together sugar and cinnamon. Roll muffins in butter, then sugar mixture. Cool on wire racks.

Yield: approximately 3 dozen small muffins

OATMEAL BANANA MUFFINS

These nutritious muffins are good for breakfast and also great packed in your children's lunch for dessert.

½ cup sugar
1 stick margarine, softened
2 eggs
3 medium bananas, mashed
¾ cup honey
1½ cups flour

1 teaspoon baking soda
¾ teaspoon salt
1 teaspoon baking powder
1 cup quick cooking rolled oats

Preheat oven to 375°. Grease medium muffin tins or use paper liners. Cream together sugar and margarine in a medium mixing bowl. Beat in eggs, bananas, and honey. In a separate bowl, stir together the dry ingredients. Add to the creamed mixture, beating until just blended. Stir in oats. Fill muffin tins ⅔ full. Bake for 18 to 20 minutes. Remove and cool on wire racks.

Yield: 24 medium muffins

ORANGE BRUNCH MUFFINS

Try these muffins split in half, spread with quince jelly and thin slices of smoked turkey or country ham.

2 sticks butter, softened
1 cup sugar
2 eggs
1 teaspoon soda

1 cup buttermilk
2 cups flour, sifted
Grated rind of 2 oranges
½ cup golden raisins

Sauce:
Juice of 2 oranges or ½ cup orange juice

1 cup brown sugar

Preheat oven to 375°. Grease miniature muffin tins. Cream butter and sugar together in a mixing bowl. Add eggs and blend well. Dissolve soda in buttermilk. Add flour and buttermilk alternately to creamed mixture, mixing thoroughly. Add orange rind and raisins. Fill muffin tins ½ full and bake for 15 minutes. Mix orange juice and brown sugar thoroughly and spoon about 1 teaspoon of sauce on warm muffins.

Yield: approximately 36 small muffins

EASY CARAMEL ROLLS

1 cup pecans, chopped
1 24-count package frozen
  dinner rolls
1 3-ounce package regular
  butterscotch pudding mix

¾ cup brown sugar
1 stick butter

Generously butter a bundt pan. Sprinkle nuts in the bottom of the pan.
Place frozen rolls on top of nuts, narrow end down, side by side, but do
not stack. There will be an inner and outer ring. Mix pudding and
brown sugar together and sprinkle over rolls. Cut butter into cubes
and place on top. Cover with a towel and allow to rise overnight. Bake
for 30 minutes in a preheated 350° oven. Turn out of pan onto serving
platter. If not serving immediately, rub a small amount of butter over
the cake to keep the sugar from crystalizing.

Yield: 24 rolls

FUNNEL CAKES

*Delicious for breakfast. If you add 1 cup of chopped apples to the
batter, you have apple fritters.*

1¼ cups flour
⅛ teaspoon salt
1 egg, slightly beaten
1 teaspoon vanilla
1 cup apple juice

1 teaspoon baking powder
Oil
1 cup confectioners sugar
1 tablespoon cinnamon

Mix first six ingredients together in a large mixing bowl to make batter.
Heat two inches of oil to about 400°. Take ½ cup of batter, place in a
small funnel while holding index finger over the funnel hole. Hold over
skillet of hot oil and release finger and swirl funnel around and across
to form a circle. Turn when golden brown. Place on plate to drain. Sift
together confectioners sugar and cinnamon and sprinkle over tops of
cakes.

Yield: 3 cakes

MOTHER'S PANCAKES

Why buy a mix when this is so easy to prepare and delicious?

2 cups flour, unsifted
1½ teaspoons salt
4 teaspoons baking powder, heaping
2 tablespoons sugar

2 eggs, beaten
1½ cups milk
4 tablespoons oil or melted shortening

Preheat griddle or skillet to medium-high. Sift dry ingredients together and set aside. Beat eggs in separate bowl. Add milk and oil blending well. Stir in dry ingredients. Spoon onto griddle or skillet. Flip when outside edges turn lightly brown.

Yield: 4 servings

STEVE'S FAVORITE WAFFLES

2 egg whites
2 cups flour
4 teaspoons baking powder
½ teaspoon salt

2 tablespoons sugar
1¾ cups milk
2 egg yolks, beaten
1 stick butter, melted

Preheat waffle iron. Beat egg whites until stiff and set aside. Sift dry ingredients together. Gradually add milk, egg yolks, and butter. Stir well. Fold in egg whites. Pour into waffle iron and bake until golden brown.

Yield: 6 servings

BAKED APPLE PANCAKES

2 eggs, separated
3 tablespoons sugar
3 tablespoons flour
3 tablespoons milk
Dash of salt

1 cup pared apple, finely
  diced
1 tablespoon lemon juice
2 tablespoons sugar
1 teaspoon cinnamon

Preheat oven to 400°. Butter 10-inch iron skillet and place in oven to heat, taking care not to burn butter. Beat egg whites until frothy and gradually add 3 tablespoons sugar, beating until stiff. In a separate bowl, beat egg yolks; add flour, milk, and salt. Fold in apple, lemon juice and egg whites. Pour into hot pan. Mix 2 tablespoons sugar and cinnamon; sprinkle on top. Bake 10 minutes until glazed and puffy. Serve immediately.

Yield: approximately 4 servings

HEAVENLY FRENCH TOAST

Make this the night before and cook the next morning. It is delicious made with homemade bread or frozen loaf bread, baked and sliced.

2 tablespoons corn syrup,
  light or dark
1 stick butter or margarine
1 cup brown sugar, firmly
  packed

10-12 slices white bread
5 eggs
1½ cups milk
1 teaspoon vanilla

Combine first three ingredients in a small saucepan and simmer over low heat until syrupy. Pour in the bottom of a 9x13 inch pyrex dish. Place bread on top. Beat together eggs, milk, and vanilla in a small bowl. Pour eggs over the bread. Cover dish and place in refrigerator overnight. Uncover and bake in a preheated oven at 350° for 45 minutes. Serve hot or warm. Slice into squares to serve.

Yield: approximately 8 servings

LYNN'S LEMON OR ORANGE BISCUITS

These biscuits are great for breakfast or brunch. They are easy to pre-pare, and the ingredients are things you normally have on hand.

1 stick butter, melted
¾ cup sugar
3-4 tablespoons lemon or
orange juice
½ teaspoon lemon or orange
peel, grated

2 10-count cans refrigerated
biscuits
½ teaspoon nutmeg
⅛ cup sugar

Preheat oven to 375°. Combine butter, ¾ cup sugar, lemon juice, and lemon peel in a saucepan and heat until sugar has dissolved. Pour sauce into a 9x13 inch baking dish. Cut biscuits into fourths. Place biscuit pieces into dish, rolling them in butter mixture so they are covered. Combine nutmeg and sugar. Sprinkle over top of biscuits. Bake for 25 minutes or until brown on top.

Yield: approximately 10 servings

CUISINART BEATEN BISCUITS

These are traditionally served with Virginia ham during the holidays; however, your family might just as soon forget the Virginia ham and stuff themselves with these instead. They make good Christmas treat gifts; they keep in tins for a long time and may also be frozen.

2 cups unbleached flour,
sifted
1 teaspoon salt

1 stick butter, softened
½ cup ice water

Preheat oven to 350°. Place flour and salt in cuisinart bowl. Using steel blade, blend briefly. Cut butter into small pieces and process until butter and flour are mixed. Pour cold water through the cuisinart tube and blend until dough forms a ball on the blade.

Roll dough out on a floured surface, placing a fold in the dough to make 2 layers. Roll as thin as possible using additional flour (as little as possible). Cut with a small biscuit cutter. Pierce the tops with a fork several times to prevent puffing. Place on baking sheet two inches apart. Bake 30 to 40 minutes or until lightly browned.

Yield: 32 small biscuits

IRRESISTIBLE BACON CORNBREAD MADELEINES

The name says it all. They are pretty and unusual baked in the madeleine pans but work just as well in muffin tins.

4 slices bacon
3 green onions with tops,
  minced
Shortening, melted
1 cup white cornmeal
1 cup flour

½ cup sugar
4 teaspoons baking powder
¼ teaspoon salt
1 cup milk
1 egg, slightly beaten

Preheat oven to 350°. Grease madeleine pans. Fry bacon and drain. Crumble and set aside. Saute onions in the bacon drippings. Remove and drain on paper towels. Pour bacon drippings into a measuring cup. Add melted shortening to equal ½ cup. Combine cornmeal, flour, sugar, baking powder, and salt. Add milk, egg, and the reserved bacon drippings. Beat until fairly smooth. Add crumbled bacon and sauteed onion. Pour batter into madeleine pans, filling ½ full. Bake for 12 to 15 minutes or until golden brown.

Yield: 2 dozen

HOT WATER CORNBREAD

Hot Water Cornbread is hard to beat. Keep the family out of the kitchen when you're making it, or you might find the whole pan gone before you can get it to the table.

Oil
1 stick margarine
3 tablespoons sugar
3½ cups boiling water

2 cups white cornmeal
1 teaspoon baking powder
1 teaspoon salt

Preheat oven to 450°. Pour small amount of oil in jelly roll pan and heat. Place margarine and sugar in water and let come to a boil. Mix cornmeal, salt, and baking powder together; add all at once to the boiling water, stirring constantly until it leaves the side of the pan, 2 or 3 minutes. Remove from heat and allow to cool before shaping into patties. Roll mixture into small patties and place on hot pan. Bake for 45 minutes to 1 hour, turning about halfway through to brown both sides.

Yield: approximately 24 muffins

BUTTERMILK BREAD, LOVE JAN

If you prefer whole wheat bread, substitute half of the flour with whole wheat flour. This bread makes excellent toast for breakfast.

1½ cups buttermilk
¾ cup sugar
2¾ teaspoons salt
1 stick margarine
1½ cups very warm water

1½ packages dry yeast
8 cups flour
¼ plus ⅛ teaspoon baking
  soda

Preheat oven to 350°. Grease three 9x5 inch loaf pans. Scald milk, stir in sugar, salt, and margarine. Cool to lukewarm. Measure warm water into a large bowl, add yeast. Add scalded milk. Stir in 3 cups flour and the soda. Beat until smooth, then add the rest of the flour and beat until flour is absorbed. Cover and let rise in the same bowl until double in size, about 1 hour.

Shape and place into pans. Let rise until double, about 1 hour. Bake for 25 to 30 minutes or until golden brown.

Yield: 3 loaves

WONDERFUL WHITE BREAD

A bread that requires no kneading.

2 packages dry yeast
1 cup water, tepid
¾ cup sugar
¾ cup shortening

1½ teaspoons salt
1 cup water, boiling
2 eggs, beaten
6 cups flour

Preheat oven to 350°. Grease four 7x5 inch loaf pans. Soften yeast in tepid water with 1 teaspoon sugar for 5 minutes. Combine sugar, shortening, and salt in a large bowl and pour boiling water over mixture. Blend with an electric mixer and allow to cool. Add beaten eggs. Add softened yeast and gradually add flour with mixer until dough becomes too stiff; blend in remaining flour by hand.

Cover bowl with an inverted plate in the refrigerator so dough may rise. Let rise until double in size, about 3 to 4 hours. Separate into four portions and place in loaf pans. Let rise again until doubled, about 30 to 45 minutes. Bake for 35 minutes. If browning too fast, cover with a paper towel.

Yield: 4 loaves

PITA BREAD

5 cups flour	⅛ cup oil
2 teaspoons salt	1½ packages dry yeast
2 teaspoons sugar	2½ cups lukewarm water

Preheat oven to (gas) 425° or (electric) 550°. Mix first three ingredients together in a mixing bowl. Make a well in the center and pour oil into the center. Dissolve yeast in lukewarm water and pour into flour mixture. Mix well, adding more water if the mixture is too dry. Place dough on a lightly floured surface and knead for 5 to 7 minutes until dough is smooth and elastic and does not stick to your hands. Cover with a tea towel or sheet and let rise in a warm place until double in size, about 45 minutes.

Shape dough into 4 or 5 large balls or 8 to 10 small balls, the size of an orange. Roll out the first ball into a round flat loaf. Place loaf on a tea towel or sheet and keep covered. Continue rolling the rest of the balls into flat loaves and covering after each one. Starting with the first loaf, place on a cookie sheet on bottom rack of oven; bake for 3 to 5 minutes until puffed and brown on the bottom. Place cookie sheet on the top shelf of the oven and bake or broil until brown. Cook large loaves one at a time and smaller ones 3 to 4 at a time. Allow to cool for an hour; stack together and press the air out. Store in a plastic bag. Can be refrigerated for 2 to 3 days or frozen.

Yield: 4-5 large or 8-10 small loaves

FRENCH BREAD WITH GARLIC BUTTER

Mix all the herbs into softened butter and store in an airtight container in the refrigerator. Use as a spread on bread or on fish, steaks, or vegetables.

½ teaspoon oregano	¼ teaspoon garlic salt
⅛ teaspoon sweet basil	½ teaspoon minced onion
1 teaspoon garlic powder	1 pound butter or margarine
½ teaspoon parsley	1 large loaf French bread

Preheat oven to 325°. Finely crush the oregano and sweet basil. Combine all ingredients in a microwave safe container or saucepan. Melt the butter with the added spices in microwave or on stove. Cut the bread into slices and spread the slices with the melted butter. Wrap in aluminum foil and bake until warm.

Yield: 1 loaf

MONKEY BREAD

The smell of this bread will make your mouth water. It is light and has a wonderful flavor. Best served the day it is baked.

1 tablespoon dry yeast	1 cup milk
½ cup warm water	3-4 cups flour
½ cup sugar	1 stick margarine or
1 teaspoon salt	butter, melted
½ stick margarine or butter, softened	

Preheat oven to 400°. Dissolve yeast in warm water in large bowl. Combine next 4 ingredients in a saucepan and heat until warmed. Add to the yeast. Beat in flour to make the dough stiff. Place in a greased bowl and grease top of dough. Let rise for 2 hours. Punch down. Roll out on floured surface into ¼ to ½ inch thickness. Cut into squares or break into small pieces. Dip each piece in melted butter. Place side by side in a tube pan making two layers. Pour remaining butter over dough. Let rise until doubles in size, about 45 minutes. Bake for 25 minutes.

Yield: 1 large round loaf

WHOLE WHEAT DILLY BREAD

This hearty bread is great for sandwiches, stews or with cheese instead of crackers.

2 tablespoons butter, melted	1 teaspoon dillweed
2 cups cottage cheese	1 tablespoon onion, grated
2 eggs	¾ cup Cheddar cheese, shredded
2 packages dry yeast	½ teaspoon baking soda
½ cup warm water	5-6 cups whole wheat flour
½ teaspoon sugar	Butter
2 teaspoons salt	Salt
4 tablespoons sugar	
1 tablespoon dill seed	

Grease three 9x5 inch loaf pans. Combine butter, cottage cheese, and eggs. Bring to room temperature. Dissolve yeast in warm water with ½ teaspoon sugar for 10 minutes. Combine cottage cheese mixture and yeast. Add salt, 4 tablespoons sugar, dill seed, dillweed, onion, cheese, and soda. Mix in flour until it forms a stiff dough. Knead on floured surface about 10 minutes until dough is elastic.

Divide into 3 loaves and place in pans. Let rise until double in size, about 1 hour. Bake for 25-30 minutes in 350° oven. Remove from pan and cool on wire racks. While loaves are still warm brush with melted butter and salt.

Yield: 3 loaves

ONION BATTER BREAD

This bread can be made in a round casserole or a round pan.

1 package dry yeast
½ cup warm water
1 cup creamed cottage
  cheese, heated to
  lukewarm
2 tablespoons sugar
1 tablespoon instant minced
  onion
1 tablespoon butter, softened

2 teaspoons dill seed
1 teaspoon salt
¼ teaspoon baking soda
1 egg
2½ cups flour
Butter
Salt

Soften yeast in water. Combine next 7 ingredients to yeast. Add flour in 3 additions to make the dough stiff. Use a low speed on the mixer for the first addition. Cover and let rise in warm place about 1 hour or until doubled in size. Stir down dough. No kneading is necessary. Turn dough into well-greased 8 inch round or 9x5 inch loaf pan. Let rise again. Bake at 350° for 40-50 minutes until golden brown. Brush with melted butter and sprinkle with salt while still warm.

Yield: 1 loaf

HERBED ROLLS

You won't believe these are canned biscuits!

1 stick margarine or butter
1½ teaspoons parsley flakes
½ teaspoon dillweed
1 teaspoon onion flakes

2 teaspoons Parmesan
  cheese, grated
1 10-count can buttermilk
  biscuits

Melt margarine in 9 inch pan and add herbs and cheese. Mix and let stand 30 minutes. Cut each biscuit in half lengthwise. Place in pan coating all sides. Bake 12-15 minutes in 425° oven.

Yield: 6-8 servings

SYDNE'S EASY CHEESY ROLLS

Don't let the simplicity of this recipe fool you; these are very good. Be sure and make plenty because guests have been known to eat three of these at a time.

1 5-ounce jar Old English
   cheese spread, softened
1 stick butter, softened

2 drops Tabasco sauce
1 8-12 count package Vienna
   or other large dinner rolls

Preheat oven according to package directions on rolls. Stir together cheese spread, butter, and Tabasco sauce. Cut slices down middle of bread. Spread cheese mixture onto and inside slits of rolls. Bake according to directions on rolls.

Yield: 8-12 rolls

BRAN ROLLS

These rolls are a hit with everyone and are almost impossible to ruin. Any leftovers are great buttered and toasted for breakfast.

2 yeast cakes
1 cup lukewarm water
1 cup shortening
⅔ cup sugar
1 cup bran
1½ teaspoons salt

1 cup boiling water
2 eggs, beaten
6 cups flour, sifted
1 stick butter, melted to
   grease pan

Dissolve yeast cakes in lukewarm water in a large bowl. Place shortening, sugar, bran, and salt in a small mixing bowl. Add boiling water. Cover the bowl and let it stand 5 to 10 minutes. Add beaten eggs to this mixture. Pour combined mixture into large bowl with softened yeast and water. Add flour, one cup at a time, stirring with a spoon until all has been added. Cover and put in refrigerator overnight.

Place the dough on a floured pastry cloth. Knead several times and roll to about ¼-inch thickness. Cut with a 1½ inch cutter. Place on a jelly roll pan that has been greased with melted butter. Allow to rise about two hours. Bake for 15 to 20 minutes in preheated 400° oven.

Yield: approximately 4 dozen small rolls

MOTHER'S EASY HOT ROLLS

This dough will keep several days in the refrigerator.

1 package dry yeast
2 cups lukewarm water
1 teaspoon salt
3 tablespoons butter-flavored
  shortening, melted

½ cup sugar
1 egg, beaten
6-7 cups flour

Dissolve yeast in warm water. Add remaining ingredients except flour. Beat in flour one cup at a time until dough is stiff. Place dough in a greased bowl and allow to rise in a warm place until doubled. Place in refrigerator until needed. About 2 hours before baking, pinch off dough and shape into rolls. Place into greased pans and let rise until doubled. Bake at 350° for 10-12 minutes

Yield: 3 dozen rolls

BUTTERFLAKE BUTTERMILK ROLLS

1 package active dry yeast
2 tablespoons warm water
1 tablespoon sugar
4 tablespoons butter
½ cup warm, mashed
  potatoes

1 cup buttermilk, room
  temperature
1 egg
1½ teaspoons salt
3½-4 cups unbleached flour,
  sifted

Preheat oven to 425°. Grease muffin pans. Dissolve yeast in warm water with ½ teaspoon sugar. Set aside until foamy. In a bowl, stir butter into hot potatoes. Cool to tepid. In a large bowl, combine potatoes, yeast, buttermilk, egg, remaining sugar, and salt until well blended. Beat in about 2½ cups flour to make a smooth batter. Then add the remaining flour to make a soft dough. Knead, either by hand or in an electric mixer with a dough hook, until smooth and elastic.

Grease a large bowl. Put dough in the prepared bowl turning to butter the top; let rise in a warm place until doubled in bulk, 1 to 1½ hours. Punch down the dough and shape as desired. Place in pans. Cover loosely and let rise until double in bulk. To freeze for future use, seal tightly with waxed paper, then foil. Bake 12 to 15 minutes until golden brown.

Yield: approximately 20 rolls

CAPPY'S ROLLS

Wait until you taste these! You only touch the dough once.

¼ cup shortening
¼ cup sugar
½ tablespoon salt
¼ cup water
2 eggs

1½ packages dry yeast
¾ cup ice water
3 cups flour
1 stick butter, melted

Preheat oven to 375°. Grease a deep baking pan. Melt shortening, sugar, salt, and water in a saucepan over medium heat, stirring until dissolved. Remove from heat and cool to lukewarm.

Place eggs and yeast in a mixing bowl and mix with an electric mixer on medium speed until yeast is dissolved. Add shortening and ice water and blend well. Add flour slowly to mixture and mix slowly with dough hooks, until dough pulls away from sides of mixer. Cover with plastic wrap and refrigerate for 2 hours. Remove from refrigerator 2 hours before baking. Use mixer to bring back to dough consistency. Roll dough out on floured board and cut with biscuit cutter, dipped in melted butter and place in pan. Fold once and punch with one finger to secure fold. Cover with cardboard, let rise in a warm place until dough doubles in size. Bake for 10 to 15 minutes or until lightly browned.

Yield: 30 rolls

GRANDMA'S YORKSHIRE PUDDING

Serve with roast beef and gravy.

Shortening
1 egg
1 cup milk

1 cup flour
½ teaspoon salt

Melt shortening in jelly roll pan at 475°. Shortening should be ½ inch thick and heated to smoking. Combine egg, milk, flour, and salt in a blender. Pour mixture evenly and quickly into pan. Do not remove pan from oven; just open oven door, pull out shelf, pour batter, and close door quickly. Bake 15 minutes until batter is puffed and nicely brown. Pour off grease immediately after pan is removed from oven.

Yield: approximately 6 servings

POPOVERS

Serve these right out of the oven with butter and Peachy Keen Preserves.

1 cup flour, sifted	**2 eggs**
1 cup milk	**½ teaspoon salt**

Do not preheat oven. Grease medium size muffin tins. Mix all ingredients by hand until smooth. Fill muffin tins ⅔ full. Place on bottom rack of the oven. Bake for 40 minutes at 400°.

Yield: 8 popovers

CRANBERRY BUTTER

Spread on hot rolls or biscuits. You may substitute cranberries with fresh strawberries.

1½ cups confectioners sugar	**1 stick butter, softened**
1 cup cranberries, fresh or frozen	**1 teaspoon lemon juice**

Combine all ingredients together in a food processor. Process with the chopping blade until berries are chopped.

Yield: 1 cup

CALICO EGGS

A tasty and easy breakfast dish that is perfect for spur of the moment weekend company.

12 eggs	**1-2 avocados, chopped**
3 ounces cream cheese, softened	**1-2 tomatoes, chopped**

Scramble eggs in a large skillet over medium heat. When eggs are almost done, add cream cheese, stirring to heat. Remove from heat and add avocado and tomato.

Yield: 6 servings

SCRAMBLED EGGS
AND MUSHROOMS AU GRATIN

The rave reviews you receive from your guests on this dish will be well worth your effort.

1 pound fresh mushrooms, sliced	2½ cups milk, heated
1½ sticks butter	½ cup whipping cream
2 tablespoons shallots, minced	Fresh lemon juice to taste
Salt and pepper to taste	16 eggs
6 tablespoons flour	1 cup combined Parmesan, Cheddar, and Swiss cheese, grated

In a small skillet saute mushrooms in 3 tablespoons butter for 5 to 6 minutes or until barely beginning to brown. Stir in shallots and toss over moderate heat for 1 to 2 minutes. Season to taste with salt and pepper and set aside. This can be done a day ahead; bring to room temperature before using.

To prepare sauce, melt 5 tablespoons butter in a heavy saucepan. Blend in flour and stir over moderate heat until butter and flour froth together without coloring. Remove from heat and vigorously beat in milk with a wire whisk until thoroughly blended. Beat in half the cream; salt and pepper to taste. Boil slowly, stirring for 4 to 5 minutes. Thin sauce with additional cream, beaten in by driblets. Sauce should coat the spoon but not be thick. Season to taste. Beat in drops of lemon juice to taste. Remove from heat and float a tablespoon of cream on top to prevent a skin from forming.

Beat eggs in a bowl until just blended. Melt 3 tablespoons butter in a large skillet. Pour eggs into skillet and cook slowly for 2 to 3 minutes, stirring rapidly until they scramble into very soft curds. The eggs need to be slighty underdone; they will finish cooking under the broiler. Remove from heat.

To assemble casserole, spoon a layer of the sauce in a 9x12 inch baking dish. Sprinkle one-third cheese mixture over sauce and top with half of the eggs. Fold one cup of the sauce into the mushrooms and spoon over the eggs, top with one-third more of the cheese. Cover with remaining eggs and sauce. Sprinkle with cheese and dot with butter. At this point eggs can set an hour or so at room temperature. Preheat broiler to very hot and broil until lightly browned. Serve immediately.

Yield: 8 servings

EGGS GRUYERE CASSEROLE

Prepare your casserole by layering cheese and bacon before you go to bed. Half of your work is done before the next morning.

1 6-ounce package Gruyere
   cheese wedges
10 slices bacon, crisply
   cooked and crumbled

10-12 eggs
½-¾ cup whipping cream
Pepper to taste

Preheat oven to 350°. Generously grease 9x13 inch baking dish. Cut five cheese wedges into 4 slices each, reserving one wedge, and cover bottom of baking dish. Sprinkle bacon on top of cheese. Carefully crack eggs over top of bacon and cheese as uniformly as possible. Spoon cream carefully over top of egg yolks. Shred reserved cheese wedge and sprinkle over top. Sprinkle lightly with pepper. Bake uncovered for 25 to 30 minutes or until eggs are set.

Yield: 12 servings

SAUSAGE-CHEESE SQUARES

Serve this for breakfast or brunch with hot fruit and muffins.

2 cups Bisquick baking mix
½ cup cold water
¼ pound spicy bulk sausage
¼ cup green onions with
   tops, finely chopped

¾ cup mayonnaise
35 medium mushrooms
2 cups Cheddar cheese,
   shredded
Dash of paprika

Preheat oven to 350°. Grease 9x13 inch casserole dish. In a bowl mix Bisquick and water until soft dough forms; beat vigorously 20 strokes. Press dough into bottom of dish with floured hands. Cook sausage in a skillet until browned and drain well.

In a large bowl mix together sausage, onions, and mayonnaise. Remove stems from mushrooms and finely chop stems. Stir stems into sausage mixture. Fill mushroom caps with sausage. Place mushrooms in rows on dough; sprinkle with cheese and paprika. Cover pan loosely with foil and bake for 20 minutes. Remove foil and continue baking until cheese is bubbly, about 5 to 10 minutes. Cut into squares.

Yield: approximately 35 small squares

EGG AND CHEESE PUFF

This is an old favorite that is great for overnight company or a brunch.

16 slices bread, crust
  removed
Butter or margarine
½ pound Cheddar cheese,
  shredded

2 tablespoons chives
6 eggs
1 quart milk
1½ teaspoons salt
¼ teaspoon white pepper

Grease 9x13 inch baking dish. Butter each slice of bread. Arrange 8 slices of bread in baking dish with buttered sides down. Cover with cheese and chives. Top with remaining bread with buttered sides up. Combine eggs, milk, salt, and pepper in a mixing bowl. Pour over bread. Cover with foil and refrigerate overnight. Remove foil and place in a pan of hot water to bring to room temperature. Bake in oven at 350° for 1 hour or until lightly browned and puffed. Can be frozen, thawed, and reheated.

Yield: 8 servings

SHERRIED EGGS

This egg dish can be made up to 2 days ahead of time. Try adding chopped green onion for extra color and flavor.

1 cup fresh mushrooms,
  sliced or 4 ounces of
  canned
4 tablespoons butter
1 10¾-ounce can cream of
  mushroom or cream of
  chicken soup

1½-2 cups mild Cheddar
  cheese, shredded
12 eggs
½ cup Half and Half
Salt and pepper to taste
¼ cup sherry

Saute mushrooms in 2 tablespoons butter. Add soup and cheese. Set aside. Scramble eggs with 2 tablespoons butter. Add Half and Half and seasonings. Stir sherry into soup, add eggs, and blend. Pour into 9x13 inch casserole and bake in 350° oven until hot and bubbly. Add more cream if needed to keep from drying.

Yield: 8 servings

CHEESE SOUFFLE

4 tablespoons margarine	1½ cups Cheddar cheese,
2 tablespoons flour	shredded
1 cup milk, scalded	4 egg yolks, slightly beaten
½ teaspoon salt	4 egg whites, stiffly beaten

Preheat oven to 350°. Butter a 3 quart souffle dish. Melt margarine in a saucepan; stir in flour. Gradually add milk until smooth and thickened, stirring constantly. Add salt and cheese and remove from heat. Quickly stir in egg yolks. Allow to cool and fold in egg whites. Pour into dish. Bake for about 30 minutes or until lightly browned on top.

Yield: 6 servings

BREAKFAST SOUFFLE

Consider this recipe next time you take a dish to a friend.

8 bread slices, crust removed	2½ cups milk
½ pound Cheddar cheese,	5 eggs, beaten
shredded	½ cup evaporated milk
½ pound bulk sausage,	1 cup cream of mushroom
browned and drained	soup
¾ teaspoon dry mustard	

Line a 9x13 inch buttered baking dish with bread. Sprinkle top with cheese and sausage. Mix mustard, milk, and eggs; pour over cheese and sausage. Place in refrigerator overnight.

Combine evaporated milk and soup. Pour over eggs and bake at 300° for 1½ hours.

Yield: 6 servings

MINIATURE QUICHE

These are perfect to serve at a coffee.

Pastry:
2 sticks butter or margarine, softened

2 3-ounce packages cream cheese, softened
2 cups flour

Filling:
¼ pound bacon
1 10-ounce package frozen chopped broccoli, thawed and well drained
2 cups milk
¾ teaspoon salt

Dash of dry mustard, onion powder, and Cavender's seasoning
4 eggs, beaten
½ pound Swiss, Cheddar, munster, or Monterey Jack cheese, shredded

Mix pastry ingredients with electric mixer. Roll into balls and pat into miniature non-greased muffin tins, covering bottom and sides completely. Preheat oven to 350°. Fry bacon, drain, crumble, and sprinkle in bottom of pastry shells. Saute broccoli in bacon grease, slowly adding milk and seasonings. Pour over eggs and add cheese. Stir until melted. Spoon liquid over bacon in shells to fill. Bake for 15 to 20 minutes.

Yield: 3 dozen

QUICHE LORRAINE

Nutmeg and cayenne pepper will give this a different twist.

10-12 slices bacon, cooked and crumbled
⅓ cup onions, minced
1 cup Swiss cheese, shredded
2 cups whipping cream, whipped for 1 minute on high speed

4 eggs, slightly beaten
¼ teaspoon sugar
¾ teaspoon salt
1 9-inch deep dish frozen pie shell

Preheat oven to 425°. Layer crumbled bacon, onion, and cheese in frozen pie shell. Combine whipping cream, eggs, sugar, and salt in a small mixing bowl. Pour egg mixture over cheese layer. Bake for 15 minutes, then turn oven down to 300° and bake for an additional 30 minutes, or until knife inserted one inch from edge comes out clean.

Yield: approximately 4 servings

QUICK MOZZARELLA QUICHE

4 eggs
1 cup milk or Half and Half
¼ teaspoon nutmeg
⅛ teaspoon cayenne pepper
½ teaspoon salt, optional
2 tablespoons green onion, chopped
1 tablespoon butter or margarine

1 10-ounce package frozen spinach cooked according to directions
10 slices bacon, fried crisp and crumbled
1 cup mozzarella cheese, shredded
1 9-inch pie shell, unbaked

Preheat oven to 425°. Combine eggs, milk, and spices. Saute onion in butter. Combine spinach, onion, and bacon with eggs. Stir in cheese. Pour in pie shell and bake for 15 minutes. Reduce heat to 350° and bake for another 30 minutes.

Yield: 6 servings

QUICHE EVEN A MAN WOULD LOVE

The name says it all. Serve with confidence to men; all who have tried it have loved it.

5 slices bacon, cooked and crumbled, reserve grease
1 small onion, finely chopped
⅓ medium green bell pepper, finely chopped
1 4-ounce can chopped mushrooms
4 large fresh mushrooms, sliced, reserve one for garnish

4 eggs, beaten
½ teaspoon salt
¼ teaspoon pepper
½ teaspoon oregano
½ teaspoon basil
3 cups Swiss cheese, shredded
1 9-inch deep dish frozen pie shell

Preheat oven to 325°. Saute onion, bell pepper, and mushrooms in bacon grease in a medium skillet. Beat eggs in a mixing bowl and add spices. Mix all ingredients together. Pour into pie shell and bake for 40 minutes until crust is golden brown.

Yield: 6 servings

FRENCH CREPES

This is a good basic crepe recipe.

½ cup flour
½ teaspoon salt
1 cup milk

4 eggs
3 tablespoons butter, melted
Cooking oil

Mix all ingredients together in the blender until smooth. Allow to stand in refrigerator until ready to make crepes.

Place ½ to 1 teaspoon oil in an 8-inch frying pan and heat over medium heat until hot (375°-400°). Pour crepe mixture slowly, spreading thin and evenly. Cook until done; top batter will look dull. Stack crepes between waxed paper.

Yield: 20 crepes

CREPES FLORENTINE

An elegant and delicious "ladies'" entree. Fresh fruit salad is a nice accompaniment.

8-10 crepes
1 medium onion, chopped
7 tablespoons butter
6 tablespoons flour
3 cups milk
1 teaspoon salt
⅛ teaspoon Tabasco
2 cups Monterey Jack cheese, shredded

½ pound fresh mushrooms, sliced
2 10-ounce packages fresh spinach; chopped, cooked, and drained
¼ cup whipping cream, whipped
Paprika

Saute onions in 4 tablespoons of butter in a large saucepan. Add flour and milk, stirring constantly until mixture thickens. Remove from heat and stir in salt, Tabasco, and cheese. Set aside ½ cup of the sauce for topping. Saute mushrooms in remaining butter in a small skillet over medium heat. Stir into cheese mixture, adding spinach. Fold whipped cream into reserved ½ cup cheese sauce.

Preheat oven to 425°. Butter 9x13 inch baking dish. Spread ¼ cup of the filling in each crepe, roll it up, and place seam side down in the baking dish. Spread reserved sauce over top. Bake for 15 minutes or until hot and cheese topping is slightly brown. Sprinkle top with paprika.

Yield: 8 servings

CHICKEN CREPES

This is wonderful at a ladies' luncheon, but men also love it.

14 crepes
6 tablespoons onion, chopped
1½ sticks butter
1 cup flour
4 cups milk
6 tablespoons chives, chopped
¾ cup sherry
2 4-ounce cans sliced mushrooms, drained

Salt and pepper to taste
¼ teaspoon paprika
2 cups Swiss cheese, shredded
3 cups chicken, cooked and diced
⅔ cup milk
½ cup chicken broth
Parmesan cheese, grated

Saute onions in butter in a large skillet over medium heat. Blend in flour. Add 4 cups milk cooking and stirring until mixture boils. Add remaining ingredients except chicken, ⅔ cup milk, broth, and Parmesan. Allow to simmer for a few minutes. Divide mixture into two saucepans, one for sauce and one for filling. Gradually add chicken and broth to the filling. Remove from heat and chill for 30 minutes. Thin sauce mixture with ⅔ cup of milk and set aside till ready to use.

Preheat oven to 375°. Butter 9x13 inch baking dish. Spoon 1 tablespoon of filling into center of each crepe and roll up. Place rolled crepes seam side down in the baking dish. Cover with sauce. Bake for 15 to 20 minutes. Sprinkle with grated Parmesan cheese.

Yield: 14 servings

A Texas Sampler

Thank you for your financial support
of the following Junior League of Waco project:

Children's Exhibit
The Downtown Art Center Annex

A hands-on exhibit—especially for children—
demonstrating all the elements of art.

HOT PEPPER PASTRIES

Serve these at your next fiesta.

1 5-ounce jar sharp cheese
  spread
1 stick butter, softened

1 cup flour
1 tablespoon cold water
2 tablespoons jalapeno jelly

Preheat oven to 375°. In medium size mixing bowl, cut cheese and butter into flour until mixture resembles cornmeal. Sprinkle in cold water and stir with fork until all ingredients are moist. Shape dough into a ball and chill several hours.

Divide dough in half and roll out on floured surface to ¼ inch thickness. Cut dough with 3-inch round cutter. Place one teaspoon jelly in the center of each dough circle. Fold over and seal completely with fork, moistening edges with water. Bake on lightly greased cookie sheets for 10 to 12 minutes. Cool on wire racks.

Yield: 2 dozen

JALAPENO JELLY

Serve over a block of cream cheese with assorted crackers.

¾ cup green bell pepper,
  ground
¼ cup fresh jalapeno
  peppers, ground
1 cup cider vinegar

5 cups sugar
1 6-ounce box Certo
Green food coloring
Sterilize and keep hot, five
  6-ounce jelly jars

In large heavy saucepan, combine and bring to a boil the first four ingredients. Boil four minutes and remove from heat. Cool one minute. Stir in Certo and a few drops of green food coloring. Pour into jelly jars and seal.

*Note: Use Saran wrap or wear rubber gloves when handling jalapenos so the juice will not burn your hands.

Yield: Five 6-ounce jars

MARVELOUS MUSHROOM EMPANADES

For a quicker appetizer, substitute three boxed Pillsbury pie crusts for pastry.

Pastry:
3 3-ounce packages cream
  cheese, softened
1 stick butter, softened

1½ cups flour
½ teaspoon salt

Filling:
3 tablespoons butter
1 large onion, minced
½ pound fresh mushrooms,
  chopped
¼ teaspoon thyme

½ teaspoon salt and pepper
2 tablespoons flour
¼ cup sour cream
1 egg
1 teaspoon milk

Combine pastry ingredients in medium bowl with electric mixer. Chill 30 minutes. Roll dough out to ⅛ inch thickness on a floured surface. Cut dough with 3-inch round biscuit cutter.

Preheat oven to 450°. Melt butter in a large skillet. Add mushrooms and cook 3 minutes. Add the seasonings. Sprinkle in the flour and stir. Add sour cream and cook until thickened. Place 1 teaspoon filling in the middle of cut pastry. Fold over and seal edges. Place on ungreased cookie sheet. Beat egg and milk slightly and brush tops of pastry with egg. Bake for 10 to 15 minutes or freeze for later use.

Yield: approximately 3 dozen

GUACAMOLE PIE

This can be made ahead as it will not turn dark.

4 ripe avocados
Juice of 1 lemon
Grated onion to taste
Tabasco sauce to taste
Salt to taste

1 cup sour cream
Picante sauce
2 tablespoons ripe olives,
  chopped

Mix avocado and lemon juice together. Mash well. Add onion, Tabasco sauce, and salt. Spread guacamole evenly in a pie plate. Cover with sour cream. Dribble picante sauce over the top. Add olives. Chill.

Yield: approximately 2 cups

TEXAS TORTILLAS

A bit of lime juice and garlic powder give this a different flavor.

1 8-ounce package cream cheese, softened
1 8-ounce carton sour cream
5 green onions with tops, finely chopped or 1 small onion
3 jalapenos, finely chopped or a 4-ounce can chopped green chilies

2 tablespoons black olives, chopped (optional)
½ cup sharp Cheddar cheese, shredded (optional)
1 12-count package large flour tortillas
Picante sauce

Place all ingredients except tortillas and picante in a food processor. Process until smooth. Spread mixture on flour tortillas and roll up. Roll tortillas in damp paper towels and place in ziploc storage bags. Chill. To serve, cut tortillas into 1-inch pieces. Place on a tray with a bowl of picante sauce and toothpicks.

Yield: approximately 5 dozen

SHRIMP PADRE ISLAND

As a variation, serve the shrimp over rice for an entree.

2 tablespoons Worcestershire sauce
2 tablespoons lemon juice
½ stick butter or margarine, melted
½ teaspoon garlic salt

¼ teaspoon pepper
10-12 slices bacon, cut in half
1 pound large shrimp, peeled and deveined

Combine all ingredients except bacon and pour over shrimp. Allow to marinate in refrigerator for 2 hours. Remove shrimp from marinade and wrap with half a slice of bacon. Secure with a toothpick. Place shrimp on a broiler pan and pour marinade sauce over shrimp. Broil 10 minutes. Serve.

Yield: 8 servings

TEXICAN OLÉ

So good it's addictive!

1 16-ounce can refried beans
½ cup picante sauce
1 cup mayonnaise
1 cup sour cream
1 package taco seasoning
   mix
3 avocados, mashed
2 tablespoons lemon juice
½ teaspoon salt

1 8-ounce medium or sharp
   Cheddar cheese, shredded
3 tomatoes, chopped
1 bunch green onions,
   chopped
2 4-ounce cans chopped ripe
   olives, drained
Optional: 1 pound ground
   beef

Mix together beans and picante sauce in a small bowl. In another bowl mix mayonnaise, sour cream, and taco seasoning. Mash avocados. Add lemon juice and salt. Layer ingredients in order in a 9x13 inch pyrex dish beginning with beans, sour cream, avocado, cheese, tomato, onions, and ending with olives. Chill. Serve with tortilla chips.

*Note: You may add a layer of meat to this dip. Brown meat with a package of taco seasoning and spread on top of the beans. Layer remaining ingredients in order and bake at 350° for 20 minutes.

Yield: 20 servings

WACO QUESO DIP

This is wonderful with a half pint of whipping cream added to it. For a different flavor add one pound browned bulk sausage and one package each of bleu cheese and garlic cheese salad dressing mix.

2 pounds Velveeta cheese,
   cubed
1 stick margarine
2 large tomatoes, chopped
1 large green bell pepper,
   chopped

1 large onion, chopped
2 jalapenos, chopped or two
   4-ounce cans chopped
   green chilies

Melt Velveeta over low heat in saucepan, stirring occasionally. Melt margarine in large skillet. Add remaining ingredients and saute until tender. Combine vegetable mixture with melted cheese and stir well. Serve hot in chafing dish with tortilla chips.

Yield: 6 cups

HEART O' TEXAS "CAVIAR"

Drain the dip well and serve on a bed of lettuce as a cold salad.

2 4-ounce cans chopped
  green chilies
2 4½-ounce cans chopped
  ripe olives
2 large tomatoes, chopped
6 green onions with tops,
  chopped
1 15-ounce can jalapeno
  pinto beans

2 tablespoons garlic flavored
  red wine vinegar
2 tablespoons olive oil
Juice of 1 lime
¼ cup cilantro, finely
  chopped
1 avocado, coarsely chopped

Combine first four ingredients in medium mixing bowl. Place beans in colander and wash off juice. Drain and add to above mixture. Add vinegar, oil, juice of ½ lime, and cilantro. Chill overnight. Just before serving; mix avocado with remaining lime juice, and add to beans mixing gently. Serve with tortilla chips.

*Note: Chop cilantro in food processor to get the correct texture.

Yield: 10 servings

TEXAS FAVORITE PICADILLO

This dip is so delicious you cannot get enough of it.

2 large onions
2 cloves fresh garlic
2 fresh jalapenos
3 stems cilantro
2 large tomatoes, peeled and
  cubed
2 large potatoes, peeled and
  cubed
2 pounds lean ground beef

1 tablespoon vegetable oil
1 tablespoon olive oil
1½ teaspoons cumin, ground
1-2 tablespoons flour
2 beef bouillon cubes
1½ cups hot water
Salt and pepper to taste
Accent to taste

In a food processor chop first four ingredients. In a large skillet brown meat in vegetable and olive oil. Add onion mixture and cumin. Saute until onions are limp. Stir in flour to thicken. Add tomatoes and potatoes. Saute for 5 to 10 minutes. Dissolve bouillon in water. Add to meat and season. Simmer slowly on top of stove for 1½ to 2 hours in a covered skillet; stirring occasionally. Serve hot with tortilla chips.

Yield: 8 servings

CINCO DE MAYO DIP

Great with Four Star Fajitas and Margarita's Magnifico.

8 large tomatoes, peeled and chopped
5 large onions, peeled and chopped
1 pound carrots, peeled and sliced ⅛ inch thick
½ bunch cilantro, chopped (stems removed)
3 cayenne peppers, cut in rings
3 jalapeno peppers, cut in rings

1½ teaspoons salt
1 teaspoon Accent
1 teaspoon heaping chili powder
½ teaspoon black pepper
1 teaspoon ground cumin
½ teaspoon garlic powder
2 teaspoons honey
2 ripe avocados, peeled and chopped (optional)

Combine all ingredients except avocados together in a large pot and bring to a boil. Reduce heat and simmer 1 hour. Add avocados before serving.

Yield: 4 cups

LAYERED FIESTA SHRIMP

1 8-ounce package cream cheese, softened
2 tablespoons mayonnaise
Worcestershire sauce to taste
1 clove garlic, minced
2 medium avocados
1 tablespoon lemon juice
½ teaspoon salt

¾ cup mild picante sauce
1 8-ounce can baby shrimp
3 green onions, chopped
1 4-ounce can chopped ripe olives
1 cup Monterey Jack cheese, shredded

Cream together first four ingredients. Spread in the bottom of a 9 or 10 inch pie pan. Mash avocados. Add lemon juice and salt. Layer on top of cream cheese. Spread the picante sauce on top of avocado. Arrange the shrimp over picante. Layer remaining ingredients in order. Chill. Serve with tortilla chips.

Yield: 12 to 14 servings

BRAZOS RIVER FESTIVAL CHEESE BALL

Be creative by using different condiments to decorate the sections of the cheese ball. We suggest black olives, green olives, capers, parsley, pimentos, or crumbled bacon.

1 3-pound loaf cream cheese, softened

½ pound Roquefort cheese, crumbled

½ pound sharp Cheddar cheese, shredded

½ cup chives or green onion, chopped

1 clove garlic, minced

8 tablespoons red caviar

8 tablespoons black caviar

Divide cream cheese into three parts. Mix one part with Roquefort, one part with Cheddar, and one part with chives and garlic. Pile each part on top of another and shape into a ball. Mark the ball with a knife into eight sections. Cover each section with caviar, alternating between the red and black. Chill.

Yield: approximately 50 servings

CATHY'S COUNTRY COOLER

So pretty to float fresh strawberries, lemon, or orange slices in the glass.

1 12-ounce can frozen pink lemonade, thawed

12 ounces white table sherry

Dilute lemonade with 3½ cans water. Add sherry. Stir and serve over ice.

Yield: approximately ½ gallon

MARGARITA'S MAGNIFICO

A must with Mexican food.

12 ounces limeade
6 ouncess tequila
6 ounces triple sec

12 ounces water or ice cubes
Margarita salt
Lime slices

Mix first four ingredients and serve over ice. To make frozen Margaritas combine first three ingredients in a blender. Add ice cubes until blender is full; process until smooth. Garnish glass with salt and lime slice.

Yield: 6 servings

BLOND SANGRIA

1 fifth white wine
1 cup pineapple juice
⅓ cup orange juice
3 tablespoons lemon juice
1 tablespoon lime juice

¼ cup sugar
1 10-ounce bottle club soda
    or a 12-ounce can of 7-Up
Lemon, lime, and orange
    slices

Combine wine, fruit juices, and sugar in a pitcher. Stir in soda. Serve over ice. Garnish with slices of citrus.

Yield: 8 servings

SANGRIA MARIA

This is also good with Burgundy wine and Sprite.

2 6-ounce cans frozen pink
    lemonade, thawed
4½ cups rose wine, chilled
Juice of 1 lime
2 cups club soda, chilled

1 lemon, lime, and orange,
    thinly sliced
½ cup maraschino cherries,
    optional

Combine lemonade, wine, and lime juice in a pitcher. Stir until blended. Slowly stir in club soda. Serve over ice. Garnish with citrus and cherries.

Yield: 2½ quarts

SUMMER GIN SLUSH

A wonderful cool drink to beat the Texas heat. Try this with Bourbon and add a bit of cherry juice.

¾ cup sugar
4½ cups water
1 6-ounce can frozen
  lemonade
1 6-ounce can frozen orange
  juice

2 tablespoons fresh lemon
  juice
1 cup gin
7-Up or Sprite

Heat sugar and water in a saucepan until sugar dissolves. Mix remaining ingredients except 7-Up in a large container. Add sugar water stirring until juices are melted. Freeze overnight. To serve, scoop desired amount of mixture into a glass and crush to a slushy consistency. Add 7-Up to fill glass and stir.

Yield: approximately 6 servings

GLUWEIN

Guaranteed to give you a warm feeling, "Deep in the Heart".

1 cup red wine
1 clove
1 cinnamon stick

1 teaspoon sugar
1 lemon wedge

Combine first four ingredients and bring to a boil in a medium saucepan, stirring constantly. Place lemon in the bottom of a mug and pour in the hot wine.

Yield: 1 cup

BOURBON ON THE BRAZOS

1½ gallons vanilla ice cream,
  softened
1 gallon milk
1 fifth Bourbon
1½ cups rum
½ cup creme de cacao

1 pint whipping cream
  whipped with 5 table-
  spoons confectioners sugar
  and 1 teaspoon vanilla
Nutmeg

Mix ice cream and next four ingredients until a smooth consistency. Whip cream until soft peaks form. Add sugar and vanilla. Blend until smooth. Fold whipped cream into ice cream mixture. Sprinkle with nutmeg.

Yield: approximately 35 servings

TEXAS TUMBLEWEED

A delicious after dinner drink.

Vanilla ice cream
¼ cup Kahlua
¼ cup creme de cacao
½ cup milk

Crushed ice, optional
½ cup whipping cream,
  whipped

Fill blender ⅔ full with ice cream. Add liqueurs and milk. Process in blender until smooth, adding crushed ice if desired. Pour mixture into serving glasses and top with a dollop of whipped cream.

Yield: 4 servings

TEXAS TEA PUNCH

This tea is also delicious when orange juice is added.

1½ cups sugar
3 quarts water
½ cup loose tea
4 large stalks of mint

1 6-ounce can frozen
  lemonade, thawed
1½ cups pineapple juice

Boil sugar and water for 5 minutes in a medium saucepan. Pour sugar water over tea and mint. Allow to stand for 5 minutes, covered. Strain twice. Add fruit juices and chill. Serve over ice.

Yield: ½ gallon

AVOCADO SOUP

3 cups chicken broth
1 cup Half and Half
2 large avocados, peeled and
  chopped
1 clove garlic, crushed

1 tablespoon onion, chopped
½ teaspoon salt
¼ teaspoon cilantro, minced
Dash of pepper

Heat broth in saucepan over medium heat. Place half of the broth and remaining ingredients in blender and puree. Stir in the remaining broth. Cover and chill for 2 to 3 hours. To serve garnish with sour cream, paprika, and avocado slices.

Yield: 6 servings

MOMMA MIA, IT'S BEAN SOUP

Tastes great on a cold, rainy day served with warm flour tortillas, butter, and hot sauce.

Beans:
1 pound pinto beans
6 cups water
6 ounces beer
1 cup onion, chopped
3 cloves garlic, minced

1 cup tomatoes, chopped
1½ cups cabbage, chopped
1 tablespoon cilantro,
  chopped
Salt and pepper to taste

Soup:
½ cup vegetable oil
10 slices bacon, cut in 1 inch
  pieces
1 cup onion, chopped
1 cup green bell pepper,
  chopped

1 cup tomatoes, chopped
2 tablespoons cilantro,
  chopped
1 tablespoon garlic powder
1 teaspoon black pepper

In a large pot, soak beans overnight in 6 cups of water. Add remaining bean ingredients and cook 1 hour, stirring occasionally. Brown bacon in oil. Add remaining ingredients and cook until green pepper is tender. Set aside. Ladle beans in a large bowl and measure bean juice. Add enough water to make 9 cups of liquid, then add beans, garlic powder, salt, and pepper. Bring to a boil. Mash beans slightly, then add reserved vegetable and oil mixture. Simmer for 20 minutes and serve.

Yield: approximately 8 servings

BRAZOS BELLES' BROCCOLI AND CHEESE SOUP

A thick, rich soup. Easy to prepare, particularly if you cook the vegetables in the microwave. Try it with cauliflower.

1 10-ounce package chopped
  broccoli
½ cup carrots, grated
½ cup celery, chopped
½ cup onion, chopped
½ stick butter

¼ cup flour
2 cups milk
1 pound Velveeta cheese,
  cubed
Pepper to taste

Combine vegetables in a saucepan and cook until nearly done. Melt butter in a medium saucepan; stir in flour until smooth. Add milk; stirring constantly. When mixture becomes thick; add cheese and stir until melted. Add vegetables and pepper, mixing well. Heat thoroughly. If you prefer a thinner soup, add additional milk.

Yield: approximately 6 servings

MCLENNAN COUNTY MUSHROOM SOUP

4 tablespoons butter
1 medium onion, finely
  chopped
1 pound fresh mushrooms,
  chopped

3 tablespoons flour
4 cups beef bouillon
⅛ teaspoon white pepper
⅛ teaspoon nutmeg
1½ cups whipping cream

Melt butter in a large saucepan and saute onions until transparent. Add mushrooms and cook until tender. Add flour, stirring constantly. Stir in beef bouillon; bring to a boil. Add pepper and nutmeg. Remove from heat and stir in cream. Serve immediately.

Yield: approximately 4 servings

CAPPY'S GAZPACHO WITH KICKAPOO JOY JUICE

¾ green bell pepper
1 small rib celery
2 ounces lemon juice

2 small cucumbers
Cappy's Kickapoo Joy Juice

Slightly chop vegetables in a blender with lemon juice. Add Joy Juice to fill blender and blend for a few seconds. Chill and serve cold.

Yield: 4 servings

CAPPY'S KICKAPOO JOY JUICE

Add two tablespoons Thousand Island dressing, salt to taste, and serve with chips, or leave as is and serve as a hot sauce.

10 jalapeno peppers,
  chopped with juice
6 16-ounce cans tomatoes,
  chopped
2 tablespoons Accent
4 large white, sweet onions,
  chopped

1 whole pod garlic, minced
3 bay leaves
2 2½-ounce jars mushrooms,
  stems and pieces

Combine ingredients in a large saucepan and bring to a boil over medium heat. Cook until onions turn clear. Chill immediately for 24 hours before serving.

Yield: 1 gallon

POBLANO SOUP GRATINEE

A Texas substitute for French onion soup.

3 tablespoons butter
1 tablespoon vegetable oil
3 cups onion, thinly sliced
3 tablespoons flour
2 quarts chicken stock
Salt to taste
1-2 fresh Poblano chilies
1 cup corn, fresh or frozen

1 cup chicken, cooked and
  diced
½ teaspoon ground cumin
  seed
Toast rounds
Monterey Jack cheese,
  shredded

Heat butter and oil in skillet. Cook onions over low heat for about 15 minutes. Sprinkle with flour and stir for 3 to 4 minutes. Add chicken stock and salt; cook over medium heat. Over an open flame or under the broiler, roast Poblano peppers until skins are charred. After placing peppers in a sealed plastic bag for 10 minutes, carefully peel and seed under cold running water. Cut peppers into ⅛ inch strips. Add to the stock and simmer 20 to 30 minutes. Stir in corn and chicken; cook an additional 4 minutes before seasoning with cumin. Pour into ovenproof bowls and float toast rounds on top. Sprinkle with cheese. Place under the broiler until cheese is bubbly and golden.

Yield: 6 servings

WILD WEST RICE SOUP

1 cup wild rice
2 ribs celery, diced
1 large onion, chopped
½ green bell pepper, diced
½ pound fresh mushrooms,
  sliced

1 stick butter
½ cup flour
8 cups chicken broth
Salt and pepper to taste
1 cup Half and Half
3 tablespoons white wine

Cook rice according to package directions. Saute celery, onion, bell pepper, and mushrooms in butter until barely tender. Sprinkle with flour and stir until blended. Do not brown. Add broth and stir in rice. Season to taste and heat thoroughly. Stir in Half and Half and add wine just before serving.

Yield: 6 servings

TORTILLA SOUP

This is very spicy; you may want to leave out the Tabasco.

3 cloves garlic, chopped
1 onion, chopped
1 4-ounce can green chilies,
  chopped
3 tablespoons olive oil
1 16-ounce can stewed
  tomatoes, chopped
1 10-ounce can Rotel
  tomatoes, chopped
6 cups chicken stock
1 10¾-ounce can tomato
  soup

1 tablespoon cumin
1 tablespoon chili powder
½ tablespoon salt
1 teaspoon pepper
1 tablespoon lemon pepper
¼ teaspoon Tabasco
2 teaspoons Worcestershire
  sauce
6 corn tortillas, cut into
  strips

Garnish:
Monterey Jack cheese,
  shredded
Sour cream

Avocado, chopped
Tortilla chips

Simmer garlic, onion, and green chilies in oil in a large soup pot until onions are tender, about 3 minutes. Add remaining ingredients except seasonings and tortilla strips; bring to a boil. Add seasonings and simmer 1 hour. Fifteen minutes before done, add tortilla strips. Serve with garnish of your choice.

Yield: approximately 12 servings

IT'S SLAW YA'LL

1 teaspoon salt
⅓ cup sugar
½ cup oil
½ cup white vinegar
1 head cabbage, shredded

½ cup onion, chopped
1 green bell pepper, chopped
3 carrots, shredded
1 teaspoon celery seed
Pepper to taste

Combine first four ingredients in a saucepan and bring to boil over medium heat, allowing sugar to dissolve. Combine next six ingredients in a large salad bowl. Pour hot liquid over cabbage and stir. Chill overnight.

Yield: 8 servings

DOVE SALAD

Just as good when prepared with chicken.

1 6½-ounce box chicken
flavored Rice-a-Roni
12 doves or 6 chicken breasts
⅓ cup mayonnaise
1 green bell pepper, chopped
4 green onions, chopped

2 6½-ounce jars marinated
artichokes, drain and
reserve juice
1 4-ounce can ripe olives,
chopped and drained

Cook Rice-a-Roni according to package directions. Boil doves in slightly salted water until tender. Remove meat from bones and cut into bite size pieces. Blend mayonnaise and ¼ cup artichoke juice together. Combine all ingredients in a large bowl and toss well. Serve on a bed of lettuce.

*Note: If using chicken, increase the amount of mayonnaise.

Yield: 8 servings

LOLA'S EAST TEXAS POTATO SALAD

Serve this potato salad at your next outdoor barbecue.

6 large new potatoes
½ bag fresh spinach
2 bunches green onions,
chopped
1 cup cottage cheese
1 cup mayonnaise

Salt and pepper to taste
Red pepper to taste
Accent to taste
2 teaspoons Dijon mustard
Bacon crumbled to sprinkle
on top

Place potatoes in a large saucepan, cover with water, and boil in jackets. Drain and cool. Peel potatoes and dice. Break spinach leaves into bite size pieces. Mix potatoes, spinach, onions, cottage cheese, mayonnaise, salt, pepper, red pepper, Accent, and mustard together in a large salad bowl. Sprinkle bacon on top.

Yield: 8 servings

HEART OF THE SOUTH SALAD

Light, crunchy, and tasty.

4 tablespoons sesame seeds
3 ounces slivered almonds
½ cup chow mein noodles
1 head iceberg lettuce

4 green onions, chopped
1 11-ounce can Mandarin
  oranges, drained

Dressing:
4 tablespoons sugar
½ cup oil
1½ teaspoons salt

1 teaspoon Accent
1 teaspoon pepper
1 tablespoon white vinegar

Preheat oven to 250°. Place sesame seeds, almonds, and noodles on a cookie sheet and toast in oven for 12 to 15 minutes. Combine lettuce, onions, sesame seeds, almonds, chow mein noodles, and Mandarin oranges in a salad bowl. Combine dressing ingredients in a blender and process. Pour over salad before serving.

Yield: 6 servings

CASA MIA SALAD DRESSING

1 medium onion, chopped
3 medium cloves garlic
2 teaspoons parsley, chopped
1 teaspoon celery, chopped
1 tablespoon salt, or less if
  desired
¼ teaspoon dry mustard

¼ teaspoon paprika
⅛ teaspoon pepper
3 tablespoons sugar
¾ cup apple cider vinegar
¼ cup water
2 cups oil

Place first four ingredients in a food processor with metal blade and blend about 2 to 3 seconds. Add salt, mustard, paprika, pepper, and sugar; continue processing adding vinegar and water. Gradually add oil in a slow stream through the feed tube while blending. Dressing will thicken. Refrigerate in a closed container.

Yield: approximately 4 cups dressing

MEXICAN FIESTA SALAD
WITH CILANTRO DRESSING

This colorful salad makes a great entree. Prepare the beans and dressing the day before and marinate overnight.

Beans:

⅔ cup black beans, dried, rinsed, and picked over

2 tablespoons olive oil

2 tablespoons white wine vinegar

½ teaspoon salt

Cilantro Dressing:

3-5 jalapenos, seeded

¼ cup white wine vinegar

1 clove garlic

1 teaspoon salt

⅔ cup olive oil

½ cup fresh cilantro, packed

Salad:

½ cup red onion, chopped

2 cups iceburg lettuce, thinly sliced

1½ cups tomatoes, seeded and chopped

1 cup corn

½ cup green bell pepper, chopped

1 cup Monterey Jack cheese, shredded

1 avocado

4 slices lean bacon, cooked and crumbled

Cilantro sprig for garnish

Cover beans with two inches cold water in a large pot, and bring to boil for 3 minutes. Remove from heat and let beans soak for 10 minutes. Drain beans and cover with two inches cold water. Bring to a boil and simmer for 45 minutes, or until just tender. Drain and refresh under cold water. Transfer beans to a bowl and add oil, vinegar, and salt. Cover and chill 2 to 24 hours. Make dressing while beans are chilling. In a blender, puree the jalapenos with the vinegar, garlic, and salt. Continue processing and add the oil in a steady stream, blending until emulsified. Add the cilantro and blend until finely chopped.

To assemble: Drain beans and toss with onion. In the bottom of a 2-quart souffle dish or a bowl, arrange the lettuce; top it with the beans, reserving 2 tablespoons, and layer tomatoes on top reserving 1 tablespoon. In a small bowl toss together the corn and bell pepper; top the tomatoes with the corn, reserving 1 tablespoon; and top the corn with cheese. (The salad may be prepared up to this point 8 hours in advance and kept covered and chilled.) Halve the avocado lengthwise, reserving one-half; peel the remaining half and cut it into six slices. Arrange the avocado slices like the spokes of a wheel on top of the

(continued)

cheese. Fill in the spaces between the avocado alternately with reserved beans, tomatoes, corn, and the bacon. Garnish salad with cilantro sprig and serve with cilantro dressing.

Yield: 4 servings

TUMBLIN T CHERRY MUFFINS

These wonderful muffins get better with age. They also freeze well so you can keep some on hand for unexpected company.

¾ cup pecans, finely ground
4 tablespoons butter,
  softened
½ cup sugar
½ cup brown sugar
2 eggs, separated

1 cup flour
¼ teaspoon baking powder
2 tablespoons maraschino
  cherry juice
36 maraschino cherries
Confectioners Sugar

Preheat oven to 400°. Grease miniature muffin tins. Sprinkle bottom of each muffin tin with ½ teaspoon pecans. Cream together butter and both sugars in a medium mixing bowl. Add beaten egg yolks until well blended. Mix together flour and baking powder; add gradually to butter. Beat egg whites. Add cherry juice and fold egg whites into batter. Place 1 teaspoon of batter in prepared muffin tins, then a cherry. Add another teaspoon of batter on top of cherry. Sprinkle top with ½ teaspoon pecans. Bake for 10 minutes. Roll muffins in powdered sugar while still warm. Cool and store in tin box or can covered tightly for several days.

Yield: 3 dozen miniature muffins

BLUEBONNET BLUEBERRY MUFFINS

Cover batter and store in refrigerator for three to four weeks. For a different flavor add ¼ cup fresh squeezed orange juice and 1 tablespoon grated orange peel.

⅔ cup shortening
1½ cup sugar
3 eggs
3 cups flour
2 heaping teaspoons baking
  powder

1 teaspoon salt
1 cup milk
1½ cups frozen blueberries,
  thawed

Preheat oven to 375°. Line muffin pans with paper liners. Cream shortening and sugar together. Add eggs, one at a time, and continue to blend. Sift dry ingredients together; add alternately with milk to batter. Fold in blueberries. Bake for 15-20 minutes.

Yield: 3 dozen medium muffins

BUTTERMILK BISCUITS

These are wonderful for breakfast served with sausage and cream gravy. Leftovers can be used as a topping for chicken pie.

¼ cup shortening
2 cups flour
1 teaspoon salt

¼ teaspoon baking soda
3 teaspoons baking powder
1 cup buttermilk

Preheat oven to 450°. Grease 8x8-inch cake pan. Place shortening in a cuisinart bowl with the steel blade, or use mixer with dough hook. Add all ingredients except buttermilk; cut into the shortening until it looks like cornmeal. Add buttermilk and mix with the steel blade until dough forms a ball. Remove from the cuisinart to a floured bread board. Knead biscuit dough on the bread board ten times, then roll the dough out to ½-inch thick and cut with a biscuit cutter. Place biscuits in the pan and brush the tops with melted shortening. Bake for 12 to 15 minutes.

Yield: 1 dozen

GINGERBREAD PANCAKES

Serve with Lemon Hard Sauce and maple syrup or melted butter with honey.

2¼ cups flour
½ teaspoon salt
1 teaspoon cinnamon
1 teaspoon nutmeg
1 teaspoon ginger
½ teaspoon cloves
1½ teaspoons baking powder

1½ teaspoons baking soda
1 tablespoon instant coffee
½ stick butter, melted
1 egg, beaten
¾ cup buttermilk
¼ cup brown sugar
¾ cup water

Sift first nine ingredients together in a large mixing bowl. Stir in butter and remaining ingredients. Blend well. Pour about ¼ cup batter per pancake onto hot non-stick skillet. Brown on both sides.

Yield: approximately 8 servings

LEMON HARD SAUCE

Serve with Gingerbread Pancakes.

1 stick butter, softened
2½ cups confectioners sugar

3 tablespoons fresh lemon
   juice
Grated lemon rind

Cream butter, add sugar, and beat well. Stir in the lemon juice and grated lemon rind. Beat until it has the consistency of whipped cream.

Yield: 2 cups

LONE *STAR BREAD

This bread is fun to make and is very good with B-B-Q. Make just prior to serving and serve warm.

1 12-ounce can beer (Lone
   Star preferred)
½ cup sugar

3 cups self-rising flour
Butter

Preheat oven to 350°. Grease a 9x5 inch loaf pan. Mix all ingredients well and place in pan. Bake for 1 hour. Every 10 minutes butter top of bread with small pieces of butter.

Yield: 1 loaf

HEART OF TEXAS KOLACHES

2 packages dry yeast	2 egg yolks
¼ cup lukewarm water	2 teaspoons salt
1 teaspoon sugar	6 cups flour
¾ cup sugar	2 cups milk or one 13-ounce
¾ cup shortening or 1½	can evaporated milk plus
sticks margarine	hot water to equal 2 cups

Topping:

1 cup flour	½ stick butter, softened
⅔ cup sugar	

Dissolve yeast in ¼ cup warm water, sprinkle with 1 teaspoon sugar and set aside in a warm place and allow to foam about 10 to 15 minutes. Cream together sugar and margarine in a large mixing bowl with electric mixer. Add egg yolks and salt; mix well. Add dissolved yeast and ½ cup flour. Mix slowly with mixer. Add milk and continue adding the remaining flour, using mixer or stirring by hand, until dough is glossy. Cover and let rise in a warm place until dough has doubled in bulk, about 1 hour.

After dough has risen, cut off small portions of dough about the size of an egg. Using a tablespoon, shape into balls and place on greased cookie sheet about an inch apart. Butter tops with butter or shortening. Let rise until light (unless you are making cottage cheese or sausage filled kolaches). For fruit filled kolaches make an indentation in each and fill with your choice of fillings below. Mix topping ingredients together with a fork until it crumbles. Sprinkle over top of fruit and cottage cheese kolaches. Bake for 15 minutes in a preheated 425° oven. Butter tops upon removing from oven. Cool on wire racks.

Cherry filling:

1½ cups sugar	1 quart fresh or frozen
1 tablespoon almond extract	cherries
	4 tablespoons tapioca

Cook cherries in saucepan for 10 minutes over medium heat. Drain and reserve ½ cup juice and add tapioca. Cook over low heat for 15 to 20 minutes or until tapioca is cooked. Add cherries and almond extract to tapioca. Allow to cool before filling kolaches.

(continued)

Pineapple filling:
1 8-ounce can crushed   ½ cup sugar
   pineapple   3 tablespoons lemon juice
4 tablespoons minute tapioca

Combine ingredients together in a saucepan and bring to boil slowly for 15 to 30 minutes until tapioca is cooked, stirring to keep from sticking. Allow to cool before filling.

Prune filling:
1 pound pitted prunes   ½ teaspoon cinnamon
½ cup sugar

Cook prunes in enough water to cover in a medium saucepan over medium heat until soft and tender. Add sugar and cinnamon and mix well. Cool before filling.

Apricot filling:
1 10-ounce package apricots   1½ cups sugar

Cook apricots in enough water to cover in a medium saucepan over medium heat until soft and water has cooked out. Add sugar and blend well. Cool before filling.

Cottage cheese filling:
1½ cups cottage cheese,   ¼ cup sugar
   drained   ½ teaspoon lemon extract
¼ teaspoon salt   1 teaspoon lemon rind,
⅓ cup raisins, optional   grated
2 tablespoons flour   4 tablespoons sweet cream
2 egg yolks

Mix all ingredients together in a mixing bowl, blending well. Fill kolaches. Seal, following same directions as sausage-filled kolaches.

Sausage kolaches:
Polish style pork sausage,
   cut into 2-inch pieces

Cut the sausage into 2-inch pieces, then cut the pieces in half lengthwise. Spread small pieces of dough and place sausage on dough. Pinch all sides together. Place sealed side down on pan and butter all sides. Let rise and bake until golden brown.

Yield: approximately 3 dozen

MEXICAN SPOON BREAD

A great accompaniment for taco salad or beef brisket. If you like it more spicy, add chopped jalapenos instead of green chilies.

1 cup yellow cornmeal
1 17-ounce can cream style corn
⅓ cup corn oil, peanut oil, or bacon drippings
¾ cup milk
2 eggs, beaten

1 teaspoon salt
½ teaspoon baking soda
1 8-ounce can chopped green chilies, drained
1½ cups Cheddar cheese, shredded

Preheat oven to 375°. Grease a 3-quart casserole with a lid. Mix first seven ingredients together thoroughly in a large mixing bowl. Turn half of the mixture into casserole. Spread chilies evenly over mixture. Add one-half of the cheese and sprinkle evenly. Spoon remaining corn mixture into casserole. Sprinkle with remaining cheese. Cover with lid. Bake for 45 to 50 minutes.

Yield: 6 servings

NEVER FAIL TEXAS CORNBREAD

Ditch the cornbread mix and try this! It's so easy and tastes so good, you'll never buy another mix.

¼ cup bacon drippings, melted
1 cup yellow cornmeal
½ cup flour
1 teaspoon salt

½ teaspoon baking soda
1 cup buttermilk
½ cup sweet milk
1 egg
1 tablespoon baking powder

Preheat oven to 450°. Place 3 tablespoons bacon drippings in iron skillet and heat in oven until hot. Combine next three ingredients in a large mixing bowl. Dissolve baking soda in buttermilk. Combine milk, egg, baking powder, and 1 tablespoon bacon drippings in a small mixing bowl. Add both milk mixtures to the cornmeal and stir until just combined. Pour batter into skillet and bake for 25 to 30 minutes or until browned.

Yield: approximately 8 servings

PEACHY KEEN PRESERVES

2 cups fresh peaches, peeled   1 cup sugar
  and chopped   2 tablespoons lemon juice

Mix ingredients together in a saucepan. Stir constantly over medium heat until peaches are clear and sugar is dissolved. Pack while hot, leaving ¼ inch space at top, into sterile canning jars. To seal, follow directions on canning jar box.

Yield: 3 cups

WILD PLUM JELLY

Wild plums are available in May and June.

Wild plums   Water
Sugar   Jars

Wash plums well, removing leaves and stems. Add ½ cup water for every pound of fruit. Cook in a deep kettle in amounts not more than 8 quarts. Cook until soft and mushy. Working with a small amount at a time, strain juice and pulp through a coarse material, such as unbleached muslin. Squeeze hard until juice is extracted. Strain again through a fine cloth, such as a man's handkerchief. For every 3 cups of juice, add 2 cups of sugar. Stir only until sugar is dissolved. Do not cook more than 4 cups at a time. Cook to 219° on candy thermometer, skimming often, until liquid falls in a sheet from the spoon. Jelly will become clear when cooked. Pour into hot, sterilized jars and seal.

Yield: Depends on amount of plums

SCRAMBLED EGGS IN TORTILLAS

6-8 large flour tortillas
½ pound ground sausage
¼ cup green onion, chopped
¼ cup green bell pepper, chopped
2 tablespoons butter

4 large eggs, slightly beaten
2-3 tablespoons milk
Salt and pepper to taste
½ cup sharp Cheddar cheese, shredded
Picante sauce

Preheat oven to 350°. Wrap tortillas tightly in foil and heat in oven for 15 minutes. Brown sausage in a large skillet over medium heat. Add onions and bell pepper. Drain well and set aside. Mix eggs with milk, salt, and pepper in a mixing bowl. Pour into skillet and cook, stirring occasionally. Add sausage mixture to eggs while they are still slightly moist and stir well. Spoon sausage egg mixture into middle of tortillas. Top with cheese and picante sauce and roll up to serve.

Yield: approximately 6 servings

VENISON AND EGG CASSEROLE

Butter
1 pound venison sausage
6 slices whole wheat bread, torn in pieces
1½ cups smokey sharp Cheddar cheese, shredded

5 eggs
2 cups Half and Half
1 teaspoon salt
1 teaspoon dry mustard

Preheat oven to 350°. Butter 9x13 inch dish. Cook sausage over medium heat in skillet and drain well. Lay bread in bottom of dish. Mix sausage and remaining ingredients together in a mixing bowl. Pour into casserole over bread. Bake for one hour.

Yield: approximately 10 servings

BRAZOS BAKED BEANS

1 pound bacon
1 large onion, chopped
1 medium green bell pepper, chopped
5 16-ounce cans pork and beans, drained
1 14-ounce bottle catsup

2½ cups brown sugar, firmly packed
¼ teaspoon mustard
¼ cup Worcestershire sauce
2 teaspoons Liquid Smoke seasoning
Tabasco sauce to taste

Preheat oven to 300°. Fry bacon in a large skillet. Add onion and bell pepper and cook until tender. Drain excess bacon grease and add all remaining ingredients. Pour in a baking dish and bake for about 2 hours.

Yield: approximately 12 servings

BEANS A LA CHARA

Serve with Fajitas!

½ pound pinto beans
1 slice salt pork, about ½ inch wide
Salt and pepper to taste
½ teaspoon oregano
1 tablespoon chili powder
4 slices bacon, chopped

1 large onion, chopped
2 cloves garlic, minced
1 tomato, chopped
1 Poblano pepper, seeded and chopped
2 tablespoons cilantro, chopped

Soak beans, cover with water in a medium kettle for 2 hours. Add salt pork and bring to a boil over medium heat. Reduce heat, cover, and cook for 1½ to 2 hours. Add salt, pepper, oregano, and chili powder and continue to simmer. Saute bacon, onion, garlic, tomato, Poblano pepper and cilantro for approximately 10 minutes. Add to beans and simmer an additional 30 minutes.

Yield: approximately 8 servings

BAYERISCHES KRAUT

An old Bavarian dish that has been passed down through generations.

2 tablespoons bacon drippings	¼ cup apple cider vinegar
4 cups shredded red cabbage	¼ cup water
¼ cup sugar	1¼ teaspoons salt

Heat bacon drippings in a skillet. Add remaining ingredients and cover. Simmer for 15 to 30 minutes until cabbage is tender.

Yield: 4 servings

CENTRAL TEXAS CELERY

A fast and easy microwave veggie.

4 cups celery, diagonally sliced	½ cup pecan pieces
1 10¾-ounce can cream of celery soup	1 cup buttery crackers, crushed
½ cup milk	3 tablespoons butter, melted

Place celery in an even layer in a 1½-quart casserole dish. Cover and microwave on High for 5 to 6 minutes, stirring once midway through cooking. Drain. Add soup, milk, and pecans to celery and stir until well blended. Sprinkle crushed crackers over top and drizzle with butter. Microwave on Medium-High for 6 to 8 minutes or until thoroughly heated.

Yield: 6 servings

"DOWN HOME" COLLARD GREENS

Serve with baked corn, grits, black-eyed peas, ham, and cornbread for a real "down home" meal.

2 bunches fresh collard
  greens
2 10½-ounce cans chicken
  broth
2 soup cans water
1 large onion, chopped
1 tablespoon seasoning salt

1 teaspoon fresh cracked
  pepper
3 tablespoons bacon grease
  or 4 strips of raw bacon
8 good shakes Tabasco sauce
1 tablespoon butter

Cut stems off of collard greens. Wash and drain well. Coarsely chop and place in a large soup pot. Add soup and water to cover. Add onion, salt, pepper, and bacon grease. Bring to a full boil over medium-high heat. Cover and reduce to simmer for 1 hour. Add Tabasco sauce and simmer for a few more minutes. Drain partially and place in a bowl with butter to serve.

Yield: 6 servings

GRILLED CORN WITH CUMIN BUTTER

Serve with Sweet and Sour Mustard Glazed Spare Ribs for a great grilled dinner.

2 small red bell peppers,
  seeded and cut into 1½
  inch squares

4 small ears of corn, cut into
  1 inch thick rounds

Cumin Butter:
1½ sticks butter
1 teaspoon cumin
½ teaspoon dried red pepper
  flakes

Salt and pepper to taste
3 tablespoons fresh cilantro,
  chopped

Prepare barbecue grill. Alternate vegetables on 4 skewers. Melt butter with cumin, red pepper flakes, salt and pepper in a small heavy sauce pan. Remove from heat and stir in cilantro. Arrange skewers on barbecue rack and brush with cumin butter. Grill until vegetables are crisp and tender and beginning to char, turning and basting occasionally, about 15 minutes. Remove from grill and brush with more butter.

Yield: 4 servings

SOUTHERN STYLE GREEN BEANS AND POTATOES

Country cooking at its best.

1½ pounds fresh green
   beans, washed and
   snapped into 1½-inch
   pieces
8 slices bacon, quartered
1 medium onion, chopped

6 cups water
1 ham hock
2 teaspoons salt
1 teaspoon pepper
1 pound new potatoes,
   cubed

Fry bacon until crisp in a Dutch oven. Remove bacon and set aside. Saute onions in ¼ cup bacon drippings until tender. Add water and ham hock to onions and bring to a boil. Add bacon, beans, salt, and pepper and bring to a boil. Cover and simmer for 15 minutes. Add potatoes and cook for 15 minutes or until potatoes are tender.

Yield: 6 servings

TRUE GRIT CASSEROLE

If you prefer a less spicy taste, omit green chilies and add ½ cup milk.

6 cups boiling water
1½ cups quick grits
1½ sticks butter
1 pound Cheddar cheese,
   shredded
2 teaspoons salt

2 teaspoons seasoned salt
4 tablespoons green chilies,
   chopped
2 tablespoons pimento,
   chopped
3 eggs, beaten

Preheat oven to 350°. Grease a 3-quart casserole. Cook grits in boiling water until thick. Stir in butter, cheese, seasonings, green chilies, and pimento. Continue to stir and cook slowly until cheese melts. Remove from heat and fold in eggs. Pour into casserole and bake for 1 hour.

Yield: approximately 10 servings

MAMA MAKE ME SOME MACARONI AND CHEESE

Smooth, creamy, and oh so good!

1 12-ounce package macaroni	2 cups milk
¼ cup flour	12 ounces Velveeta cheese, cubed
½ stick butter	

Preheat oven to 350°. Cook macaroni according to package directions and drain. Butter a 9-inch square baking dish. Melt butter in a saucepan and stir in flour until well blended. Add milk and heat until it begins to thicken. Add cheese and stir until cheese melts. Add macaroni and mix well. Pour in baking dish and bake for about 30 minutes.

Yield: 6 servings

PEARLIE'S SWEET POTATOES

2 yams, boiled and chopped	1 teaspoon nutmeg
2 eggs	½ stick butter
1 cup sugar	1 teaspoon cinnamon
1 5¾-ounce can evaporated milk	1 jigger Bourbon
	Miniature marshmallows

Optional Topping:
1¼ cups brown sugar	1 stick butter, melted
¾ cup flour	1½ cups pecans, chopped

Preheat oven to 325°. Butter baking dish. Mash yams and mix with next six ingredients. Pour into baking dish. Bake in oven for 30 to 45 minutes. Remove from oven and poke holes deep into the yams and pour Bourbon over the yams. Mix topping ingredients and add at this point, if desired. Return to oven and bake for 10 minutes. Top with marshmallows and bake until marshmallows start to brown.

Yield: approximately 4 servings

TEXICAN RICE

3 tablespoons olive oil
2 cloves garlic, crushed
1 onion, chopped
1 large tomato, chopped
1 cup uncooked long grain
rice
1 Poblano pepper, seeded
and chopped

1 13-ounce can chicken
broth
¼ teaspoon crushed red
pepper
½ teaspoon cumin
½ teaspoon oregano
1 teaspoon salt
1 avocado for garnish

Preheat oven to 400°. Heat oil in a Dutch oven over medium heat. Add garlic, onion, and tomato. Cook until onion is transparent. Add the rice and cook, stirring until rice is hot and shiny, about 5 minutes. Stir in the remaining ingredients except avocado. Bring to a boil, cover and bake for 20 minutes. Garnish with avocado slices.

Yield: 6 servings

TEXAS HOT RICE

This has a delightful texture and flavor.

1 cup onion, chopped
½ stick butter
4 cups rice, cooked
2 cups sour cream
1 cup creamy cottage cheese
Salt and pepper to taste

3 4-ounce cans mild green
chilies
2 cups Monterey Jack cheese
or sharp Cheddar cheese,
shredded

Preheat oven to 375°. Lightly grease a 2-quart baking dish. Saute onion in butter in a medium saucepan until tender. Remove from heat; stir in rice, sour cream, cottage cheese, salt, and pepper. Layer ½ rice mixture, ½ chilies, and ½ cheese in baking dish. Repeat layers. Bake uncovered for 25 minutes or until bubbly.

Yield: 10 servings

JALAPENO SPINACH CASSEROLE

2 10-ounce packages frozen chopped spinach
½ stick butter, melted
2 tablespoons onion, chopped
3 tablespoons flour
½ cup milk or evaporated milk
½ cup liquid from cooked spinach

½ teaspoon each salt and pepper
¾ teaspoon celery salt or celery seed
¾ teaspoon garlic salt
1 teaspoon Worcestershire sauce
1 6-ounce roll jalapeno cheese
Breadcrumbs

Preheat oven to 350°. Cook spinach according to package directions and drain well reserving ½ cup liquid. Cook onions and flour in butter until onions are soft. Add to cooked spinach. For sauce, combine remaining ingredients, except breadcrumbs. Cook over medium heat until cheese is melted. Mix sauce and spinach together and pour into a 9x13 inch casserole. Sprinkle with breadcrumbs. Bake for 20 minutes.

Yield: approximately 8 servings

TEXAS PEAR CHUTNEY

Watch your favorite soap opera while peeling the pears.

10 pounds Texas hard green pears; peeled, cored, and sliced
1½ cups onions, diced
1½ pounds dark raisins
3 tablespoons ground ginger

3 pounds brown sugar
4 cups vinegar
1½ tablespoons mustard seed
1½ tablespoons salt
1½ tablespoons chili powder

Preheat oven to 400°. Combine all ingredients together in a large bowl. Pour into two 17x12-inch pans. Bake for 2 hours. Add water if needed to cover pears while baking. Store in jars according to canned directions.

Yield: approximately 8 quarts

KING FAMILY SAUSAGE DRESSING

This dressing is very easy to make and freezes well. The sausage adds a wonderful flavor and is a great accompaniment to your holiday turkey.

4 medium onions, chopped
1½ stalks celery, chopped
2 tablespoons butter
2 6-ounce packages cornbread mix or 2 pans Never Fail Texas Cornbread
1 8-count can biscuits
2 10¾-ounce cans cream of mushroom soup

1½ soup cans water
2 pounds seasoned bulk sausage
Salt and pepper to taste
1 tablespoon sugar
Sage, optional

Preheat oven to 325°. Saute onions and celery in butter until tender and clear. Bake cornbread and biscuits according to directions. Crumble cornbread and biscuits into a large mixing bowl. Mix soup and water; add to cornbread. Stir in sausage, onion, celery, salt, pepper, and sugar. Add sage to taste if desired. Bake covered for 1 hour or steam for 3 hours.

Yield: approximately 8 servings

BARBECUE BRISKET ON THE BRAZOS

This marvelous sauce can be served with other meats as well.

1 2½ to 3 pound boneless
   brisket, well trimmed
1 teaspoon seasoned salt

1 teaspoon lemon pepper
¼ cup Liquid Smoke

Smokey Sauce:
1 tablespoon Liquid Smoke
1½ tablespoons brown sugar,
   firmly packed
½ cup catsup
¼ cup water
1 teaspoon celery seed

3 tablespoons butter
2 tablespoons Worcestershire
   sauce
1½ teaspoons dry mustard
Dash of pepper

Sprinkle brisket with salt and pepper and pour Liquid Smoke over top. Wrap in foil and seal. Marinate in refrigerator overnight. Preheat oven to 300°. Remove brisket from refrigerator and bake for 2½ to 3 hours or until desired doneness. Uncover for last 30 minutes of baking. Combine all sauce ingredients together in a saucepan and simmer for 5 minutes over low heat. This makes about 1¼ cups. Serve over thinly sliced brisket.

Yield: approximately 8 servings

DOSSETT McCULLOUGH'S BARBECUE SAUCE

This is especially wonderful for ribs, chicken, and pork chops.

1 onion, chopped
1 clove garlic, chopped
½ stick butter
½ cup red wine vinegar
½ cup honey
2 tablespoons Worcestershire
   sauce

1 teaspoon soy sauce
Marjoram, black pepper, and
   rosemary to taste
1 cup chili sauce

Mix all ingredients together in a saucepan and simmer about 30 minutes.

Yield: 3 cups

COUNTRY TAVERN BARBECUE SAUCE

Wonderful on hamburgers.

1 32-ounce bottle catsup
1 cup brown sugar
1 cup sweet pickle juice
1 medium onion, grated
1 cup water
Juice of 2 lemons
1 tablespoon prepared
   mustard

2 tablespoons Worcestershire
   sauce
1 tablespoon salt
1 tablespoon red pepper, less
   for a milder sauce

Blend all ingredients together in a mixing bowl using a wire whisk.
Serve over brisket or chicken.

Yield: 8 cups

BEST IN TEXAS CHICKEN FRIED STEAK

Flour
2-3 cups buttermilk
4-6 cubed steaks
Salt to taste

Lemon pepper to taste
Cooking oil or melted
   shortening

Gravy:
Pan drippings
3 tablespoons flour

1½ cups milk
Salt and pepper to taste

Place flour in a shallow bowl. Pour buttermilk in a separate shallow
bowl. Dip steaks in buttermilk and roll in flour. Season with salt and
pepper. Repeat dipping and rolling process again. Fry steaks in a cast
iron skillet in oil over medium heat until golden brown. Oil should be
deep enough to cover the steak. Keep warm while preparing gravy.

Gravy: Pour all but 2 tablespoons of oil from skillet. Add flour and stir
with a wooden spoon over medium heat. Scrape and stir until the mixture is blended and beginning to brown. Add milk and stir until thickened. Add salt and pepper to taste. Pour over chicken fried steak and
serve immediately.

Yield: approximately 4 servings

BLUE RIBBON MEAT LOAF

The vegetables and gravy make this a very special meat loaf. Serve with mashed potatoes and your favorite green vegetable.

¾ cup yellow onion, minced
¾ cup shallots, minced
½ cup celery, minced
½ cup carrots, minced
¼ cup green bell pepper, minced
¼ cup red bell pepper, minced
2 teaspoons garlic, minced
3 tablespoons unsalted butter
1 teaspoon salt

¼ teaspoon cayenne pepper
1 teaspoon black pepper
½ teaspoon ground white pepper
½ teaspoon cumin
½ teaspoon nutmeg
½ cup Half and Half
½ cup catsup
1½ pounds lean ground beef
½ pound ground pork
3 eggs, beaten
¾ cup breadcrumbs

Meat loaf gravy:
2 tablespoons shallots, minced
½ teaspoon dried thyme
1 bay leaf
¼ teaspoon black pepper
2 tablespoons unsalted butter

1 cup dry white wine
1 cup beef stock
1 cup chicken stock
Salt and pepper to taste

Preheat oven to 350°. Saute onions, celery, carrots, bell peppers, and garlic in butter until softened. Cool to room temperature. Combine salt, cayenne, black and white pepper, cumin, and nutmeg. Stir into cooled vegetables. Add Half and Half, catsup, ground beef, pork, eggs, and breadcrumbs. Form into 8 loaves. Place on a baking sheet with sides, and bake for 45 to 50 minutes. Reserve juices and scrape baking sheet for all bits of meat. Remove loaves to cutting board. Cut each meat loaf into slices and serve with gravy.

Gravy: Saute shallots, thyme, bay leaf, and pepper in one tablespoon butter until shallots are soft. In separate saucepan boil reserved juices and scraps of meat with wine for about 5 minutes. Strain. Add sauteed vegetables and stocks. Boil, reducing liquid by ½. Then swirl in remaining tablespoon butter. Season to taste with salt and pepper. Serve as glaze on meatloaf.

Yield: 8 loaves

LONE STAR LASAGNA

If you like the flavor of ricotta cheese, you may want to mix an 8-ounce container of ricotta cheese and cottage cheese when you make this lasagna.

6 tablespoons butter
½ cup onions, chopped
3 cloves garlic, minced
2 14½-ounce cans Italian
  tomatoes, sliced
1½ pounds ground meat
½ cup dry bread crumbs
¼ cup milk
2 eggs, slightly beaten
1 cup Parmesan cheese,
  grated
½ cup fresh parsley,
  chopped

2½ teaspoons salt
¼ teaspoon pepper
2 6-ounce cans tomato paste
3 cups water
1 tablespoon sugar
1½ teaspoons basil
1 pound lasagna noodles,
  cooked and drained
1 pound mozzarella cheese,
  sliced or shredded
1 pound cottage cheese

Preheat oven to 350°. Spray two 9x11 inch casserole dishes with Pam. Melt 4 tablespoons butter in a large saucepan. Saute onion and garlic until tender. Add tomatoes and simmer until liquid has evaporated. Combine ground meat, bread crumbs, milk, eggs, ¼ cup Parmesan cheese, ¼ cup parsley, 1½ teaspoons salt, and pepper in a large bowl, mixing well. Melt remaining 2 tablespoons butter in a large skillet; add meat mixture and cook over medium-high heat until brown. Drain and add meat to cooked tomato sauce. Mix in tomato paste, water, sugar, ¼ cup parsley, basil, ¼ cup Parmesan cheese, and 1 teaspoon salt. Simmer 1 hour. Pour 1 cup sauce into each pan. Top with a layer of noodles, ⅓ of mozzarella cheese (2 slices), ⅓ cottage cheese, and 2 tablespoons Parmesan cheese. Repeat layers. Bake for 30 minutes.

Yield: approximately 24 servings

*FOUR*STAR*FAJITAS*

Beef flank skirt steak or chicken, ⅓ to ½ pound per person.

*Marinade Number One:

1 cup soy sauce
½ cup teriyaki sauce
2 tablespoons lemon juice
3 tablespoons corn oil

1 teaspoon garlic salt
½ can beer
¼ teaspoon black pepper
1 teaspoon meat tenderizer

*Marinade Number Two:

1 8-ounce bottle Italian
  dressing
2 cups Herdez green sauce

½ cup green bell pepper,
  chopped
Salt and pepper to taste

*Marinade Number Three:

1 12-ounce can beer
Lemon pepper to taste

Garlic powder to taste
Meat tenderizer

*Marinade Number Four:

1 8-ounce bottle Italian
  dressing
1 13-ounce bottle Woody's
  marinade
1 12-ounce can beer

Juice of 3 lemons
1 teaspoon vinegar
Garlic salt to taste
Meat tenderizer

Remove fat from meat and choose your favorite marinade to marinate steak for 8 hours or overnight: Combine marinade ingredients from one of the four choices and pour over steak in a shallow pan. Cover with foil and refrigerate.

Prepare grill. When coals are hot, grill meat for about 15 minutes on each side. Remove from heat and place in a 9x13 inch aluminum pan. Pour marinade over meat and cover with foil. Cook for an additional 40 minutes on indirect heat. Remove from heat and slice meat in ¼ inch pieces on crossgrain. Serve meat on warmed flour tortillas and garnish with guacamole, chopped tomatoes, hot sauce, refried beans, and sauteed slices of onions and green peppers.

Yield: approximately 8 servings

JEWEL'S CHILI

Serve in a bowl with beans, rice, cheese, onions, and crackers.

5 pounds lean chili meat	2 cups water
1 pound bulk sausage	2 teaspoons salt
1 pound ground meat	1 teaspoon pepper
1 tablespoon garlic, chopped	1 teaspoon oregano
8 tablespoons chili powder	1 tablespoon sugar
3 tablespoons ground cumin	1 tablespoon paprika
2 6-ounce cans tomato paste	¼ cup flour
2 dried chili pods	½ cup warm water

Brown meats together in a large pot over medium heat. Add next eleven ingredients to pot and simmer approximately 1 to 2 hours. Place flour and water in a bowl and stir until smooth. Add flour paste to chili and cook an additional 15 minutes to thicken.

Yield: 1½ gallons

CHANDLER'S HEARTBURN CHILI

To prevent heartburn, cut down on the amount of Tabasco and cayenne pepper.

6-10 large dried chilies	3 tablespoons comino seeds
4 pounds coarsely ground beef	2 teaspoons oregano
2 tiny green chilies, very hot	7 dashes Tabasco sauce
1 large onion, chopped	¼ teaspoon cayenne pepper
1 16-ounce can tomatoes	1-2 Jalapeno peppers, seeded
1 3-ounce bottle chili powder	2 tablespoons powdered cocoa
2 teaspoons salt	2 teaspoons instant coffee
5-7 cloves garlic, minced	3-4 tablespoons Masa Harina or cornmeal

Seed and wash dried chilies, place in pot and cover with water. Boil 10 to 15 minutes or until chilies are tender. Place cooked chilies in a blender or food processor and puree with a little water. Brown ground beef in a large chili pot. Drip off excess fat. Add pureed chilies and remaining ingredients except Masa Harina. Cover with water and bring to a boil. Cover with lid and simmer for 2 to 3 hours. Mix Masa Harina with a small amount of cold water and stir into chili to thicken. Add water if too thick.

Yield: approximately 12 servings

MEXICAN FIESTA

A good dish for serving a large crowd.

Chili:

4 pounds ground beef, browned

3 large onions, chopped

2 15-ounce cans tomato puree

1 15-ounce can tomato sauce

4 tablespoons chili powder

1 teaspoon garlic powder

2 teaspoons cumin

5 teaspoons salt

1 30-ounce can Ranch Style beans

Fiesta ingredients:

1 48-ounce package corn chips, crushed

6 cups rice, cooked

Chili

2 large onions, chopped

2 heads iceberg lettuce, chopped

8 tomatoes, chopped

2 16-ounce cans large ripe olives, pitted

1 pound Cheddar cheese, shredded

4 cups pecans, chopped

4 cups coconut

1 32-ounce jar picante sauce

Sour cream

Guacamole

Chili: Brown beef in large Dutch oven with onions. Stir in remaining chili ingredients and simmer 30 minutes.

Fiesta: Layer on a large plate the ingredients listed in order. Don't be afraid of the pecans and coconut - they are surprisingly good!

Yield: 20 servings

SOUR CREAM ENCHILADA CASSEROLE

This is wonderful for a Mexican supper.

1 12-count package corn
  tortillas

1 16-ounce jar picante
  sauce

Meat Sauce:

1 tablespoon oil
1½-2 pounds ground meat
1 medium white onion,
  chopped
1 green bell pepper, chopped
1 teaspoon salt
½ teaspoon black pepper
½ teaspoon seasoned salt

2 tablespoons picante sauce
½ teaspoon cumin
½ teaspoon garlic powder
1 teaspoon Worcestershire
  sauce
2 tablespoons chili sauce
¼ cup ripe olives, chopped
1 tablespoon chili powder

Sour Cream Sauce:

1 stick butter, melted
2 tablespoons flour

2 cups milk
1 pint sour cream

1 8-ounce package Cheddar
  cheese

Preheat oven to 375°. Cut tortillas in strips. Pour all but 2 tablespoons picante over tortillas in a bowl and allow to soak in refrigerator.

Meat sauce: Heat oil in Dutch oven or skillet. Brown ground meat. Add onion, green pepper and seasonings. Simmer over medium heat.

Sour Cream Sauce: Melt butter in a saucepan, stir in flour. Add milk and sour cream. Heat but do not boil.

Place ½ Sour Cream Sauce in a 9x13 inch baking dish. Layer softened tortillas on top of sour cream. Follow with meat, ½ cheese, and remaining Sour Cream Sauce. Place cheese on top and garnish with ripe olives. Bake for 30 minutes.

Yield: 12 servings

BEEFILADAS

Use your own chili to top these off if you prefer.

1½ pounds ground beef
½ teaspoon salt
¼ teaspoon pepper
2 15-ounce cans of chili,
  without beans
¼ cup water

10-12 corn tortillas
Cooking oil
6 ounces Cheddar cheese,
  shredded
1 small onion, chopped

Preheat oven to 350°. Brown ground meat seasoned with salt and pepper. Heat cans of chili with water. Fry tortillas in a small skillet in oil until just hot. Place tortillas in a 9x13 inch pyrex dish and fill with ground meat, cheese, onion, and one tablespoon chili. Roll each tortilla up and place seamed side down. Pour remaining chili over top of beefiladas. Sprinkle with cheese and onions. Cover with foil and bake for 30 minutes.

Yield: 6 servings

TACO MIX

1 tablespoon chili powder
2 teaspoons onion powder
1 teaspoon ground cumin
1½ teaspoons garlic powder
1 teaspoon paprika

1 teaspoon ground oregano
1 teaspoon salt
1 teaspoon sugar
½ teaspoon Accent

Mix all ingredients together and store in an airtight container.

Yield: 3 tablespoons or equivalent to 1½-ounce packaged mix

C.C.'S CHEESE ENCHILADAS

1 onion, coarsely chopped
2 cloves garlic, coarsely
 chopped
1 Poblano pepper, seeded
 and coarsely chopped
½ jalapeno pepper, seeded
 and coarsely chopped
2 tomatoes, quartered
1 6-ounce can tomato paste
1 teaspoon salt
½ teaspoon oregano
1 teaspoon cumin

2 tablespoons vegetable oil
2 cups chicken broth
6 cups Monterey Jack cheese,
 shredded
1 4-ounce can mild chopped
 green chilies
½ cup green onions,
 chopped
½ cup sour cream
18 fresh corn tortillas
½ cup vegetable oil

Garnish:
1 avocado, sliced
1 cup green onions, chopped

2 cups sour cream

Preheat oven to 350°. Puree in a food processor or blender, onion, garlic, Poblano pepper, jalapeno pepper, tomatoes, tomato paste, salt, oregano, and cumin. Saute the puree in a heavy skillet with oil about 5 minutes. Add chicken broth and simmer 20 minutes. Mix together 4 cups cheese with green chilies, chopped green onions, sour cream, and 2 tablespoons of the sauce.

Heat ½ cup oil in a skillet. Dip each tortilla in the oil to cook briefly on each side. Dip each tortilla in the sauce and place one large spoonful of cheese mixture in each. Roll up and place in an ungreased 3-quart oblong baking dish. Cover with remaining sauce. Sprinkle with remaining cheese and bake for 20 minutes or until bubbly. Garnish with avocados, sour cream, and chopped green onions.

Yield: 6 servings

TANGY SMOKED CHICKEN

This chicken comes out slightly hot, not too hot. A favorite with men.

2 chicken fryers, quartered
  or halved
Tabasco sauce to taste
Lemon pepper to taste

Salt to taste
Garlic powder to taste
1 stick butter, melted

Prepare smoker or grill. Cover chicken heavily with Tabasco sauce. Sprinkle with lemon pepper, salt, and garlic powder. Place chicken bone side down in smoker or on grill. Do not place directly over coals! Smoke for 3½ to 4 hours. Chicken should be very tender. Coals may have to be added to keep fire going. Brush chicken every 30 minutes during cooking with butter to keep moist, careful not to wash off seasoning.

Yield: 8 servings

BARBECUED CHICKEN SEASONING

A low-calorie idea!

2 tablespoons salt
1 tablespoon black pepper
2 teaspoons garlic powder
2 teaspoons ground bay
  leaves

1 teaspoon paprika
1 teaspoon dry mustard

Mix all ingredients together and sprinkle over chicken before barbecuing.

Yield: 2 ounces

TEXAS STYLE CHICKEN AND DUMPLINGS

1 chicken, cut in pieces
1 10½-ounce can chicken
   broth
¼ teaspoon salt
¼ teaspoon pepper

¼ teaspoon celery salt
¼ teaspoon minced onion
¼ teaspoon sage
¼ teaspoon garlic salt

Dumplings:
1 cup milk
1 egg
¼ cup shortening

1 teaspoon salt
2½ cups flour

Gravy:
¼ stick butter
¼ cup flour

1 10½-ounce can chicken
   broth

Stew chicken in a large pot, barely covered with water and chicken broth. Add seasonings. Make dumplings while chicken is cooking. Combine all ingredients, adding enough flour to make a soft dough. Roll out on floured board, cut dough in strips about 1x2 inches. Remove chicken from broth. Combine ingredients for gravy together in a saucepan. Heat until thickened and add to chicken liquid. Drop in dumplings while boiling and cook covered 10 to 15 minutes. Add chicken and serve with cranberry sauce.

Yield: 6 servings

TEXAS TERIYAKI

1 cup soy sauce
1 cup brown sugar
1½ cups water
6 cloves garlic, crushed
1 medium onion, sliced

¼ teaspoon ginger
2 flank steaks cut in 1½ inch
   slices across the grain, or 2
   packages chicken breasts
   with bones

Mix first six ingredients. Add flank steak or chicken and marinate in refrigerator overnight. Grill over hot coals until done.

Yield: approximately 4 servings

CURRIED AWAY WITH TEXAS CHICKEN CREPES

10 crepes
2 tablespoons butter
1 heaping teaspoon curry
 powder
½ teaspoon paprika
2 pounds chicken, cooked
 and cubed

2 cups Half and Half, heated
4 tablespoons sherry
2 teaspoons cornstarch
Salt and pepper to taste
⅓-½ cup golden raisins,
 optional
Gruyere cheese, shredded

Melt butter; add curry and paprika and saute 1 minute. Add chicken and stir. Add hot cream and sherry mixed with cornstarch. Cook until thickened. Add raisins if desired.

Fill crepes with chicken. Place sauce in middle of crepe and roll up. Place with seam side down in a 9x13 inch casserole. Pour remaining sauce over crepes. Top with Gruyere cheese. Place under broiler to melt cheese, taking care not to burn.

Yield: approximately 10 crepes

LAYERED CHICKEN ENCHILADA CASSEROLE

1 medium onion, chopped
1 small green bell pepper,
 chopped, optional
1 4-ounce can green chilies,
 chopped
3 tablespoons butter or
 margarine
¾ cup chicken broth
1 10¾-ounce can cream of
 mushroom soup
1 10¾-ounce can cream of
 chicken soup

1 5¾-ounce can evaporated
 milk
1 10-ounce can Rotel
 tomatoes and green chilies
2½ cups chicken, cooked
 and chopped
1 teaspoon chili powder
1 12-count package corn
 tortillas
½ pound Cheddar or
 Monterey Jack cheese,
 shredded

Preheat oven to 250°. Grease a 9x13 inch casserole dish. Brown onion, green pepper, and chilies in butter. Add next seven ingredients and simmer 10 minutes. Line casserole with tortillas. Layer with ½ sauce and ½ cheese. Repeat layers. Cover and bake for 45 minutes. Serve with tostados and hot sauce.

Yield: 8 servings

SOUR CREAM CHICKEN ENCHILADAS

1 medium onion, chopped
1 tablespoon butter or
  margarine, melted
3 cups chicken, cooked and
  chopped
2½ cups sour cream
2 10¾-ounce cans cream of
  chicken soup
2 4-ounce cans mushroom
  stems and pieces
1 4-ounce can chopped
  green chilies, drained

1 teaspoon chili powder
½ teaspoon salt
½ teaspoon garlic powder
¼ teaspoon pepper
1 teaspoon ground cumin
20 corn tortillas
Salad oil
1 cup Monterey Jack cheese,
  shredded
1 cup Cheddar cheese,
  shredded

Preheat oven to 400°. Saute onion in butter until tender. Stir in chicken and add ½ cup sour cream, 1 can chicken soup, mushrooms, green chilies, and seasonings. Cook over low heat and stir until well heated. Soften tortillas by frying each side in oil in a large skillet. Fill tortillas with a scant ¼ cup mixture and top with Monterey Jack cheese. Roll up and place seam side down in a 9x13 inch baking dish that has been spread with 1 cup sour cream.

Combine the remaining can of chicken soup with remaining sour cream and shredded cheese. Spoon over tortillas and bake uncovered for 35 minutes.

Yield: 8 servings

JUAREZ CHICKEN ENCHILADAS

1 onion, coarsely chopped
2 cloves garlic, coarsely
chopped
1 4-ounce can mild chopped
green chilies
1 Poblano pepper, seeded
and coarsely chopped
1 1-pound can green
tomatoes, undrained, or 4
tomatillos and ½ cup
chicken broth
½ jalapeno, seeded and
coarsely chopped

1 teaspoon cumin
1 teaspoon salt
½ teaspoon oregano
2 tablespoons oil
4 cups chicken breasts,
cooked and chopped
4 cups Monterey Jack cheese,
shredded
Salt and pepper to taste
1½ cups heavy cream,
warmed
½ cup vegetable oil
1½ dozen fresh corn tortillas

Preheat oven to 350°. Puree in food processor or blender the first
nine ingredients. Saute the puree in a heavy skillet with 2 tablespoons
vegetable oil for about 10 minutes. Combine chicken with 2 cups
cheese, salt, and pepper. Remove sauce from heat and allow to cool
slightly. Mix in cream.

Heat ½ cup oil in a skillet large enough for the tortillas. Dip each tortilla in the oil to cook briefly on each side. Dip each tortilla into the
sauce and place one large spoonful of chicken mixture in each and roll
up. Place in an ungreased 3-quart casserole dish, seam side down.
Cover with remaining sauce and sprinkle remaining cheese over top.
Bake for 20 minutes or until bubbly.

Yield: 6 servings

SALSA VERDE

Very good served over chicken enchiladas.

1 cup onion, chopped
½ cup vegetable oil
10 ounces spinach, washed and chopped
1 13-ounce can green Spanish tomatoes

1 4-ounce can chopped green chilies
2 cloves garlic, crushed
2 teaspoons oregano
1 cup chicken broth

Saute onion in oil in a heavy saucepan. Add spinach and next four ingredients. Cover and cook for 5 to 10 minutes over medium heat. Remove from heat and process ingredients in a blender or food processor until smooth. Return to saucepan and add broth. Bring to a boil. Reduce heat and simmer for 15 minutes uncovered. Will keep for a week in the refrigerator.

Yield: approximately 5 cups

CHICKEN TACOS

2½ cups chicken, cooked and shredded
1 bunch green onions, chopped (chop green ends separately)
1 cup medium or hot taco sauce
1 4-ounce can whole green chilies
3 tablespoons vegetable oil
3 ounces cream cheese

½ teaspoon dried cilantro
¼ teaspoon garlic powder
½ teaspoon cumin
Salt and pepper to taste
12 taco shells
Cheddar cheese, shredded
Shredded lettuce
Additional taco sauce
Sour Cream
Sliced avocados

Preheat oven to 350°. Saute chicken, whites of onion, taco sauce, and chilies, in oil. Blend in cream cheese and seasonings. Heat taco shells for 5 minutes in oven. Spoon cheese into each taco shell and top with chicken mixture. Top tacos with lettuce, taco sauce, and green onion. Serve with sour cream and avocados.

Yield: 12 tacos

SOUTH TEXAS GRILLED DOVE

This method of cooking is equally good for quail or dove. Stuffing with a jalapeno takes the wild taste out of the bird. Bacon keeps them tender.

Doves, three or four per
  person
Seasoned salt
Black pepper
Canned mild jalapeno
  peppers, deveined

Bacon
Corn oil
Butter, melted

Pick the entire bird. Using field shears, split the bird down the back and dress. Salt and pepper in and out generously. Place a jalapeno pepper in the cavity and wrap bird with one slice of bacon securing with a toothpick. Place birds on very hot grill with fire close to the cooking surface. Do not close the top. Brown the doves, careful not to overcook. Baste with a mixture of ½ corn oil and ½ butter.

Yield: 3 to 4 per person

VENISON SHISH-KA-BOB

This is also good with beef chunks

Marinade:
¾ cup hot water
⅓ cup soy sauce
¼ cup honey
3 tablespoons vegetable oil
2 tablespoons lemon juice
1 clove garlic, minced

Venison backstrap, about 2
  pounds, cut in 1 inch
  cubes
1 green bell pepper, cut in 1
  inch chunks
1 onion, cut in 1 inch
  chunks

Mix marinade ingredients together and pour over venison in a large bowl. Marinate 24 hours in refrigerator.

Parboil green peppers and onion for 3 to 5 minutes. Alternate meat, onion, and green pepper chunks on meat skewers. Cook on grill until desired doneness, taking care not to dry out.

Yield: 6 servings

CHORIZO

Good for breakfast with huevos rancheros.

2 tablespoons chopped green
  chilies
½ teaspoon garlic powder
3 teaspoons oregano

½ cup white vinegar
½ cup chili powder
Scant ¼ cup water
2½ pounds ground pork

Combine all ingredients except the ground pork in a blender and mix well. Place meat in a ceramic casserole dish or a bowl and pour chili sauce over meat. Cover with a plate and allow to marinate at room temperature overnight or 12 hours. Pour off any water which accumulates. Chili prevents spoiling.

Yield: 4 cups

APRICOT RIBS

1 17-ounce can apricot halves
⅓ cup brown sugar, firmly
  packed
3 tablespoons vinegar

1 clove garlic, chopped
4 teaspoons soy sauce
⅛ teaspoon ground ginger
1 slab pork ribs

Prepare grill. Drain apricots, reserving ⅓ cup syrup. Puree apricots with ⅓ cup reserved syrup in blender. Pour into small saucepan. Add brown sugar, vinegar, garlic, soy sauce, and ginger. Stir and simmer over medium heat uncovered 10 to 15 minutes. Prepare grill and cook ribs slowly about 50 minutes. Baste with apricot sauce last 30 minutes of cooking.

Yield: approximately 6 servings

HAM AND RED EYE GRAVY

Ham steaks, ¼ to ½ inch
  thick
1 tablespoon butter or
  margarine
1 small onion, chopped
1 clove garlic, chopped
1 10½-ounce can beef
  bouillon

1 heaping tablespoon
  cornstarch
¼ cup strong coffee
2 squeezes lemon
Cooked grits

Fry ham steaks in butter in a heavy skillet. Saute on one side and add onion and garlic. Turn ham slice, saute with drippings and remove. Mix together bouillon, cornstarch, and coffee with drippings. Add lemon juice to cut the salty taste. Place ham back in skillet for a minute. Serve gravy over grits.

Yield: 1 steak per person

HEART AND SOLE

6 fillets of sole or flounder,
  washed
Salt and pepper to taste
3-4 tomatoes, thinly sliced
½ cup breadcrumbs

¾ cup white wine
¾ stick butter
2 teaspoons fresh lime juice
¼ cup Parmesan cheese,
  grated

Preheat oven to 400°. Season fillets with salt and pepper. Cover bottom of 9x13 inch baking dish with tomato slices. Sprinkle with breadcrumbs. Place fillets on top. Combine wine, butter and lime juice in a saucepan. Simmer until butter is melted. Pour over fillets and sprinkle with cheese. Bake in oven for 10 to 15 minutes or until fillets flake with a fork. Do not overcook.

Yield: Approximately 4 servings

BRAZOS RIVER OVEN BAKED FISH

1 stick butter, melted
⅔ cup buttery flavored
  crackers, crushed
¼ cup Parmesan cheese,
  grated

½ teaspoon basil
½ teaspoon oregano
½ teaspoon salt
¼ teaspoon garlic powder
Catch of the day, cut into
  fillets

Preheat oven to 350°. Mix ingredients together. Coat fish thoroughly and bake for 25 to 30 minutes.

Yield: approximately ½ cup

BAR-B-QUED SHRIMP

These are also delicious wrapped in bacon and served as an appetizer.

2 pounds fresh or frozen
  shrimp, shelled and
  deveined
2 cloves garlic, mashed
½ teaspoon salt
½ cup oil
¼ cup soy sauce

½ cup lemon juice
3 tablespoons parsley, finely
  chopped
2 tablespoons onion, finely
  chopped
½ teaspoon pepper

Arrange shrimp in a shallow baking dish. Combine remaining ingredients and pour over shrimp. Cover and refrigerate for 2 to 3 hours. Place on skewers leaving a space between shrimp. Grill over medium heat with hood down for 3 minutes. Turn and continue cooking for 5 minutes. Baste with marinade occasionally.

*Note: You may leave shrimp in pan, cover, and grill for 20 to 30 minutes.

Yield: approximately 4 servings

AUNT MATTIE'S TEA CAKES

Use big cookie cutters when cutting out this dough. We prefer a Texas-shaped cutter!

2 sticks butter, softened
2 cups sugar
3 eggs, well beaten
3 tablespoons milk

2 teaspoons vanilla
4 cups flour
4 teaspoons baking powder
½ teaspoon salt

Cream butter and sugar. Add eggs, milk, vanilla, flour, baking powder, and salt, mixing well. Chill dough for easier handling and cutting. Preheat oven to 375°. Roll dough thin, about ¼ inch thick. Cut with cookie cutter and place on ungreased baking sheet. Bake for 8-10 minutes or until lightly browned.

Yield: 3 dozen

PECAN HARVEST CAKE

3 tablespoons butter, melted
1 cup pecans, coarsley
  chopped
⅔ cup butter, softened
1⅓ cups sugar
1½ teaspoons vanilla

2 eggs
2 cups cake flour, sifted
1½ teaspoons baking powder
¼ teaspoon salt
⅔ cup milk
Cream Cheese Icing with ⅓
  cup chopped pecans added
  (see desserts)

Preheat oven to 350°. Grease and flour three 8-inch round pans. Mix 3 tablespoons butter and 1⅓ cups pecans in a jelly roll pan. Toast until golden brown. Allow to cool.

Cream butter and sugar beating until light and fluffy. Add vanilla. Add eggs, one at a time, beating well after each addition. Sift dry ingredients together and add alternately with milk, beginning and ending with flour mixture. Fold in 1 cup of toasted pecans. Divide mixture into three cake pans and bake 20 to 30 minutes. Cool in pans for 10 minutes and finish cooling on wire racks. Ice and refrigerate.

Yield: 8 servings

GRANNY'S FRIED PIES

Fruit:
2 cups dried apples, peaches,   Water to cover
  or apricots   ¾ cup sugar

Crust:
2 cups flour   ¾ cup buttermilk
1 teaspoon salt   Pinch of baking soda
⅓ cup shortening   Shortening, melted

Glaze:
1 cup confectioners sugar   1-2 tablespoons milk

Cover fruit with water in a saucepan. Cook until fruit is tender. Add sugar and cook an additional five minutes. Drain and mash with a fork or potato masher. Mix flour, salt, and shortening together. Add baking soda to buttermilk then add to flour, blending well. Do not make it too stiff. More buttermilk may be added. Roll dough onto a floured board to ⅛ inch thickness. Cut a rounded circle using an inverted saucer as a guide. Place 1 tablespoon fruit in the center of one side of circle. Fold over the other side and seal by pressing edges with a fork. Prick top 3 to 4 times. Melt shortening in an iron skillet and fry pies until brown, turning once.

Glaze: Combine sugar and milk by adding milk slowly to reach a glaze consistency. Spread over each pie.

Yield: approximately 8 pies

MAMA'S FLAKY PIE CRUST

2⅔ cups flour, sifted   1 cup shortening
1 teaspoon salt   6 tablespoons ice water

Mix flour with salt. Cut in shortening until mixture looks like small peas. Add water, 1 tablespoon at a time, tossing flour mixture with a fork. Mixture should leave sides of bowl when all water has been added and mixed in. Roll crusts on floured board.

Yield: 2 crusts

CRANBERRY-RAISIN PIE WITH WALNUT CRUST

The cranberry filling glistens a beautiful red, and the crunchy walnut crust makes this a festive dessert for a holiday table. Whipped cream with 1 tablespoon of framboise or kirsh adds a nice taste to this dessert.

Crust:

1 cup walnuts, coarsely
   chopped
½ cup flour

⅓ cup sugar
½ stick butter, melted

Filling:

1½ cups sugar
6 tablespoons flour
¼ teaspoon salt
4 cups fresh cranberries
   (1 pound)

1½ cups raisins
½ stick butter
1½ cups water
1 teaspoon almond extract

Preheat oven to 350°. Grease a 9-inch pie plate. Combine in food processor, walnuts, flour, sugar, and melted butter, until you have a fine, silky crumb mixture. Press the crumbs firmly over the bottom and sides of the pie plate and bake until slightly brown, about 12-15 minutes. Combine all the filling ingredients except the almond extract in a large saucepan. Cook over low heat stirring often, until the mixture becomes thick and glossy, about 20 minutes. Remove from heat and stir in almond extract. Cool to room temperature. Pour filling into crust and bake 30 minutes. Top with ice cream or whipped cream.

Yield: 8 servings

TEXAS PECAN PIE

1 9-inch pie crust
1 cup Karo syrup
1 cup dark brown sugar
⅓ cup butter, melted

⅓ teaspoon salt
1 teaspoon vanilla
3 eggs, slightly beaten
1 heaping cup pecans

Preheat oven to 350°. Mix Karo syrup, brown sugar, butter, salt, and vanilla. Add eggs and blend well. Pour into pie crust and top with pecans. Bake for 45 minutes.

Yield: 8 servings

MOTHER'S PUMPKIN PIE WITH PECAN TOPPING

1 9-inch pie shell

Filling:

½ cup sugar
1 heaping teaspoon flour
1 rounded tablespoon butter, softened
3 egg yolks

1 cup fresh or canned pumpkin (puree fresh pumpkin with ¼ teaspoon of salt)
1 cup milk
¾ teaspoon cinnamon
¾ teaspoon allspice

Topping:

⅔ cup brown sugar
¼ cup flour

1 cup pecans, chopped
½ stick butter, softened

Preheat oven to 375°. Bake pie shell in oven for approximately 10 minutes. Allow to cool. Cream together sugar, flour, butter, and egg yolks until well blended. Add pumpkin, milk, cinnamon, and allspice. Mix well. Pour the filling into pie shell. Bake approximately 40 to 50 minutes or until filling is firm and cake tester inserted in the middle comes out clean.

Mix brown sugar, flour, and pecans together for topping. Cut in butter and sprinkle over pie 15 minutes before pie is done.

Yield: 8 servings

DINNY'S PECAN PIE

1 9-inch pie crust
⅓ cup sugar
2 tablespoons flour
½ teaspoon salt
1 cup light corn syrup

1 cup dark corn syrup
3 eggs, beaten
1½ cups pecans
1 teaspoon vanilla

Preheat oven to 400°. Add first five ingredients to beaten eggs and mix well in a medium mixing bowl. Add pecans and vanilla. Pour mixture into your favorite pie crust. Bake for 10 minutes at 400°, then reduce heat to 350° and bake an additional 35 minutes. Will continue to cook after it comes out of oven.

Yield: 8 servings

BRAZOS BLACKBERRY COBBLER

2 pie crust sticks
6 cups fresh blackberries,
  washed

¾ cup sugar
½ stick butter

Preheat oven to 425°. Prepare pie crust and roll into circle large enough to fit a 2-quart round deep ovenproof dish, allowing edges to hang over about 2 inches. Add blackberries. Add leftover pieces of crust here and there in the blackberries. Sprinkle sugar over berries and dot with butter. Fold excess dough over top (will not meet). Bake for 45 minutes and serve warm with cream.

Yield: 8 servings

"DOWN HOME" PEACH COBBLER

Pie crust pastry for 2 pies
5 cups fresh peaches, peeled
  and sliced
1¼ cups sugar
¼ cup water

3 tablespoons flour
⅛ teaspoon salt
½ teaspoon almond extract
½ stick butter

Preheat oven to 375°. Prepare pastry. Roll out ½ pastry in floured surface. Line bottom of 2-quart Pyrex dish with pastry. Roll out the other half of dough. Cut into 2-inch strips. Bake half strips in oven until lightly brown. Break cooked strips into three inch pieces. Mix peaches, 1 cup sugar, and water in a saucepan and cook over medium heat until fruit is soft. Mix flour, ¼ cup sugar, and salt; add fruit. Cook, stirring occasionally until slightly thickened. Stir in almond extract and cooked pastry strips. Pour into crust lined baking dish. Cover with unbaked strips of dough. Dot with butter and sprinkle with sugar if desired. Bake at 400° for 35 to 40 minutes until browned. Serve with ice cream.

Yield: 8 servings

OLD FASHIONED APPLE PIE

2 9-inch pie crusts

Filling:

¼ cup brown sugar, packed
½ cup sugar
2 tablespoons flour
¼ teaspoon salt
¾ teaspoon cinnamon
¼ teaspoon nutmeg

5-7 firm green apples or pears; peeled, cored, and sliced
¼ stick butter, cut in small dabs

Preheat oven to 425°. Mix all filling ingredients together in a mixing bowl except apples and butter. Layer pastry in pie plate. Heap apples and filling onto crust and dot top with butter. Top with remaining pastry. Flute the edges and slit the top crust to allow steam to escape. Bake 40-45 minutes. Place on wire rack to cool.

Yield: 8 servings

BRAZOS PEACH PIE

It is delicious served warm and topped with ice cream. This reheats well.

1 9-inch pie crust

4 cups fresh peaches, peeled and sliced

Custard:
1 cup sugar
2 tablespoons flour

2 tablespoons butter or margarine, melted
2 eggs, beaten

Preheat oven to 350°. Place peaches in crust. Mix custard ingredients together. Pour over the peaches. Bake for about 1 hour or until firm.

Yield: 6 servings

FLAN

1-2 tablespoons butter	1 13-ounce can evaporated
1 cup sugar	milk
1 14-ounce can sweetened	1 teaspoon vanilla
condensed milk	4 eggs, beaten

Preheat oven to 325°. Carmelize sugar by rubbing a heavy saucepan lightly with butter. Place ½ cup sugar in pan and cook over moderate heat. Stir constantly until sugar melts. Add the other ½ cup sugar and continue stirring until you have a clear brown syrup.

Mix canned milks, vanilla, and eggs in bowl. Pour in pan with carmelized sugar and place pan in a separate pan of water. Bake for 1 hour. Refrigerate in pan overnight. Invert and serve.

Yield: 6 servings

MANN CENTURY PEACH ICE CREAM

Leave out the peaches for a wonderful vanilla ice cream.

6 eggs, separated	½ teaspoon salt
3 cups sugar	3 cups water
3 tablespoons cornstarch	1 tablespoon vanilla
3 13-ounce cans evaporated	6 cups fresh peaches, sliced
milk	

Beat egg yolks with a wire whisk. Add sugar, cornstarch, milk, salt, and water, mixing well. Place in a sauce pan and simmer for 1 to 1½ hours until thickened, like custard. Strain custard after allowing to cool. Add vanilla, beaten egg whites, and peaches. Place in ice cream freezer and freeze.

Yield: approximately 10 servings

SWEET LIL'S FAMOUS SUGAR COOKIES

4¼ cups flour	1 cup confectioners sugar
1 teaspoon baking soda	2 sticks butter, softened
1 teaspoon salt	¾ cup oil
1 teaspoon cream of tartar	2 eggs, slightly beaten
1 cup sugar	1 tablespoon vanilla

Combine 1 cup flour, baking soda, salt, and cream of tartar in a mixing bowl and set aside. Combine sugars, butter, and oil; cream well. Add egg and vanilla to sugar and fold in all flour. Cover and chill overnight. Preheat oven to 375°. Shape dough into walnut size balls. Place on an ungreased cookie sheet. Flatten with the bottom of a glass dipped in sugar. Bake for 12 to 15 minutes or until lightly browned. Watch closely. Cool on wire racks.

Yield: 12 dozen small cookies or 6 dozen large

LYNN'S CARMELITAS

Crust:

1 cup flour	½ teaspoon baking soda
¾ cup brown sugar	1½ sticks butter or
⅛ teaspoon salt	margarine, melted
1 cup quick oats	

Filling:

1 6-ounce package chocolate chips	¾ cup caramel ice cream topping
½ cup pecans, chopped	3 tablespoons flour

Preheat oven to 350°. Combine all crust ingredients together in a large mixing bowl, blending well with a mixer to form crumbs. Press ½ of crumbs into a 9-inch square pan. Bake 10 minutes. Remove from oven and sprinkle with chocolate chips and pecans. Blend caramel topping with flour. Spread over chips and nuts. Sprinkle with remaining crumb mixture. Bake 15 to 20 minutes or until golden brown. Chill for 1 to 2 hours. Cut into squares to serve.

Yield: 36 squares

BRAZOS BROWNIES

Be sure you cover these tightly!

1 8-ounce package
    unsweetened baking
    chocolate, 8 squares
2 sticks butter, softened
5 large eggs
3 cups sugar
1 tablespoon vanilla

1½ cups flour
4 tablespoons cocoa
1 stick butter
⅓ cup milk
1 16-ounce box
    confectioners sugar

Preheat oven to 375°. Grease a 9x13 inch baking pan. Melt chocolate and butter together. Allow to cool. Beat eggs, sugar, and vanilla on high speed with electric mixer for 10 minutes. Blend in chocolate and mix well. Fold in flour and stir until just blended. Pour into baking pan. Bake for 35 minutes.

Mix together cocoa, butter and milk in a saucepan and cook, stirring until bubbly and butter is melted. Add to confectioners sugar in a mixing bowl; blend. Ice brownies while warm. Cool completely before cutting.

Yield: approximately 24 brownies

TEXAS MILLIONAIRES

1 pound pecan halves
2 12-ounce packages
    chocolate chips
1 7-ounce jar marshmallow
    cream

4½ cups sugar
1 stick butter or margarine
1 13-ounce can evaporated
    milk

Mix pecans, chocolate chips, and marshmallow together. Mix sugar, butter, and milk together in a heavy saucepan. Bring to a rolling boil and cook for 7 minutes, stirring constantly. Pour over pecan mixture and stir until smooth and blended. Drop by teaspoonfuls onto waxed paper and allow to set until firm. Store in an airtight container in refrigerator.

Yield: 120 pieces

EL PRESIDENTE PRALINES

2 cups sugar
1 teaspoon baking soda
1 cup buttermilk
¼ teaspoon salt

2 tablespoons butter
2⅓ cups pecan halves
1 teaspoon vanilla

Stir together first four ingredients in a saucepan. Cook briskly stirring frequently until mixture reaches 210° on a candy thermometer. Stir in butter and pecan halves. Stir until 230°. Remove from heat and add vanilla. Cool for 1 to 2 minutes, then beat by hand with a wooden spoon until candy changes color slightly and looks creamy instead of clear and "strings" start to form behind the spoon. This usually takes 3 to 4 minutes of hard stirring. Drop by tablespoonfuls onto waxed paper and allow to harden.

Yield: approximately 2 dozen

TRIED AND TRUE MICROWAVE PRALINES

1½ cups brown sugar,
    packed
⅔ cup Half and Half
2 tablespoons butter

⅛ teaspoon salt
2 cups pecans, halves and
    pieces
1 teaspoon vanilla

Place first four ingredients together in a 2-quart glass mixing cup and stir to mix. Place in microwave for 9 minutes on High setting. At 4½ minutes remove, and add 1½ cups pecans and vanilla. Stir well. Cook remaining 4½ minutes. Let mixture set one minute. Beat with a wooden spoon for 3 minutes. Drop mixture by tablespoonfuls onto waxed paper. Add remaining pecans when ¼ mixture remains.

*Note: After dropping first 2 or 3 and they don't seem to be setting, place back in microwave for 30 seconds.

Yield: approximately 2-3 dozen

Side Dishes and Condiments

Thank you for your financial support
of the following Junior League of Waco project:

"Education and Parents Meeting Today's Challenge"
A Conference on Teen Sexuality

A conference for parents and youth professionals
on the issues of adolescent sexuality.

ASPARAGUS CASSEROLE

1 16-ounce can cut
  asparagus, drained
½ teaspoon salt
½ teaspoon white pepper
1 2-ounce jar diced pimento,
  drained
2 eggs, beaten

1 cup buttery cracker
  crumbs
1 cup milk
1 cup Cheddar cheese,
  shredded
½ stick butter, melted

Preheat oven to 400°. Grease an 8-inch square baking dish. Combine all ingredients together in a mixing bowl. Spoon into baking dish and sprinkle additional cracker crumbs on top. Bake uncovered for 25 to 30 minutes.

Yield: 6 servings

4-BEAN BAKE

3 medium onions, chopped
3 tablespoons margarine,
  melted
1 16-ounce can navy beans,
  drained
1 16-ounce can green lima
  beans, drained
1 16-ounce can butter beans,
  drained

1 16-ounce can baked beans
½ cup catsup
3 tablespoons vinegar
1 tablespoon brown sugar
1 teaspoon salt
1 teaspoon dry mustard
¼ teaspoon black pepper
4 slices of bacon, cooked and
  crumbled

Preheat oven to 325°. Saute onions in margarine in a medium skillet until tender. Place beans in a large bowl; add onions and remaining ingredients except bacon. Mix together and pour into a 2½ quart casserole dish. Bake uncovered for 1 hour. Top with bacon.

Yield: approximately 12 servings

MAMA BOYCE'S PINTO CHILI BEANS

Beans can be made into a soup by adding a bit more liquid.

1 pound pinto beans
1 pound salt pork
1 large onion, chopped
1½ large cloves garlic,
  mashed
½ large green bell pepper,
  chopped

1 16-ounce can tomatoes
1 16-ounce can enchilada
  sauce
½ box whole comino seed

Cover beans with boiling water and soak for 30 minutes. Simmer salt pork in 2-3 cups water for 30 minutes in a large pot. Add beans to salt pork mixture. Simmer for several hours or until beans are tender. Add remaining ingredients and continue cooking over low heat for 1 to 2 hours or until desired consistency is reached. If beans need more liquid, add boiling water.

Yield: approximately 6 servings

DRUNK BEANS

These beans are not only wonderful by themselves, but are perfect to put in a taco salad or for making bean dip.

2 pounds pinto beans
½ teaspoon garlic salt
1 teaspoon chili powder
1 teaspoon cumin
1 tomato, quartered
1 onion, quartered
1 rib celery, chopped
2 jalapeno peppers, chopped

1 small green bell pepper,
  chopped
5 quarts water
⅓ pound salt pork, cut in
  small pieces
½ can beer
Salt to taste

Combine all ingredients except beer and salt in a large pot. Cover. Cook over low heat for 6 hours. Add more water if needed when cooking. When beans are done, add beer and salt. Simmer 30 minutes.

Yield: 1 large pot

PAM'S SCRUMPTIOUS BROCCOLI-ARTICHOKE BAKE

1 20-ounce package frozen chopped broccoli
1 8-ounce package cream cheese
1 stick margarine
1 8-ounce can sliced water chestnuts
2 4½-ounce jars marinated artichoke hearts, drained
3-4 tablespoons Italian bread crumbs
3-4 tablespoons Parmesan cheese, grated

Preheat oven to 350°. Cook broccoli according to directions and drain. Melt cheese and butter together in a saucepan. Add broccoli and water chestnuts. Place artichokes in the bottom of a large baking dish. Pour broccoli mixture over artichokes. Sprinkle with bread crumbs and cheese. Bake for 30 minutes.

Yield: approximately 6 servings

COMPANY BROCCOLI CASSEROLE

1 large sweet onion, chopped
½ stick margarine
2 10-ounce packages frozen chopped broccoli
1 10¾-ounce can mushroom soup
1 4-ounce can sliced mushrooms, drained
2 6-ounce rolls garlic cheese, cubed
1 8-ounce can water chestnuts, drained and chopped
⅛ teaspoon cayenne pepper
1 16-ounce package frozen broccoli cuts
1 2½-ounce jar sliced pimento, drained

Preheat oven to 350°. Grease a 2-quart casserole dish. Saute onions in margarine in a saucepan until onions are tender and translucent. Cook chopped broccoli according to package directions and drain well, squeezing out all of the moisture. Add cooked broccoli, mushroom soup, mushrooms, cheese, water chestnuts, and cayenne pepper to onions. Heat until cheese melts over medium heat.

Cook broccoli cuts according to package directions and drain well. Pour broccoli-cheese mixture in casserole and place broccoli cuts on top. Garnish with sliced pimentos. Bake for 20 to 30 minutes.

Yield: 10 servings

CABBAGE SURPRISE

You won't even know this is cabbage.

4 cups shredded cabbage
1 teaspoon salt
3 tablespoons butter
3 tablespoons flour
½ cup onion, chopped
1 teaspoon Worcestershire
  sauce

1 28-ounce can tomatoes, cut
  up
1 teaspoon sugar
2 cups plain croutons
¼ pound sharp Cheddar
  cheese, shredded

Preheat oven to 375°. Lightly grease a 9x13 inch casserole. Cook cabbage in salted water in a large saucepan for 10 minutes and drain. Melt butter in a skillet and add flour and blend well. Add onion, tomatoes, Worcestershire sauce, and sugar and cook until blended. Layer cabbage, sauce, croutons, and cheese in casserole and bake for 30 minutes.

Yield: 8 servings

LEMONY CARROTS

For a variation add a bit of garlic and sprinkle with Parmesan cheese.

1 pound carrots
½ teaspoon sugar
1 teaspoon salt
½ cup onion, finely chopped
½ stick butter

1-1½ tablespoons lemon
  juice
2 tablespoons parsley flakes
  or 4 tablespoons fresh
  parsley, chopped

Scrape carrots and slice into sticks 3 inches long. Cover with water and bring to a boil with sugar and salt. Boil for 15 minutes. Drain and keep warm. Saute onion in butter in a skillet over medium heat until tender and transparent. Add lemon juice and parsley, blending well over very low heat. Pour over warm carrots. These carrots are best made ahead of time and then gently reheated to allow seasonings to meld.

Yield: 8 servings

CARROTS AU GRATIN

4 cups carrots, sliced
Salt to taste
½ cup water
2 tablespoons butter
2 tablespoons flour

1 cup milk
1 cup sharp Cheddar cheese,
   shredded
1 3½-ounce can French fried
   onions

Boil carrots in salted water for 5 minutes and drain. Melt butter in saucepan over medium heat. Slowly add flour, stirring constantly. Gradually add milk. Cook until thickened. Add cheese, and stir until melted.

In a 1½ quart casserole, layer carrots and onions twice, reserving some onions. Pour sauce over all. Bake for 15 minutes in 350° oven. Top with remaining onions and bake an additional 5 minutes.

Yield: 6-8 servings

SWEET CARROT SOUFFLE

An interesting change from sweet potatoes.

2 cups carrots, cooked
3 eggs
¼ teaspoon cinnamon
2 tablespoons flour

½ cup sugar
1 cup milk
½ stick butter

Preheat oven to 350°. Mix all ingredients together in a blender until smooth. Spoon into a 9x13 inch baking dish and bake for 45 minutes.

Yield: 6 servings

CREAMY BAKED CORN

12 ears corn
1 teaspoon salt
1 tablespoon flour, heaping
2 tablespoons sugar

1 stick butter, chunked
2 tablespoons bacon
  drippings
¼ cup water

Cut kernels off cob without coming too close to cob. Scrape juice from cob. Mix all ingredients in a greased 3 quart casserole. Cover and bake at 350° for 1 hour, stirring occasionally.

Yield: 10-12 servings

CORN CASSEROLE

Corn lover's delight.

1 stick butter
¾ cup green bell pepper,
  chopped
1 clove garlic, chopped
¼ cup flour
⅔ cup milk
¾ teaspoon each salt,
  pepper, basil, and oregano

1 teaspoon sugar
1 cup Cheddar cheese,
  shredded
1 17-ounce can whole kernel
  corn, drained
2 cans onions, drained
2 16-ounce can tomatoes,
  drained

Preheat oven to 325°. Melt butter in a large skillet; saute bell pepper and garlic for a few minutes. Stir in flour, milk, salt, pepper, basil oregano, and sugar. Add ½ cup cheese and canned corn. Cook until cheese is melted. Add onions and tomatoes. Pour into a 9x13 inch casserole and top with ½ cup cheese. Bake for 50 minutes.

Yield: 8 servings

GREEN AND GOLD CORN CASSEROLE

Add a little more color to this casserole by adding a 4-ounce jar of drained chopped pimentos.

1 16-ounce can cream style corn
1 16-ounce can whole kernel corn, drained
¼ cup onion, chopped
1 4-ounce can chopped green chilies
2 tablespoons butter, melted
2 eggs, slightly beaten
½ teaspoon sugar
½ teaspoon salt
¼ teaspoon black pepper
1 cup buttery cracker crumbs, crushed
¼ cup cream
1 tablespoon Parmesan cheese, grated
1 cup Cheddar cheese, shredded

Topping:
½ cup buttery cracker crumbs
2 tablespoons butter, melted
2 tablespoons Parmesan cheese, grated
Paprika to garnish

Preheat oven to 350°. Grease a 2-quart casserole dish. Mix all ingredients together except the topping and place in casserole. Mix topping ingredients together and sprinkle over casserole. Garnish with paprika. Bake for 50 minutes.

Yield: 6 servings

PHYLLIS' CORN PUDDING

10 ears, fresh corn
2 eggs, beaten
2 tablespoons sugar
1 tablespoon flour
1 teaspoon salt
½ cup Half and Half or milk
Butter

Preheat oven to 325°. Butter a 9-inch square baking dish. Cut corn off the cob. Scrape cob with edge of knife to milk cob. Mix eggs, sugar, flour, and salt together. Add milk and mix with cut corn. Pour into baking dish and dot with butter. Bake for approximately 45 minutes.

Yield: 8 servings

PARTY BEANS

Try this with asparagus or broccoli.

2 16-ounce cans long Blue
  Lake Green Beans, drained
1 large red onion, sliced

Salt and cracked pepper to
  taste
1 tablespoon oil
1 tablespoon vinegar

Sour Cream Dressing:
1 cup sour cream
½ cup mayonnaise
1 teaspoon lemon juice

¼ teaspoon dry mustard
1 tablespoon horseradish
Onion juice to taste

Garnish: chives or fresh
  green onions, chopped

Place beans in a large serving dish. Place onions on top and sprinkle with salt and pepper. Pour oil and vinegar over bean mixture and cover. Marinate in refrigerator overnight or at least 3 to 4 hours, stirring occasionally. Combine dressing ingredients in a small bowl. Pour over marinated beans just before serving. Garnish.

Yield: approximately 6 servings

BUNDLES OF BEANS

These are wonderful to serve when fresh vegetables are out of season.

4 slices bacon, halved
2 16-ounce cans whole green
  beans, drained
½ cup brown sugar, firmly
  packed

½ clove garlic, pressed
½ stick butter, melted

Preheat oven to 350°. Divide beans into 8 portions. Wrap each portion with ½ slice bacon and secure with a toothpick. Place bean bundles in a baking dish. Combine remaining ingredients in a small mixing bowl and pour over beans. Bake for 35 minutes.

Yield: 8 servings

CHEESY GREEN BEANS

1 6-ounce can sliced
  mushrooms, drained
1 medium onion, chopped
⅓ cup butter
¼ cup flour
1 cup Half and Half
½ pound Cheese Whiz
¼ teaspoon Tabasco sauce
2 tablespoons soy sauce
½ teaspoon pepper

Dash of salt
½ teaspoon Accent
  seasoning
1 6-ounce can sliced water
  chestnuts, drained
2 16-ounce cans whole green
  beans, drained
1 2¼-ounce package slivered
  almonds

Preheat oven to 350°. Lightly grease 9x13 inch baking dish. Saute mushrooms and onions in butter. Cook until onions are tender. Add flour and cook until smooth, stirring constantly. Heat cream in a medium saucepan until warm. Add sauteed vegetables, stirring constantly. Add cheese, Tabasco, and seasonings; stir well. Add water chestnuts and green beans and mix thoroughly. Pour into baking dish and top with almonds.

Bake for approximately 20 to 25 minutes or until bubbly.

Yield: approximately 6 servings

GREEN BEANS IN MUSHROOM SAUCE

The sauce for these beans would be equally good over other vegetables such as asparagus and broccoli.

1½ pounds fresh green
  beans
2 ham hocks
1 clove garlic, minced
Salt and pepper to taste

3 tablespoons butter
½ pound mushrooms, sliced
1 cup sour cream
Salt and pepper to taste

Snap and string beans. Cook in boiling water with ham hocks, garlic, salt, and pepper about 45 minutes. Drain well and return to pan. Melt butter in skillet and saute mushrooms over medium high heat. Reduce heat and stir in sour cream, salt, and pepper, being careful not to boil. Add sauce to beans and heat thoroughly, do not boil. Serve immediately.

Yield: approximately 6 servings

SWISS GREEN BEANS

2 10-ounce packages French
  cut frozen green beans
½ stick butter
2 tablespoons flour
1 cup sour cream
1 teaspoon salt
¼ teaspoon pepper

¼ teaspoon minced onions
1 tablespoon sugar
1½ cups Swiss cheese, shredded
¼ cup buttery cracker
  crumbs

Preheat oven to 350°. Grease a 2 quart Pyrex dish. Cook green beans according to package directions and drain. Melt butter in saucepan. Stir in flour until smooth. Add sour cream and warm. Stir in salt, pepper, onions, and sugar. Combine green beans with sauce. Pour into Pyrex. Top with cheese and cracker crumbs. Bake for 25-30 minutes.

Yield: 6 servings

GREEN BEANS WITH BACON DRESSING

Try this dressing over fresh snapped green beans.

2 eggs
⅓ cup vinegar
½ cup water
3 tablespoons sugar
¼ teaspoon salt
¼ cup bacon drippings,
  reserved from bacon

2 16-ounce cans whole
  green beans
⅓ pound bacon, cooked and
  crumbled

With a fork beat first 5 ingredients together until well-blended. Heat bacon drippings in a skillet and add egg mixture. Cook over low heat, stirring constantly until thickened, 3-4 minutes. Heat beans in a separate pan. Drain and arrange on serving dish. Pour hot dressing over beans and sprinkle with bacon.

Yield: 6 servings

HOMINY AND CORN CASSEROLE

3 16-ounce cans whole white
  hominy, drained
2 12-ounce cans white
  shoepeg corn, undrained
1 4-ounce can chopped
  green chilies

½ pint sour cream
1½ cups Monterey Jack
  cheese, shredded
1½ cups Velveeta, shredded
Salt and pepper to taste
Butter

Preheat oven to 350°. Layer in a deep baking dish, ⅓ hominy and ⅓ corn. Sprinkle with salt and pepper lightly, and 3 tablespoons chilies. Dot with butter and 4 or more tablespoons sour cream. Sprinkle with ½ cup of both cheeses. Repeat layers twice. Bake for 35 to 40 minutes.

Yield: 12 servings

BAKED MUSHROOMS

3 tablespoons butter
1 pound fresh mushrooms,
  sliced
½ cup onions, finely
  chopped
¼ teaspoon salt
⅛ teaspoon pepper

1 tablespoon flour
¼ cup Parmesan cheese,
  grated
2 teaspoons dill weed
1 cup Half and Half
2 egg yolks, lightly beaten

Preheat oven to 425°. Melt butter in a large skillet and add mushrooms, onion, salt, and pepper. Cover and simmer for 8 minutes. Stir in flour and cheese and continue cooking for 3 minutes. Pour in a 1-quart baking dish or six individual ramekins. Sprinkle with dill weed. Mix cream with egg yolks. Pour over mushrooms. Bake for 15 minutes until golden brown.

Yield: 6 servings

STUFFED MUSHROOMS

Stuffed mushrooms can be served as both a sidedish and an appetizer.

24 large fresh mushrooms
½ stick butter, melted
½ pound bulk sausage, crumbled
1 onion, finely chopped
¼ cup dry sherry
½ cup white bread crumbs, finely crumbled

½ teaspoon thyme
¼ teaspoon salt
⅛ teaspoon black pepper, freshly ground
3 tablespoons fresh parsley
2 tablespoons heavy cream

Preheat oven to 375°. Remove mushroom stems and reserve. Brush caps with butter and place hollow side up in a buttered 9x13 inch baking dish. Reserve unused butter for later use. Saute sausage and onion in a skillet slowly until both are cooked and lightly brown. Add sherry and simmer mixture to evaporate liquid. Add remaining ingredients except cream. Toss lightly. Chop and add mushroom stems. Add enough cream to mixture to make it moist but still hold its shape in a spoon. Fill caps with stuffing. Drizzle reserved butter over tops. Bake for 20 minutes.

Yield: 12 servings

ONION PIE

This is best prepared with yellow onions.

1 cup saltine crackers, crumbled
5 tablespoons butter, melted
2½ cups onions, thinly sliced
2 tablespoons oil

2 eggs
¾ cup milk
Salt and pepper to taste
¼ cup Cheddar cheese, shredded

Preheat oven to 350°. Combine cracker crumbs and butter together and press into an 8-inch pan. Bake 8 minutes. Saute onions in oil until tender. Place in cracker crust shell. Mix remaining ingredients except cheese and pour over onions. Top with cheese and bake for 45 minutes.

Yield: 6 servings

BEST EVER BLACK-EYED PEAS

1 pound dried black-eyed
  peas
3 ribs celery, diced
1 green bell pepper, diced
¼ cup red bell pepper, diced
½ teaspoon black pepper
½ tablespoon salt
Scant ½ teaspoon ground
  cumin

Scant ½ teaspoon garlic
  powder
3 tablespoons butter or
  margarine
1½ teaspoons seasoned salt
Pinch cayenne pepper

Cover peas in water in a large pot and soak overnight. Preheat oven to 300°. Drain peas and place in a large baking dish. Add remaining ingredients and cover with water. Cover baking dish and simmer for 2½ to 3½ hours. Add more water if necessary.

Yield: approximately 6 servings

PEAS PTOLEMY

1 10-ounce package frozen
  green peas
1 clove garlic, attached to a
  toothpick
2 tablespoons sugar

½ teaspoon salt
¼ teaspoon pepper
¼ teaspoon tarragon
¼ teaspoon oregano
2 tablespoons butter

Cook peas according to package directions. As peas cook add remaining ingredients. Just before serving, remove garlic clove.

Yield: 4 servings

TWICE BAKED POTATOES

4 large baking potatoes,
  washed and scrubbed
8 tablespoons butter
2 teaspoons salt
¼ teaspoon black pepper
⅛ teaspoon cayenne
  pepper

Milk for creaming
2 egg yolks, beaten
1 cup sharp Cheddar cheese,
  shredded

Preheat oven to 400°. Bake potatoes in oven for 1 hour or until soft. Allow potatoes to cool slightly. Cut potatoes in half, scoop out the pulp and place in a mixing bowl, setting the skins aside. Add butter, salt, and peppers. Mash well, adding enough milk to make a fairly stiff mixture. Add beaten egg yolks and stir well. Spoon mixture into potato skins and top with shredded cheese. Place on a cookie sheet and bake for 20 minutes until well browned.

Yield: 8 servings

PATIO POTATOES

4 Idaho potatoes, scrubbed
  and unpeeled
1 large onion, chopped

Garlic salt and garlic powder
  to taste
Pepper to taste
1 stick butter

Preheat oven to 450°. Spray baking pan with Pam. Slice potatoes lengthwise into 8 slices. Place potatoes in pan and sprinkle with onions. Add seasonings. Place pats of butter on top. Cover with foil and bake for 45 minutes. Uncover and continue baking for 15 minutes or until lightly browned.

Yield: 4 servings

YOUR HEART'S DELIGHT POTATOES

4 medium potatoes
1½ cups light cream
1 stick butter
1 8-ounce medium to sharp
  Cheddar cheese, shredded
1 cup sour cream

½ cup green onions,
  chopped
6-8 strips bacon, fried and
  crumbled
Salt and pepper to taste
Paprika, optional

Preheat oven to 350°. Place potatoes in a large saucepan, cover with water and boil until tender. Allow potatoes to cool; peel and grate. Combine cream, butter, and cheese in a double boiler and stir until melted. Add mixture to potatoes; salt and pepper to taste. Spoon into a casserole and bake for 30 minutes or until bubbly. Top with 1 cup sour cream, onions, and bacon. Bake for an additional 5 minutes.

Yield: 8 servings

OLD FASHIONED RED POTATOES AND ONIONS

New twist for old-fashioned red potatoes.

1½ pounds small red
  potatoes, unpeeled and cut
  into ¼ inch slices
½ pound small onions,
  peeled and sliced
Salt to taste

Fresh ground pepper
1 tablespoon unsalted butter
½ cup whipping cream
1 tablespoon fresh parsley,
  chopped

Preheat oven to 350°. Butter a 9-inch square baking dish. Steam potatoes and onion over salted water until tender when pierced with a fork, about 10 to 15 minutes. Place steamed vegetables in baking dish and season with salt and pepper. Dot with butter and drizzle the cream evenly over the top. Bake until cream is bubbly, thick and mostly absorbed by the vegetables, approximately 15 minutes. Garnish with parsley.

Yield: 4 servings

PARTY POTATOES

You can simplify this dish by omitting the celery, green pepper, and chives.

1 stick butter, melted
1 teaspoon salt
¼ teaspoon black pepper
1 teaspoon oregano
1 10¾-ounce can cream of
  celery soup
1 pint sour cream with
  chives
2 1-pound packages frozen
  hash browns, thawed and
  chopped

½ cup onion, chopped
½ cup celery, chopped
½ cup green bell pepper,
  chopped
2 cups Cheddar cheese,
  shredded
1½ cups corn flakes,
  crushed
½ stick butter, melted

Preheat oven to 350°. Combine first 6 ingredients. In a separate bowl, combine hash browns with onion, celery, bell pepper, and cheese. Stir soup mixture into hash browns and pour into a 3 quart casserole. Top with mixture of corn flakes and ½ stick melted butter. Bake uncovered for 45 minutes.

Yield: 16 servings

SUPREME SCALLOPED POTATOES

These are also good with chopped pimento added and topped with shredded Cheddar cheese.

8 cups potatoes, peeled and
  sliced thin
¼ cup green bell pepper,
  chopped
¼ cup onion, finely chopped

1 10¾-ounce can cream of
  mushroom soup
1 cup milk
Salt and pepper to taste

Preheat oven to 350°. Grease a 2 quart casserole. Layer potatoes, bell pepper, and onion alternately. Combine remaining ingredients and pour over potatoes. Cover and bake for 45 minutes. Uncover and bake another 20-30 minutes until tender.

Yield: 8 servings

WONDERFUL AU GRATIN POTATOES

2 pounds medium potatoes,
   peeled and thinly sliced
1¼ cups cream
1 cup Cheddar cheese,
   shredded

1 cup Jarlesburg or Gruyere
   cheese, shredded
3 tablespoons Parmesan
   cheese, freshly grated
½ stick butter
Salt and pepper to taste

Boil sliced potatoes in water until almost tender. Drain well. Preheat oven to 350°. Grease a 6-cup au gratin dish with 2 tablespoons butter. Layer ½ of the potatoes in the dish, followed by ½ the cream, and ½ the cheeses. Repeat layers, season to taste, and dot top with butter. Bake for 30 minutes or until top is brown and mixture is bubbly. Cover dish with foil if top browns too quickly.

Yield: 6 servings

CANDIED YAMS

3-4 pounds sweet potatoes,
   washed and dried
2 cups sugar
Scant ¼ cup water

¼ teaspoon salt
2 teaspoons cinnamon
½ stick butter

Preheat oven to 350°. Punch holes in potato skins and bake 45 minutes to 1 hour, turning once during baking. Potatoes should be soft, not mushy. Remove from oven and peel. Cut into large chunks and place in buttered 9x9 inch baking dish. Combine sugar, water, salt, and cinnamon in a saucepan. Cook over medium heat, stirring often until sugar is dissolved and syrup is clear. Pour over potatoes. Dot with slices of butter.

Cover and bake for 30 minutes, uncover and bake an additional 15 minutes.

Yield: approximately 6 servings

RICE PILAF

1 stick butter
4 tablespoons onion, finely
  chopped
1 cup long grain rice
4 tablespoons dry white
  wine
3 cups beef stock

1¼ cups fresh mushrooms,
  sliced
½ teaspoon garlic, minced
2 tomatoes, peeled, seeded,
  and chopped
¼ teaspoon dried oregano
Salt and pepper to taste

Preheat oven to 400°. Melt ½ stick butter on stove top in a heavy casserole; add onion and saute for 1 minute. Add rice and cook, stirring over medium heat for another minute. Pour in wine and beef stock and salt to taste. Bring to boil. Cover tightly and transfer to oven. Bake for 20-25 minutes, stirring rice once with a fork halfway through baking. Saute mushrooms in 2 tablespoons butter in a small skillet for 3 minutes. Add garlic, tomatoes, oregano, and season to taste with salt and pepper. Simmer for 5 minutes. Toss rice with mushrooms and add remaining butter. Serve hot.

Yield: 4 servings

ORANGE RICE

A very pretty dish when garnished with twisted orange slices.

½ stick butter
1 cup rice, uncooked
½ teaspoon salt
2 cups chicken broth
½ cup dry white wine

Juice of one orange
1 teaspoon orange rind,
  grated
Pepper to taste
Snipped parsley

Preheat oven to 350°. Place butter, rice, salt, broth, and wine in a casserole. Cover tightly and bake for 40 to 45 minutes until rice is light and fluffy. Add orange juice and grated rind. Season with pepper and stir. Return to oven and bake for 10 minutes. Sprinkle with parsley.

Yield: approximately 4 servings

CRUNCHY CONFETTI RICE

A colorful way to serve rice.

2 cups rice, uncooked
4 cups chicken broth
1 stick butter
¾ cup celery, finely chopped
¾ cup carrot, finely chopped
¾ cup parsley, finely chopped

½ cup green onion, finely chopped
1 cup water chestnuts, sliced or chopped

Preheat oven to 375°. Cook rice, broth, and butter in a saucepan over medium heat for 25 minutes. Salt to taste. Add vegetables and mix well. Serve immediately so the vegetables will remain crunchy.

Yield: 12 servings

CROWD PLEASING RICE

This is great on a buffet table at a dinner party or a backyard cookout.

3 cups long grain white rice, uncooked
6 cups water
3 teaspoons salt, optional
1 stick butter plus 3 tablespoons
1 teaspoon salt

1 teaspoon garlic powder
1½ cups fresh parsley, chopped
1½ cups Velveeta, cubed
½ cup onion, chopped
2 cups milk
2 eggs, beaten

Preheat oven to 350°. Grease a large baking dish. Cook rice in a large pan with water, salt, and 3 tablespoons butter. To cooked rice, add 1 stick butter, salt, garlic powder, parsley, Velveeta, and onion. Slowly add milk to beaten eggs and mix well. Add to rice and pour into baking dish and bake for 1 hour.

Yield: approximately 20 servings

TURKISH PILAF

2 cups instant rice,
  uncooked
½ stick butter or margarine
1 16-ounce can tomatoes,
  chopped
2 beef bouillon cubes
1 cup boiling water
1 small onion, chopped

1 clove garlic, minced or ⅛
  teaspoon garlic powder
1 teaspoon salt
1 teaspoon sugar
¼ teaspoon pepper
1 bay leaf

Brown rice in butter in medium saucepan. Add remaining ingredients. Bring to a boil and reduce heat. Cover and simmer 15-17 minutes, stirring occasionally. Remove bay leaf before serving.

Yield: 6 servings

SPINACH STUFFED ZUCCHINI

This makes good sauce in lasagne.

3 medium zucchini
Boiling water
Salt to taste
2 tablespoons butter
2 tablespoons flour
½ cup milk
¼ teaspoon garlic powder
Salt and pepper to taste

1 10-ounce package frozen
  chopped spinach, cooked
  and squeezed dry
4 slices bacon, cooked and
  crumbled
½ cup Cheddar cheese,
  shredded

Wash zucchini. Cut off stem end and discard. Drop zucchini in boiling salted water. Cover, reduce heat and cook 10-12 minutes. Drain and cool.

Melt butter in saucepan. Add flour and stir until smooth. Add milk and garlic powder, stirring constantly. Cook until thickened.

Cut zucchini in ½ lengthwise and remove pulp, leaving a firm shell. Salt and pepper shell. Chop pulp and combine pulp and spinach with cream sauce. Stuff shells with spinach mixture. Sprinkle top with bacon and cheese. Bake at 350° for 15-20 minutes.

Yield: 6 servings

EASY SPINACH CASSEROLE

An easy spinach dish that even kids love.

1 cup herb seasoned stuffing mix
1 10¾-ounce can cream of mushroom soup
1 cup Longhorn Cheddar cheese, shredded

1 small onion, chopped
1 stick butter, melted
1 10-ounce package frozen chopped spinach, thawed and well drained

Preheat oven to 350°. Combine first five ingredients together in a mixing bowl. Place spinach in an 8-inch round glass baking dish and spread stuffing over top. Bake for 30 minutes.

Yield: 6 servings

SPINACH AND TOMATO PARMESAN

If you don't like tomatoes, omit them and mix everything together except ingredients reserved for topping.

2 10-ounce packages frozen spinach or 1½ pounds fresh spinach
3 tablespoons onion, chopped
6 tablespoons butter, melted
6 tablespoons heavy cream or ½ cup sour cream

1 teaspoon lemon rind, grated
4 firm ripe tomatoes, thickly sliced
Salt and pepper to taste
½ cup Parmesan cheese, grated
½ cup buttery cracker crumbs

Preheat oven to 400°. Butter a 9x13 inch baking dish. Cook spinach according to package directions and drain well. Chop into bite size pieces. Saute onion in two tablespoons butter. To spinach add onion, 6 tablespoons Parmesan cheese, cream, 2 tablespoons butter, and lemon rind; mix well. Arrange spinach mixture in baking dish. Sprinkle both sides of tomato with salt, pepper, and Parmesan cheese and arrange on top of spinach. Sprinkle with cracker crumbs and drizzle remaining butter over top. Bake 15 minutes or until slightly brown. Serve in squares with a tomato slice on top of each serving.

Yield: 8 servings

SPINACH WITH OYSTERS AND CHEESE

Serve with baked chicken or turkey.

1 10-ounce package frozen
  chopped spinach
3 ribs celery including
  leaves, chopped
1 small onion, chopped
½ bunch parsley, chopped
1 stick butter or margarine
1 tablespoon Worcestershire
  sauce

¼ teaspoon Tabasco
¾ cup packaged dry
  cornbread dressing
½ pint oysters, chopped
Salt and pepper to taste
1 cup Cheddar cheese,
  shredded

Preheat oven to 350°. Grease a 1½-quart casserole. Cook spinach according to package directions and drain well. Lightly saute celery, onion, and parsley in butter until tender. Combine spinach and vegetables with Worcestershire, Tabasco, cornbread dressing, chopped oysters, salt, and pepper in a mixing bowl. Place mixture in casserole and bake for 25 minutes. Top with shredded cheese and return to oven for an additional 5 minutes. Sprinkle with paprika if desired.

Yield: 6 servings

EASY BAKED SQUASH

2 pounds zucchini squash
2 pounds yellow squash
Salt and pepper to taste
1 small onion, chopped
1½ sticks butter, melted

1 8-ounce package cream
  cheese
Approximately 20 buttery
  crackers, crumbled

Preheat oven to 350°. Lightly grease a 9x13 inch baking dish. Cook zucchini and yellow squash together in a saucepan in enough water to cover, until tender. Drain and mash with a potato masher and drain again. Salt and pepper to taste. Saute onions in ½ stick butter in a small skillet until tender. Add onion to squash and place in a baking dish. Combine 1 stick butter and cream cheese and melt over medium heat. Pour over top of squash and sprinkle with cracker crumbs. Bake for 30 minutes.

Yield: approximately 8 servings

BACON CHEDDAR SQUASH

3 pounds yellow squash,
   sliced
½ teaspoon salt
1½ tablespoons sugar
1 medium onion, chopped
2 tablespoons butter
½ pound Cheddar cheese,
   shredded
3 tablespoons butter

6-8 strips bacon, cooked and
   crumbled (½ cup)
3 tablespoons flour
¼ teaspoon pepper
Accent to taste
2 eggs, beaten
1 cup milk
1 cup buttered breadcrumbs

Preheat oven to 375°. Butter a 9x13 inch casserole. Boil squash in a saucepan with two inches water, salt, and sugar until tender. Drain well and mash with a potato masher. Saute onions in butter in a small skillet until tender. Combine squash with remaining ingredients, except bread crumbs, and blend well. Place into casserole dish. Top with breadcrumbs and bake for 25 minutes or until edges are puffy and golden brown.

Yield: approximately 8 servings

SQUASH DRESSING

8-10 yellow squash, sliced
1 large onion, chopped
½ stick butter
3 6-ounce packages
   cornbread mix
1 10¾-ounce can cream of
   celery soup
1 10¾-ounce can cream of
   mushroom soup

1 10¾-ounce can cream of
   chicken soup
Salt and pepper to taste
Poultry seasoning to taste
½ cup Cheddar cheese,
   shredded

Preheat oven to 350°. Cook squash with onion in boiling water in a large saucepan for 30 minutes or until tender. Drain well and add butter. Cook cornbread mix according to package directions and allow to cool. Lightly break up cornbread; add squash and soups and mix together. Add seasonings to taste. Place in 9x13 inch casserole. Top with cheese, cover with foil and bake for 30 minutes.

Yield: 8 servings

DORTHA'S YUMMY SQUASH SOUFFLE

This is excellent for an elegant dinner party.

2 pounds yellow squash, sliced
1 large onion, chopped
½ cup Velveeta cheese, cubed
2 eggs, beaten

2 tablespoons sugar
1 4-ounce jar chopped pimento
Salt and white pepper to taste
6 tablespoons butter

Topping:
Saltine crackers, crushed
½ stick butter, melted

1 6-ounce can fried onions, optional

Preheat oven to 350°. Grease a 9x13 inch casserole. Boil squash and onion together until tender. Drain and mash with a potato masher. Add remaining ingredients except topping. Cook and stir over medium heat until cheese and butter are melted. Pour into casserole and sprinkle with cracker crumbs. Drizzle melted butter over crackers and bake for 45 minutes. Add onions to top and bake an additional 5 minutes.

Yield: approximately 10 servings

ZUCCHINI AND EGGPLANT

3 pounds zucchini squash, sliced or chopped
1½ pounds eggplant, sliced or chopped
1 24-ounce can Mountain Pass Chili
3 eggs, slightly beaten
2 tablespoons Worcestershire sauce

2 tablespoons Accent
1 tablespoon salt
2 8-ounce packages cream cheese
1 onion, finely chopped
1½ cups fine breadcrumbs
½ stick butter, melted

Boil vegetables in water until barely tender. Drain. Stir in remaining ingredients except breadcrumbs and melted butter. Pour into greased 3 quart casserole. Top with breadcrumbs and melted butter. Bake at 375° for 30 minutes.

Yield: 10-12 servings

ZUCCHINI SUPREME

3 medium zucchini, thinly
  sliced
½ cup water
½ cup sour cream
½ stick butter

1 cup sharp Cheddar cheese,
  shredded
Salt and pepper to taste
1 tablespoon chives, chopped
¾ cup buttery crackers,
  crushed

Preheat oven to 375°. Grease a 1-quart baking dish. Cook zucchini in water over low heat for 6 minutes, stirring occasionally. Drain. Combine sour cream, 2 tablespoons butter, ½ cup cheese, salt, and pepper in a medium saucepan. Stir over low heat until cheese is melted. Remove from heat and stir in chives. Gently stir zucchini into sour cream mixture. Place in baking dish and top with cracker crumbs. Dot with remaining butter and sprinkle with ½ cup cheese. Bake for 10 minutes.

Yield: 4 servings

STIR FRY ZUCCHINI

A good sidedish with Chinese food. Try this with chopped broccoli. Zucchini will be crisp if you grate it earlier and allow to drain.

2 tablespoons butter
1 tablespoon oil
1-2 cloves garlic, minced

6-8 zucchini, grated
Salt, pepper, and Parmesan
  cheese to taste

Heat butter and oil together with garlic in wok or large skillet. Stir fry zucchini over high heat for 60 seconds, until crispy, not mushy. Add salt, pepper, and Parmesan cheese. Serve immediately.

Yield: 4 servings

TURNIP GREENS

1 small piece salt pork, about ¼ inch thick	2 10-ounce packages frozen turnip greens
2 cups water	½ teaspoon salt
8 medium white turnips or 2 pounds, peeled and sliced in ¼ inch rounds	3 tablespoons sugar
	3 tablespoons bacon drippings

Place salt pork in a heavy saucepan with water. Bring to boil, turn heat to medium low and simmer approximately 30 minutes. Add sliced turnips to water and cook for 20 to 30 minutes. (Should be ¾ cup water left in saucepan.) Add frozen greens, salt, sugar, and bacon drippings. Continue to cook for 30 minutes. Season to taste.

Yield: 6 servings

LAYERED VEGETABLE CASSEROLE

A pretty company sidedish.

1 16-ounce can green beans, drained	1 8-ounce can water chestnuts, sliced
1 16-ounce can green peas, drained	½ pound Cheddar cheese, shredded
1 16-ounce can asparagus, drained	3 slices dry bread, crumbled
1 10¾-ounce can cream of mushroom soup, warmed	1 stick butter, melted

Preheat oven to 350°. Layer vegetables in a 2-quart casserole dish in above order of ingredients. Pour soup over vegetables. Place water chestnuts on top of soup and add cheese. Top with breadcrumbs and butter. Bake uncovered for 40 minutes.

Yield: approximatey 10 servings

WILD RICE AND SAUSAGE STUFFING

Especially good with roast pork.

1 6½-ounce package wild rice with herbs, cooked
1 onion, chopped
1 cup fresh mushrooms, chopped
1 green bell pepper, chopped
2 tablespoons butter
½ cup pecans, chopped
½ pounds pork sausage, cooked and drained
2 tablespoons parsley, minced
1 tablespoon sage
Salt and pepper to taste
2-3 tablespoons teriyaki sauce

Saute onions, mushrooms, and green pepper in butter until tender. Stir in remaining ingredients and simmer 15 to 20 minutes.

Yield: 8 servings

FETTUCINI

4 chicken bouillon cubes
2 sticks butter, melted
1 bunch green onions, chopped
¼ pound fresh mushrooms, sliced
1 cup whipping cream
1 cup Parmesan cheese, grated
Cracked pepper
Tabasco to taste
1 pound fettucini

Dissolve bouillon cubes in melted butter in a medium saucepan. Saute onions and mushrooms in butter. Add cream, cheese, pepper, and Tabasco. Heat thoroughly. Cook fettucini according to package directions and drain. Pour sauce over the hot pasta. Toss lightly until noodles are coated. Serve immediately.

Yield: 8 servings

BROCCOLI-MUSHROOM SPAGHETTI

Try this recipe with asparagus. It is delicious.

1 7-ounce package spaghetti
1 10-ounce package frozen
  chopped broccoli
½ stick butter
1 4½-ounce jar sliced
  mushrooms, drained

½ teaspoon salt
¼ teaspoon pepper
½ cup Parmesan cheese,
  grated
1 tablespoon lemon juice

Cook spaghetti according to directions and drain. Cook broccoli according to package directions and drain. Stir butter, mushrooms, salt, and pepper into broccoli. Heat over low heat, tossing gently until mushrooms are heated, about 5 minutes. Toss spaghetti with broccoli mixture, cheese, and lemon juice. Serve hot.

Yield: 4 servings

ASPARAGUS WITH PASTA

1 pound fresh asparagus,
  peeled and cut into 2-inch
  diagonal slices
1 cup Rotelle or Fusilli pasta
2 tablespoons butter
6 slices bacon, chopped and
  crisply cooked

2 tablespoons whipping
  cream
2 tablespoons Parmesan
  cheese, grated
3 tablespoons green onions
  with tops, chopped

In a large saucepan cook asparagus in boiling salted water until tender. Drain and reserve water. Cook pasta in asparagus water until tender. Drain and return to pan with butter and toss. Add bacon, asparagus, cream, and cheese to pasta. Toss over heat, carefully as not to break asparagus, until cream forms a coating sauce. Toss in green onions gently. Serve immediately.

Yield: approximately 4 servings

VERMICELLI

Very good with brisket and romaine salad with Mandarin oranges.

½ cup celery, chopped
3 green onions, chopped
⅓ cup green bell pepper,
  chopped
4 tablespoons olive oil
3 medium tomatoes, peeled
  and diced
3 medium zucchini, sliced
  thinly in rounds

Seasoned salt and pepper to
  taste
Garlic powder to taste
½ teaspoon oregano
½ teaspoon basil
5 ounces vermicelli
¼ cup Parmesan cheese,
  grated

Preheat oven to 350°. Saute celery, green onion, and bell pepper in olive oil until tender, about 5 minutes. Add tomatoes and zucchini and season to taste. Cover and cook until vegetables are tender, stirring occasionally, about 5 minutes. Break vermicelli into thirds; cook according to package directions. Drain well. Combine with zucchini mixture. Stir in Parmesan cheese. Turn into a baking dish and bake for 30 minutes.

Yield: 4 servings

APPLESAUCE SOUFFLE

A unique and delicious accompaniment to most meats, especially pork.

1 cup applesauce
1 cup sugar
1 cup milk
1 cup graham cracker
  crumbs

2 eggs, beaten
1 stick butter, melted
1 teaspoon cinnamon

Preheat oven to 375°. Grease a 1½-quart casserole dish. Combine all ingredients until well blended. Pour into casserole and bake for 1 hour until lightly brown.

Yield: approximately 6 servings

HOT CURRIED FRUIT

Add fresh sliced bananas just before cooking if you wish.

½ stick butter
⅔ cup brown sugar
2 teaspoons curry powder
⅓ cup brandy
1 16-ounce can peaches,
  drained and chunked
1 16-ounce can pears,
  drained and chunked

1 15½-ounce can pineapple
  chunks, drained
1 6-ounce jar maraschino
  cherries, drained
1 11-ounce can apricots,
  drained and chunked

Preheat oven to 300°. Melt butter in a medium skillet. Dissolve brown sugar, and curry powder in brandy. Add to butter and stir until blended. Arrange fruits in a 9x13 inch casserole. Pour sauce over fruit and bake for 1 hour, basting occasionally.

Yield: approximately 8 servings

HOT SPICED FRUIT

Try adding one half cup of crushed macaroons on top before baking.

1 stick butter, melted
1¼ cups brown sugar
1 25-ounce jar applesauce
¼ teaspoon cloves
¼ teaspoon cinnamon
1 16-ounce can purple
  plums; pitted, drained, and
  cut up
1 20-ounce can pineapple
  chunks, drained

1 8-ounce can pineapple
  chunks, drained
3-4 bananas, sliced
1 21-ounce can cherry pie
  filling
¼-½ cup sherry
½ cup toasted slivered
  almonds, optional

Preheat oven to 350°. Butter a 3-4 quart casserole. Mix together butter, brown sugar, applesauce, cloves, and cinnamon. Set aside. Place plums, pineapple, bananas, and pie filling in a bowl. Pour applesauce mixture over fruit and mix well. Add sherry to taste. May be refrigerated at this point until ready to bake. Place fruit in casserole; bake uncovered for 45 to 60 minutes. Sprinkle almonds on top before serving.

Yield: approximately 12 servings

APPLE-CRANBERRY RELISH

A wonderful, fresh alternative to canned cranberry sauce.

1 large orange, quartered and seeded	¼ teaspoon cinnamon
2 12-ounce bags fresh cranberries	1 large Red Delicious apple, finely chopped
1¼ cups light brown sugar, firmly packed	1 tablespoon lemon juice
	¾ cups walnuts or pecans, chopped

Finely chop oranges and cranberries together in a food processor. Place in a mixing bowl and add remaining ingredients. Mix well. Cover and refrigerate overnight. Will keep for 1 week in refrigerator.

Yield: 1½ quarts

CARRIE'S TOMATO RELISH

3 28-ounce cans tomatoes	4 large onions, chopped
4 large green bell peppers, chopped	1 cup sugar
2 large dried red chili peppers, seeded and chopped	¼ cup salt
	3 cups vinegar
	1 tablespoon cinnamon
	1 teaspoon cloves

Combine all ingredients together in a large saucepan and bring to a boil. Boil for 1½ hours. Pour into sterilized jars while hot and seal according to canning directions.

Yield: 12 pints

PICKLED BEETS

12 medium beets	1½ cups water
1 cup sugar	3½ cups vinegar

Wash and cut tops off beets leaving one inch of stem. Cover with water in a large pot and bring to boil. Boil until tender. Peel and pack in sterile jars. Combine sugar, water, and vinegar in a saucepan and bring to a boil. Pour over packed beets. Seal as directed on canning jar instructions. Chill.

Yield: 4 quarts

MIKE'S PICKLES

5 quart size canning jars
5 buds garlic
5 red chili peppers, or
  jalapeno peppers
5 large sprigs fresh dill
35 cucumber pickles, 3 to 4
  inches long

6 cups water
2 cups vinegar
½ cup sugar
½ cup salt

Place 1 garlic bud, 1 pepper, and 1 sprig of dill in each quart jar. Pack each jar with cucumbers. Combine water, vinegar, sugar, and salt; bringing to a boil in a large saucepan. Pour hot mixture over pickles leaving space of at least one-half inch at top of jar. Seal jar while hot according to directions on canning jars.

Yield: 5 quarts

BREAD AND BUTTER PICKLES

4 quarts cucumbers, sliced
  ⅛ inch thick
6 medium yellow onions,
  chopped
2 green bell peppers,
  chopped

3 cloves garlic, chopped
½ cup salt
5 cups sugar
1½ tablespoons tumeric
1½ tablespoons celery seed
3 cups vinegar

Place first four ingredients in a large pan and cover with salt. Place ice cubes on top and allow to stand for three hours. Drain well. Pack cucumbers in quart jars. Combine sugar, tumeric, celery seeds, and vinegar in a saucepan and bring to a boil over medium heat, stirring occasionally. Pour hot mixture over cucumbers. Seal jars while hot according to canning directions.

Yield: 4 quarts

Main Dishes

Thank you for your financial support
of the following Junior League of Waco project:

YWCA *Teen Parent Counseling*

A project in conjunction with the YWCA offering advice
on parenting and family planning to teenage parents.

EASY BAKE BRISKET

1 4-pound beef brisket
Salt and pepper to taste
Lemon pepper to taste
Meat tenderizer to taste
½ teaspoon green bell
   pepper, minced

1 tablespoon garlic, minced
4 small yellow onions, sliced
1 cup beef broth
1 tablespoon cider vinegar

Trim fat off brisket. Broil 10 minutes on each side in oven. Place brisket fat side up in a large roasting pan and sprinkle with salt, pepper, lemon pepper, meat tenderizer, green pepper, and garlic to taste. Place sliced onions on top. Bake in oven at 350° for 1 hour or until onions are brown. Reduce heat to 300° and add broth. Cover tightly and bake 2 hours until meat is tender. Transfer meat and two-thirds of onion to platter. Skim fat from broth. Combine juices and remaining onion in a blender. Process. Add vinegar and stir well. Serve with brisket.

Yield: approximately 10 servings

OVEN SMOKED BRISKET

1 brisket (5-8 pounds)
Seasoned salt to taste
Coarsely ground black
   pepper to taste
Garlic powder to taste
2-4 tablespoons liquid smoke
   sauce

2-4 tablespoons Worcestershire sauce
2-4 tablespoons steak sauce
   (A-1 preferred)

Preheat oven to 300°. Line baking dish with foil. Rub brisket all over with seasonings and sauces. Wrap with foil. Reduce oven temperature to 250°. Bake for 5-6 hours.

*Note be sure to turn brisket fat side up before baking.

Yield: ½ pound per person

LONDON BROIL

½ cup salad oil
2 tablespoons Worcestershire
  sauce
¼ cup soy sauce
1 bay leaf

⅛ teaspoon pepper
⅛ teaspoon ground cloves
⅛ teaspoon thyme
Dash of cayenne pepper
1½ pounds flank steak

Combine first eight ingredients for marinade. Place steak in a flat pan and pour marinade over top. Cover tightly and refrigerate overnight, turning occasionally. Heat grill to medium-high heat. Place steak on grill about 3 to 4 inches from heat. Grill 5 minutes and turn. Brush with marinade and grill 5 minutes longer. Slice diagonally at angles across grain in 6 thin strips.

Yield: approximately 6 servings

TENDERLOIN FLAMBE

A very impressive entree to serve your guests.

1 beef tenderloin

Accent to taste

Sauce:
1½ tablespoons Dijon
  mustard
1 cup beef stock
Worcestershire sauce to taste

A-1 sauce to taste
Indian chili sauce to taste
1 tablespoon brandy

Preheat oven to 325°. Brown tenderloin in skillet on both sides. Transfer to roasting pan and sprinkle with Accent. Cook 20 minutes per pound (rare) or 25 minutes per pound (medium). Combine remaining ingredients except brandy in a small saucepan and heat. Do not boil.

Place meat on a flameproof platter. Pour sauce over meat; pour brandy on top and light with a match to flame when ready to serve.

Yield: ½ pound per person

STUFFED BEEF TENDERLOIN

1 3-pound beef tenderloin
Salt and pepper to taste
½ cup onion, chopped
½ cup celery, diced
1 stick butter

1 4-ounce can sliced
  mushrooms
1½ cups soft bread crumbs
4 slices bacon

Gravy:
1½ teaspoons cornstarch
2 tablespoons cool water

Drippings from tenderloin

Preheat oven to 325°. Split tenderloin within ½ inch of edge. Salt and pepper meat to taste. Lightly brown onion and celery in butter in a small skillet. Add mushrooms and bread crumbs. Stuff mixture into tenderloin. Fasten edges with toothpicks or wrap meat with strings. Place bacon slices over top of meat. Cover and roast in oven for 20 minutes per pound for rare and 25 minutes per pound for medium meat. When meat is half done, uncover and continue baking. Let tenderloin stand 15 minutes before slicing.

Dilute cornstarch with water for each cup of pan drippings. Cook over medium heat in a saucepan until thick, stirring constantly. Serve over meat.

Yield: approximately 6 servings

HUNGARIAN BEEF CUBE PAPRIKASH

½ pound pork sausage
2 pounds boneless beef, cut
  into 1 inch cubes
3 tablespoons flour
½ cup onion, chopped
¼ cup green bell pepper,
  chopped

1½ teaspoons salt
1 teaspoon paprika
¾ cup water
1 cup sour cream
3 cups noodles, cooked
1 tablespoon butter
1 teaspoon poppy seeds

Brown sausage lightly in a skillet. Remove from pan. Dredge beef with flour and brown in sausage drippings. Add sausage, onion, bell pepper, salt, paprika, and water. Cover tightly and cook slowly for 1 hour and 15 minutes. Add sour cream when meat is done. Heat but do not boil. Mix noodles, butter, and poppy seeds together. Serve meat over noodles.

Yield: 6 servings

STEAK AND BACON TOURNEDOS
WITH HOLLANDAISE SAUCE

1½ pounds flank steak
Non-seasoned meat
  tenderizer
½ pound bacon
¼ teaspoon garlic powder

½ teaspoon garlic salt
½ teaspoon freshly ground
  pepper
2 tablespoons fresh parsley,
  chopped

Hollandaise sauce:
1 stick butter
2 egg yolks, slightly beaten

1 tablespoon lemon juice
Dash of cayenne pepper

Pound steak to ½ inch thickness. Sprinkle lightly with meat tenderizer. Cook bacon until almost done, but not crisp. Sprinkle steak with seasonings. Score diagonally, making diamond-shaped cuts. Place bacon strips lengthwise on steaks. Roll steak in a jelly roll fashion starting at the narrow end. Skewer with wooden toothpicks at 1-inch intervals and cut into 1 inch pieces. Grill over medium coals 15 minutes, turning once for rare meat. Serve with Hollandaise.

Sauce: Fill bottom half of a double boiler half way with water and bring to a boil. Reduce heat to low and allow water to quit boiling. Water should be hot with only an occasional bubble rising to the surface. Place half of butter in the top of the double boiler with egg yolks and lemon juice. Place over hot water and stir constantly until butter melts. Add remaining butter and stir until thick. Remove from heat and stir in cayenne. Serve at once. If sauce curdles, beat in 1 tablespoon of cream. To reheat, set in a pan of warm water; stir until ready to serve.

Yield: 4 serving

SAVORY PEPPER STEAK

¼ cup flour
½ teaspoon salt
⅛ teaspoon pepper
1½ pounds round steak, cut in strips
¼ cup oil
1 16-ounce can tomatoes, drained and reserve juice
1¾ cups water
½ cup onion, chopped
⅛ teaspoon garlic powder
1 tablespoon beef bouillon (granulated beef gravy base)
1½ teaspoons Worcestershire sauce
2 large green bell peppers, cut in strips
Hot cooked rice

Combine flour, salt, and pepper. Dredge steak in flour. Cook meat in oil in an electric skillet until browned. Add reserved tomato juice, water, onion, garlic powder, and bouillon. Cover and simmer 1 hour. Stir in Worcestershire sauce and bell pepper; cover and simmer 10 minutes. Add drained tomatoes and cook 5 minutes. Serve over hot cooked rice.

Yield: 6 servings

BEEF STROGANOFF

2 pounds lean steak, cut into ½ x 2-inch strips
½ cup flour
1 teaspoon salt
1 stick butter
1 cup green onions, chopped
1½ cups beef bouillon
½ teaspoon red pepper flakes, optional
1 teaspoon Dijon mustard
1 bay leaf
¼ pound fresh mushrooms, sliced
1 cup sour cream

Mix flour and salt. Dredge beef strips in flour, shaking off excess. Melt 6 tablespoons butter in a large skillet and brown meat. When meat is brown, push to one side and saute onions, cooking until slightly tender. Add one cup beef bouillon, red pepper, mustard, and bay leaf. Cover tightly and cook over low heat for 1 hour, checking every 15 minutes and scraping bottom of pan to keep from scorching. Add more bouillon if needed. Saute mushrooms until tender in remaining butter. Add mushrooms with butter and sour cream to steak, mixing thoroughly. Remove bay leaf and cook an additional 5 minutes. Serve over cooked rice or noodles.

Yield: 4 servings

STEAK SANTA FE

The green chili topping is wonderful on other charbroiled meats.

6 cloves garlic, minced
1 cup oil
4 fillets, rib eyes, or New York strips
4 bunches green onions, chopped
2 4-ounce cans chopped green chilies, with juice
2 large tomatoes, diced
1 pound fresh mushrooms, chopped
1 stick butter, melted
Salt to taste
Brown sugar, ⅓ cup per steak

Combine garlic and oil together; pour over and rub into steaks. Place meat in a container, cover tightly, and marinate in refrigerator for 8 to 10 hours. Prepare charcoal grill. Saute green onions, chilies, tomatoes, and mushrooms in butter. Remove steak from marinade, salt, and roll in brown sugar, patting so the sugar will stick to steak. Place on grill and cook as desired. Remove from grill and spoon green chili mixture over steak and serve.

Yield: 4 servings

PEPPERED STEAK

1½ tablespoons black pepper corns, crushed
2 New York strip steaks, 1-1½ inches thick
1 teaspoon salt
¼ cup brandy
2 tablespoons butter
1 clove garlic, crushed
1 teaspoon Dijon mustard
¼ teaspoon beef bouillon concentrate
½ cup heavy cream

Rub ground pepper into both sides of steaks. Cut a strip of fat from one of the steaks and render it in a heavy skillet; or coat bottom of skillet with oil and heat. Sprinkle bottom of pan with salt. Cook meat over medium high heat for 5 to 7 minutes on each side, depending on desired doneness. Pour brandy over meat and flame. Remove meat and keep warm. Melt butter in same pan; add garlic and saute, reducing liquid by half. Add remaining ingredients and cook until sauce is thickened. Serve over meat.

Yield: 2 servings

STUFFED SIRLOIN STEAK ROLLS

Wonderful served with Bearnaise sauce.

2 pounds boneless sirloin or
   round steak, sliced very
   thin lengthwise
½ pound bulk pork sausage,
   cooked and crumbled
½ cup breadcrumbs
1 egg
1½ tablespoons capers

2 cloves garlic, crushed
Salt and pepper to taste
3 tablespoons oil
½ cup water
2 teaspoons marjoram
1 medium onion, sliced
Wine, optional

Place steak slices on wax paper. Combine sausage, breadcrumbs, egg, capers, garlic, salt, and pepper together in a small mixing bowl. Spread mixture on steak slices, roll up, and fasten with toothpicks. Heat oil in heavy skillet and add the steak rolls. Saute until brown on all sides, approximately 3 to 5 minutes. Drain excess oil; add water, marjoram and onion slices. Cover and simmer 30 minutes adding water or wine if the pan dries out.

Yield: 6 servings

BEEF TIPS ON RICE

A good family meat dish that is quick and easy.

3 tablespoons flour
1 teaspoon salt
½ teaspoon pepper
½ teaspoon paprika
2 pounds sirloin, cubed

2 large onions, chopped
2 tablespoons oil
1 beef bouillon cube
¾ cup water, boiling

Combine first four ingredients together in a small bowl. Dredge steak in flour. Saute onions in oil. Add beef and cook until brown. Dissolve bouillon cube in water and add to beef. Cover and simmer 1½ hours stirring twice. Serve over cooked rice.

Yield: 4 servings

FRENCH BEEF BURGUNDY

Thin slice of salt pork
2 pounds lean beef, cubed
1 teaspoon sugar
¼ cup flour
1 cup beef bouillon or stock
1 4-ounce can button
  mushrooms with liquid
1 pound carrots
2 ribs celery

1 onion, chopped
2 bay leaves
1 tablespoon parsley
3 peppercorns
¼ teaspoon cinnamon
½ cup Burgundy or Port
  wine
1 dozen small white onions

In a deep pan, render fat from salt pork and keep very hot. Add beef, sprinkle with sugar, and brown well. Remove from heat, add flour, and stir until well coated. Return to heat. Add stock and mushrooms with liquid; stir constantly until stock thickens.

Tie in a cheesecloth bag, 1 large chopped carrot, celery, onion, bay leaves, parsley, peppercorns, and cinnamon. Add bag and wine to pot. Cover and simmer until meat is tender, approximately 2 hours. Add water if necessary to keep meat from sticking. Add carrots cut in lengthwise strips and whole small onions to meat the last 30 minutes of cooking.

Yield: 6-8 servings

RIB EYE BEEF

1 6-pound boneless rib eye
  roast
⅓-½ cup cracked pepper
½ teaspoon ground
  cardamon

1 cup soy sauce
¾ cup red wine vinegar
1 tablespoon tomato paste
1 teaspoon paprika
½ teaspoon garlic powder

Trim fat from roast. Pat pepper and cardamon into roast. Combine next five ingredients and pour over roast. Cover and marinate overnight in refrigerator, turning occasionally. Preheat oven to 325°. Remove roast and wrap in foil, discarding marinade. Place in a shallow pan. Punch a hole in the foil and insert a meat thermometer into the meat. Bake about 1 hour, until thermometer reaches 140° (rare) or 160° (medium).

Yield: 12 servings

MEETING DAY STEW

For quicker cooking, use cubed round steak, a Dutch oven, and bake at 300° for 4 hours.

2 tablespoons oil	Beef bouillon to cover
2 pounds stew meat	½ cup red wine
4 tablespoons flour	½ teaspoon pepper
4-6 carrots, chopped	¼ teaspoon thyme
3 medium potatoes, peeled and chopped	1 bay leaf
3 ribs celery, chopped	⅛ teaspoon rosemary
2 medium onions, chopped	¼ teaspoon basil
1 10-ounce package frozen green beans	¼ teaspoon oregano
1 6-ounce can mushrooms, drained	1 tablespoon Worcestershire sauce
1 16-ounce can tomatoes	Salt to taste
	1 tablespoon cornstarch, optional

Heat oil in skillet. Trim fat from meat and dust meat with flour. Sear meat in skillet. Place meat and vegetables in Crock pot. Add spices and liquid and cook over low heat for 8 to 10 hours. If thickening is desired, mix cornstarch with liquid.

Yield: 12 servings

LOVER'S STEAK AND LOBSTER BERCY

1 stick butter	1 bunch green onions, sliced
Juice of 1 lemon	1 cup dry white wine
2 6-ounce lobster tails	
2 tenderloin steaks, 2 inches thick	

Melt ½ stick butter and add lemon juice. Boil lobster tails in enough water to cover until done. Remove lobster tails from shell. Make a pocket in steaks with a sharp knife. Roll the tail up and stuff into the steak pocket. Pour lemon butter over lobster. Skewer pocket closed. Melt remaining butter in skillet. Saute steaks to desired doneness. Remove from pan. Saute onions in pan juices until tender. Add wine to hot pan, stirring to blend juices and onions. Pour sauce over steaks and serve immediately. Salt and pepper to taste.

Yield: 2 servings

INDIVIDUAL BEEF WELLINGTON

½ cup olive oil
½ cup onion, sliced
½ cup carrots, sliced
½ cup celery, sliced
¼ teaspoon thyme
¼ teaspoon sage

1 bay leaf
10 peppercorns
2 cups dry vermouth
½ cup cognac
1 large beef fillet

Duxelles:
1 pound fresh mushrooms,
    finely chopped
1 cup shallots, finely
    chopped
1 clove garlic, minced

1 stick butter
14 ounces pate de foie gras
26 ounces puff pastry
1 egg, well beaten

Two to three days before serving: Cook vegetables, spices, and herbs in olive oil until tender. Add wine, cognac, and fillet and marinate 24 hours. One to two days before serving: Cook mushrooms, shallots, and garlic in butter very slowly, stirring occasionally until all moisture has disappeared. The mixture should almost be a paste. Allow to cool to room temperature. When cooled, add pate and chill until ready to use.

Remove meat from marinade, drying excess marinade from meat. Cut into 1¼-inch thick portions. Salt and pepper to taste and brush both sides with a thin coating of vegetable oil. Sear in a medium hot skillet for a few minutes on both sides. Remove from skillet, cool, and chill for about 15 minutes. Spread mushroom pate over top of each fillet and chill for 30 minutes. Place each fillet on a 10-inch circle of puff pastry, duxelles side down and wrap puff pastry around the fillet. Seal and place on a baking sheet, seam side down. Make a small hole in the center of each pastry for steam to escape. Decorate with small pieces of left-over pastry dough. Place in freezer.

Morning before serving: Take fillets out of freezer and defrost in refrigerator at least 6 hours before cooking. Preheat oven to 400°. Brush each pastry with beaten egg. Bake fillets 12 minutes for rare, 16 minutes for medium and 20 minutes for well-done. Serve hot with Merchand de Vin Sauce.

Yield: 10 servings

MERCHAND DE VIN SAUCE

10 tablespoons butter
4 tablespoons shallots or
green onions, chopped
5 tablespoons flour
2 cups beef consomme,
boiling

2 tablespoons tomato paste
1 cup red wine
Salt and pepper to taste
4 tablespoons parsley,
chopped

Melt 6 tablespoons of butter in medium sized skillet. Add onion and saute until transparent. Add flour and cook over medium heat, stirring constantly. When roux is brown, add consomme, stirring until sauce thickens. Turn to simmer and add tomato paste and wine. Cook over low heat for 20 minutes or until desired thickness stirring occasionally. Season to taste with salt and pepper. Remove from heat and swirl in remaining 4 tablespoons butter and parsley. Serve with Beef Wellington.

Yield: 3 cups

ROAST BEEF IN MARINADE

Leftover roast makes a wonderful appetizer served with rolls and horseradish sauce.

5 pounds boneless beef roast   Salt and pepper to taste

Marinade:
1⅓ cups olive oil
1 cup red wine vinegar
2-3 cloves garlic, minced
¼ teaspoon oregano

½ teaspoon cracked pepper
2 tablespoons parsley,
minced
1 bay leaf

Preheat oven to 350°. Season roast with salt and pepper. Bake uncovered for 2 hours or until desired doneness. Refrigerate until cold. Slice thinly, removing fat. Mix all ingredients together for marinade in a small bowl. Pour over roast. Store for three days or more in a flat covered container in the refrigerator. Serve at room temperature.

Yield: 20 servings

MEAT LOAF

For a cheese-filled loaf, place ½ of the meat mixture in a loaf pan, cover with sliced American cheese, pack rest of meat on top, and bake.

1½ pounds lean ground
  meat
1 cup breadcrumbs
1 teaspoon salt

¼ teaspoon pepper
½ 8-ounce can tomato sauce
1 egg, beaten
1 medium onion, chopped

Sauce:
½ 8-ounce can tomato sauce
2 tablespoons prepared
  mustard
2 tablespoons brown sugar
  or molasses

2 tablespoons vinegar
¾ cup water

Preheat oven to 350°. Lightly mix first seven ingredients together in a mixing bowl. Form into a loaf and place in a loaf pan. Combine remaining ingredients together in a saucepan and cook over medium-high heat until it reaches a boiling point. Pour about half of the sauce over the meat loaf and bake for 1 to 1½ hours, basting occasionally. Serve with reserved sauce.

Yield: 6 servings

ONE DISH MEAL

A good choice for serving a crowd, along with salad and fresh bread.

2 pounds lean ground beef
2 small green bell peppers,
  sliced
4 medium potatoes, peeled
  and sliced
3 onions, sliced

1 8-ounce can tomato sauce
1 28-ounce can stewed
  tomatoes
1½ cups Cheddar cheese,
  shredded
Salt and pepper to taste

Preheat oven to 350°. Place meat in bottom of 9x13 inch casserole. Layer alternately with green peppers, potatoes, onions, tomato sauce, and tomatoes. Bake covered for 1½ hours. Sprinkle cheese on top and continue to bake uncovered for 30 minutes.

Yield: approximately 6 servings

COMPANY MEAT LOAF

This meat loaf is much like a terrine. It is wonderful for meat loaf sandwiches.

2 eggs, beaten
½ cup milk
1 cup breadcrumbs
1 pound ground beef
1 pound ground pork
2 onions, chopped
2 cloves garlic, minced
½-1 teaspoon salt
½ teaspoon seasoned pepper

3 tablespoons Worcestershire sauce
3 tablespoons horseradish
⅔ cup tomato sauce
2 tablespoons parsley, chopped
1 teaspoon summer savory seasoning
1 teaspoon marjoram
½ teaspoon thyme

Preheat oven to 350°. Beat eggs and milk together in a small mixing bowl, and add breadcrumbs. Mix ground beef, pork, and onions with seasonings in a medium mixing bowl. Add egg mixture to meat mixture and blend together with hands. Shape into loaves and bake for 1 hour.

Yield: 3 medium loaves or 2 large loaves

STATE FAIR CREOLE MEAT SAUCE

1 pound ground beef
2 tablespoons onion, chopped
¾ cup celery, chopped
1 tablespoon butter
2 tablespoons flour
1 16-ounce can tomatoes
2 tablespoons green bell pepper, chopped

¾ teaspoon chili powder
½ teaspoon salt
½ cup carrots, chopped
¾ cup okra, chopped
1 cup water
Cooked rice

Brown ground beef in a skillet over medium high heat and drain. Brown onion and celery in butter in a small skillet. Add flour and blend with onion and celery. Add tomatoes and stir. Add green pepper, meat, seasonings, carrots, okra, and water. Simmer 10 to 15 minutes or until vegetables are tender. A small amount of water may be added if mixture is too dry. Serve over cooked rice.

Yield: 6 servings

BROWN WINE SAUCE

Serve this over broiled rib-eye steaks

½ stick butter
1 slice onion, chopped
2 tablespoons flour
1 cup beef broth

Salt
½ pound fresh mushrooms,
  sliced
½ cup cream sherry

Melt ½ of the butter in a saucepan and saute onions until lightly brown and tender. Remove onions and cook and stir butter until golden brown. Stir in flour and cook until lightly brown. Slowly add beef broth, stirring constantly, and cook until smooth. Season with salt. Saute mushrooms in other ½ of the butter in a small skillet until tender. Add sherry and mushrooms to sauce; cook until desired consistency is reached.

Yield: 4 servings

VEAL MILANAISE

1 8-ounce can tomato sauce
3 ounces tomato paste
1 medium onion, chopped
2 cloves garlic, crushed
2 teaspoons oregano
2-3 pounds veal cutlets
Flour
3 eggs, beaten
¼ cup milk

¾ cup seasoned
  breadcrumbs
3 cups oil
¼ cup Romano cheese,
  grated
¼ cup Parmesan cheese,
  grated
Juice of 1 lemon
1 lemon, thinly sliced

Mix tomato sauce, paste, onion, garlic, and oregano together and simmer in a saucepan for 30 minutes. Pound veal cutlets to ¼ inch thickness to tenderize. Dust cutlets with flour. Combine eggs and milk together in a bowl. Dip cutlets in egg mixture and cover with breadcrumbs. Fry cutlets 2 minutes per side in oil over high heat. Remove and arrange on a serving platter. Mix cheeses together and sprinkle over top of cutlets. Squeeze lemon juice over top. Serve with tomato sauce. Garnish with lemon slices.

Yield: 6 servings

VEAL SCALLOPS IN LEMON SAUCE

1 cup Italian breadcrumbs
½ teaspoon garlic powder
½ teaspoon seasoned salt
½ teaspoon fresh cracked
  pepper
1 teaspoon dried tarragon
½ cup Parmesan cheese,
  grated
1 pound veal scallops, thinly
  sliced

1 stick butter
¼ cup dry white wine
1 teaspoon tarragon, soaked
  in white wine
1 lemon, thinly sliced
3 tablespoons fresh parsley,
  chopped

Sauce:
2 tablespoons butter, melted
1 egg yolk, beaten
2 tablespoons white wine

2 tablespoons lemon juice
1 teaspoon tarragon

Combine first six ingredients together in a shallow bowl. Lightly coat veal in mixture. Melt 1 stick butter in a large skillet and saute veal until well browned. Add wine, tarragon, lemon slices, and parsley; simmer for 10 minutes. Arrange veal on serving platter and place in a warm oven, discarding lemon slices. Beat egg yolk in wine and lemon juice; add to melted butter in a medium skillet. Add tarragon. Cook over low heat and stir constantly until desired consistency is reached. Pour over veal scallops and serve.

Yield: approximately 6 servings

MICROWAVE CORNED BEEF AND CABBAGE

2 medium potatoes, thinly
  sliced
1 medium onion, sliced
¼ cup water
¾ teaspoon salt
⅛ teaspoon pepper

2 12-ounce cans corned beef,
  crumbled
½ head cabbage, cut into 4
  wedges
½ stick butter, melted

Grease a 3-quart casserole; layer potatoes and onions. Add water, salt, and pepper. Microwave covered for 10 to 12 minutes. Add corned beef and cabbage and pour butter over cabbage. Microwave covered for 13-15 minutes or until cabbage is tender. Let stand covered for 5 minutes before serving.

Yield: 4 servings

ALMOND CHICKEN ROLLUPS

Serve this dish at your next dinner party.

3 chicken breasts, halved and deboned
1 cup very dry sherry
4 cups white breadcrumbs
½ teaspoon salt
¼ teaspoon pepper
¼ cup Parmesan cheese, grated
1-2 tablespoons dried parsley flakes
½-1 teaspoon garlic powder
1½ cups chopped almonds
2-3 sticks butter, melted
½ cup sliced almonds
6 slices thin Danish ham, (2x3 inch slices - one for each breast)
2 cups sour cream
2 tablespoons dried chives

A day ahead: Marinate chicken breasts in sherry for 5 to 6 hours. Drain and place chicken breasts in a sealed bowl overnight in the refrigerator. To prepare: Remove chicken from refrigerator and pat dry with paper towels if necessary. Combine breadcrumbs, salt, pepper, Parmesan cheese, parsley, garlic powder, and chopped almonds. Dip each breast in melted butter, roll in breadcrumb mixture, and place flat on a plate. Place a 2x3 inch slice of ham on each breast and roll in a jelly roll fashion, tucking in short ends, and fastening with a toothpick. Dip chicken in butter again, roll in crumbs, and place on a shallow baking dish. Combine sliced almonds with 3 tablespoons melted butter; spoon a few over top of each breast. Drizzle with melted butter. Bake at 350° for 1 hour.

Heat sour cream combined with chives over low heat or in the microwave. To serve, arrange chicken breasts on platter and spoon a small amount of sour cream sauce over each breast. Pour rest of sauce around chicken.

Yield: 6 servings

BRANDIED CHICKEN BREASTS

Easy and elegant! Try this with sherry.

2 tablespoons butter
6 chicken breasts, deboned
2 10¾-ounce cans of cream
  of mushroom soup
1 6-ounce can mushrooms,
  drained

1 bay leaf
1½ ounces brandy
Salt and pepper to taste
Dash of hot sauce
¼ teaspoon cayenne pepper

Saute chicken in butter in a skillet over medium-high heat until lightly browned. Add remaining ingredients and cook in a large pot over low heat on top of stove for 2 hours, until chicken is very tender. Serve over rice or mashed potatoes.

Yield: 6 servings

✳ good

HERB SEASONED CHICKEN BREAST

8 chicken breasts, skinned
  and boned
8 slices Swiss cheese
1 10¾-ounce can cream of
  chicken soup
½ small onion, finely
  chopped

¼ cup dry white wine
1 cup herb-seasoned stuffing
  mix, crushed
½ stick butter, melted

Preheat oven to 350°. Arrange chicken in a lightly greased 9x13 inch baking dish. Top with cheese slices. Combine soup, onion, and wine in a mixing bowl, stirring well. Spoon sauce evenly over chicken and sprinkle with stuffing mix. Drizzle melted butter over chicken. Bake for 45 to 55 minutes.

Yield: 8 servings

CHICKEN KIEV

4 whole chicken breasts;
  skinned, boned, and cut in
  halves
2 sticks butter
2 tablespoons chopped
  chives
2 tablespoons parsley

1 clove garlic, minced
½ teaspoon salt
½ teaspoon pepper
½ cup flour
1 egg, beaten
1 cup breadcrumbs
2-3 cups oil

Pound chicken into ½-inch thickness. Form butter into eight balls. Combine next five ingredients together and roll butter balls in mixture. Place one of the seasoned balls in the center of each half-breast and roll up so the butter is completely enclosed. Secure with toothpicks. Dust breast with flour and dip in beaten egg. Roll in breadcrumbs; fry in deep fat fryer until golden brown.

Yield: 4 servings

LEMONY CHICKEN

Serve over a bed of wild rice. The chicken broth will reduce and makes a wonderful sauce.

⅓ cup flour
1 teaspoon salt
½ teaspoon lemon pepper,
  optional
1 teaspoon paprika
3 chicken breasts, halved and
  deboned
3 tablespoons fresh lemon
  juice

½ stick butter or 3
  tablespoons shortening
1 chicken bouillon cube
1 cup water, boiling
2 tablespoons brown sugar
¼ cup green onions,
  chopped
Lemon slices for garnish

Combine flour, salt, lemon pepper, and paprika in a plastic bag. Brush chicken with 2 tablespoons lemon juice, place in plastic bag, and shake to coat. Melt butter in a large skillet and brown chicken over medium-high heat. Dissolve chicken bouillon cube in water in a small saucepan. Add brown sugar, sliced onion, and 1 tablespoon lemon juice, stirring to dissolve brown sugar. Pour over chicken and cover, reducing heat to low. Cook approximately 40 minutes or until chicken is tender. Garnish.

Yield: 6 servings

HEART OF TEXAS CHEESY CHICKEN MORNAY

½ cup flour
1 teaspoon salt
⅛ teaspoon ginger

⅛ teaspoon pepper
4-6 boneless chicken breasts
1 stick butter

Sauce:
½ cup water
½ stick butter
4 tablespoons flour
1 teaspoon salt
½ cup milk or cream
1 cup sour cream
½ cup American cheese,
   shredded

8 ounces fresh mushrooms,
   sliced or 1 cup canned
   sliced mushrooms
Top with additional shredded
   cheese
Garnish with paprika

Preheat oven to 350°. Combine first four ingredients. Coat chicken with flour mixture. Melt butter in skillet; brown chicken and cook on low heat approximately 30 minutes or until tender. Place chicken into a 9x13 inch baking dish. Add water to drippings in skillet. Add butter, flour, and salt. Blend until smooth and there are no lumps in the flour. Add milk, stirring until smooth. Stir in sour cream and cheese, until cheese is melted. Add mushrooms. Pour sauce over chicken and sprinkle with additional shredded cheese. Bake for 25 to 30 minutes. Sprinkle with paprika and serve.

Yield: approximately 6 servings

TEHUACANA CHICKEN

The first trading post in McLennan County was on Tehuacana Creek about 3 miles from Waco.

1 10¾-ounce can cream of
   mushroom soup
⅔ cup milk
½ teaspoon salt
1 cup cream-style cottage
   cheese, mashed
2 3-ounce packages cream
   cheese, crumbled
½ teaspoon poultry
   seasoning
⅓ cup onion, chopped
2 tablespoons butter or
   margarine

1 4-ounce can chopped
   green chilies
3 cups chicken, cooked and
   diced
1 6¾-ounce package Doritos
2 cups mild Cheddar cheese,
   shredded
½ cup Parmesan cheese,
   grated
½ cup buttered breadcrumbs

Heat first 5 ingredients in saucepan. Add poultry seasoning. Saute onions in butter. Add green chilies and chicken. Combine with soup mixture. In a lightly greased 3 quart casserole, layer ½ Doritos and ½ chicken. Sprinkle with 1 cup Cheddar cheese. Repeat layers. Top with Parmesan cheese and breadcrumbs. Bake for 30 minutes at 350°.

Yield: 10-12 servings

CHICKEN ITALIAN

A kid pleasing dinner item.

4 chicken breasts, skinned
   and boned
1-2 eggs, beaten
1 cup breadcrumbs or
   cracker crumbs
½ cup olive oil

2 cups pizza sauce, canned
   or bottled
4-8 tablespoons Parmesan
   cheese
4 slices mozzarella cheese

Pound chicken with a meat mallet to ¼ inch thickness. Dip into egg and dredge in breadcrumbs. Brown chicken in olive oil and drain. Place in Pyrex dish. Cover with pizza sauce. Sprinkle with Parmesan cheese. Bake at 350° for 30 minutes. Top with mozzarella and bake an additional 10 minutes or until cheese melts.

Yield: 4 servings

EASY PARMESAN CHICKEN BREAST

2-3 cups buttery flavored
   crackers, crushed
¾ cup Parmesan cheese,
   grated
¼ cup Romano cheese,
   grated
¼ cup fresh parsley,
   chopped

2 cloves garlic, crushed or 1
   teaspoon garlic powder
2 teaspoons salt
¼ teaspoon pepper
12 chicken breasts, skinned
   and boned
3 sticks butter, melted

Preheat oven to 350°. Combine crackers, cheeses, parsley, garlic, salt and pepper in a large plastic bag. Dip chicken in melted butter and coat with cracker crumbs. Place in a 9x13 inch baking dish. Pour remaining butter over chicken and sprinkle with additional cracker crumbs. Bake for 1 to 1¼ hours.

Variation: Substitute 2 cups bread crumbs for crackers. Add 1 teaspoon Worcestershire, 2 teaspoons each prepared mustard and Italian seasoning.

Yield: 12 servings

MRS. MC'S CHICKEN AND SCAMPI

1 3½-5 pound chicken fryer,
   cut up
1 tablespoon salt
½ teaspoon pepper
½ stick butter
3 small onions, finely
   chopped
1 clove garlic, minced

3 tablespoons snipped
   parsley
½ cup port wine
1 8-ounce can tomato sauce
1 teaspoon dried basil
1 pound shrimp, shelled and
   deveined
Parsley to garnish

Rub chicken well with salt and pepper. Saute chicken in hot butter in a large skillet until golden brown on all sides. Add remaining ingredients except shrimp. Simmer, covered about 30 minutes until chicken is tender. Push chicken to one side of skillet and turn heat up so tomato mixture comes to a boil. Add shrimp and cook uncovered for 3 to 4 minutes, until pink and tender. Arrange chicken on platter and top with shrimp. Skim sauce and pour over chicken and shrimp. Garnish with parsley.

Yield: 6 servings

RUSH HOUR CHICKEN

Cut up leftover chicken, add vegetables and juice, and have stew the next night.

1 4 pound whole chicken
2 teaspoons salt
1 teaspoon Accent
½ teaspoon dried thyme
2 ribs celery with leaves
1 medium onion, peeled
2 tablespoons butter
12 small white onions,
   peeled

12 small potatoes, peeled and
   cut in half
6-8 medium carrots, scraped
   and cut in 2-3 inch chunks
¼ cup dry sherry
Fresh parsley, chopped,
   optional

Preheat oven to 375°. Wash and dry chicken. Sprinkle inside of the chicken with 1 teaspoon salt, Accent, and thyme. Place celery and medium onion in the cavity of the chicken using small skewers to close cavity. Place chicken in a large heavy roasting pan. Dot chicken with butter. Cover and bake for 30 minutes. Add onions, potatoes, and carrots. Sprinkle chicken and vegetables with remaining teaspoon salt. Pour sherry over all. Cover and bake 30 minutes, basting once with juice in pan. Remove cover and continue baking for 15-30 minutes until chicken and vegetables are tender. Baste frequently with juice in pan. Sprinkle with chopped parsley and serve on a platter.

Yield: 6 servings.

DIETER'S FRIED SESAME CHICKEN

2 tablespoons flour
¼ teaspoon pepper
4 chicken breast halves,
   skinned

2 tablespoons soy sauce
2 tablespoons butter, melted
3 tablespoons sesame seeds

Preheat oven to 400°. Combine flour and pepper. Dip chicken in soy sauce and dredge in flour mixture. Place in baking dish and drizzle butter over chicken. Sprinkle with sesame seeds. Bake for 40 to 45 minutes.

Yield: 4 servings.

CHICKEN FOILED AGAIN

¾ cup uncooked rice
Salt and pepper to taste
4 boneless chicken breasts
8 fresh mushrooms, chopped
1 green bell pepper, chopped
1 medium onion, chopped

2 medium zucchini,
  chopped
1 16-ounce can tomato sauce
½ cup water or white wine
½ teaspoon dried oregano
Parmesan cheese, grated

Preheat oven to 350°. Cut four large pieces of heavy duty foil. Place 3 tablespoons of rice in middle of each piece of foil. Salt and pepper chicken and place on rice. Add equal amounts of chopped vegetables to chicken. Mix together tomato sauce, water or wine, and oregano; spoon over chicken. Top with Parmesan cheese. Seal foil tightly and bake for 1 hour.

Yield: 4 servings

CHICKEN AND BROCCOLI CASSEROLE

1 cup mayonnaise
1 10¾-ounce can cream of
  chicken soup
½ teaspoon curry powder
½ teaspoon salt
¼ teaspoon pepper
1 tablespoon lemon juice
1 4-ounce can sliced
  mushrooms
½ 8-ounce package
  cornbread stuffing mix

1 stick butter, melted
1 chicken, plus 2 breasts;
  boiled, deboned, and cut
  into pieces
2 10-ounce packages frozen
  chopped broccoli, cooked
  and drained
1 cup Cheddar cheese,
  shredded

Preheat oven to 350°. Grease a 9x13 inch baking dish. Mix mayonnaise, soup, curry, salt, pepper, lemon juice, and mushrooms. Toss stuffing mix with butter. Mix chicken, broccoli, soup, and stuffing in a bowl. Place in baking dish and top with cheese. Bake for 30 to 45 minutes.

Yield: approximately 10 servings

CREAMED CHICKEN IN PATTY SHELLS

This is good served over rice or topped with pastry.

½ green bell pepper,
  chopped
2-3 ribs celery, chopped
1 small onion, chopped
3 tablespoons butter
½ stick butter
5 tablespoons flour
1½ cups chicken broth
1 cup milk or Half and Half
3 cups chicken, cooked and
  diced

1½ cups cooked carrots,
  diced and drained
1 can green peas, drained
6 patty shells, baked
  according to package
  directions
Salt and pepper to taste
Paprika

Saute green pepper, celery, and onion in butter until tender. Drain and set aside. Melt ½ stick butter in a heavy saucepan over low heat and blend in flour. Cook one minute, stirring constantly. Gradually add chicken stock and milk and cook over medium heat, stirring constantly until thickened and bubbly. Stir in sauteed vegetables, chicken, carrots, and peas. Add salt and pepper to taste. Spoon into patty shells and sprinkle with paprika.

Yield: 6 servings

CHICKEN AND RICE ALMONDINE

½ cup slivered blanched
  almonds
1 cup fresh mushrooms,
  sliced
1 tablespoon onion, minced
½ stick butter or ¼ cup
  chicken fat
6 tablespoons flour
2 cups chicken stock or
  bouillon

1 cup whipping cream
2½ cups chicken, cooked
  and diced
3 cups cooked rice
2 tablespoons chopped
  pimentos
1 tablespoon parsley, minced
1 teaspoon salt
White pepper to taste

Preheat oven to 375°. Melt butter and saute almonds, mushrooms, and onion for 10 minutes. Stir in flour. Add stock and cream. Cook, stirring until thickened. Add chicken and remaining ingredients. Pour into a 9x13 inch baking dish. Cover and bake for 30 minutes.

Yield: 6 servings

CHICKEN CURRY CASSEROLE

1 29-ounce can peach slices
1 29-ounce can pineapple
  chunks
½ stick butter
3 teaspoons curry powder
1½ onions, chopped

¾ cup brown sugar
2 tablespoons wine vinegar
8 chicken breasts, cut into
  chunks
Condiments

Preheat oven to 350°. Drain peaches and pineapple, reserving ½ cup syrup. Melt butter in a saucepan and add curry. Simmer over low heat for 5 minutes. Remove from heat; stir in onions, reserved syrup, sugar, and vinegar. Place chicken in a shallow baking dish and cover with sauce. Bake uncovered for 1 to 1½ hours, basting occasionally. Fifteen minutes before serving, place peaches and pineapple into dish with chicken and baste with sauce. Bake an additional 10 to 15 minutes. Serve over cooked rice with your choice of condiments: chopped bananas, cashews, coconut, cooked and crumbled bacon, chutney, raisins, minced green onion, tomatoes, bell pepper, radishes, French fried onions, or hard boiled eggs.

Yield: approximately 6 servings

H.O.T. CHICKEN KABOBS

Marinade:
½-1 cup liquid from 1-pound
  can pineapple chunks
½ cup soy sauce
¼ cup cooking oil
1 teaspoon dry mustard

1 tablespoon brown sugar
2 teaspoons ground ginger
1 teaspoon garlic salt
¼ teaspoon pepper

Kabobs:
6 chicken breasts, boned and
  cut into 1 inch cubes
Sliced green bell pepper
1 1-pound can pineapple
  chunks

Cherry tomatoes
Fresh mushrooms

Combine marinade ingredients in a saucepan and simmer for 5 minutes. Allow to cool. Pour sauce over chicken and marinate for 1 hour. Alternate chicken chunks and remaining ingredients on skewers and place on grill. Cook over moderate heat for 20 minutes, turning and basting often with marinade. Serve over cooked rice.

Yield: approximately 6 servings

BELLE BAYOU CHICKEN STEW

This recipe was tested and endorsed in 1938 by "Better Homes and Gardens".

1 2½-pound chicken
4 medium red potatoes, diced
1 bunch carrots, scraped and diced
1 8¾-ounce can whole kernel corn
3 green bell peppers, chopped
1 red bell pepper, chopped or 1 2-ounce jar diced pimentos
4 medium tomatoes, peeled and diced

2 cloves garlic, pressed
2 sprigs fresh parsley, chopped
½ teaspoon thyme, ground
⅛ teaspoon sage, ground
1 teaspoon black pepper, finely ground
1 teaspoon salt
½ teaspoon red pepper
2 tablespoons olive oil
½ cup white wine, optional

Cut up chicken, place in Dutch oven and cover with water. Bring to a boil, reduce heat, and cook slowly until meat falls off the bone. Allow to cool and remove all meat from the bones. Place chicken meat back in stock in the Dutch oven. Add all remaining ingredients except wine. Cook slowly until thick, approximately 1 hour. Add wine just before serving.

Yield: approximately 8 servings

COLD CHINESE SZECHWAN CHICKEN

1 whole 2½-3 pound chicken
2 tablespoons green onion,
  finely chopped
2 tablespoons fresh ginger,
  finely chopped
1 tablespoon red oil
3 tablespoons soy sauce
1 tablespoon vinegar

2 tablespoons sesame oil
1-2 teaspoons sugar
½ teaspoon ground
  Szechwan pepper, optional
1 recipe Chinese noodles
1 6-ounce can bean sprouts
  or fresh bean sprouts
Fresh parsley

Clean chicken and place in boiling water to cover. Boil until tender. Remove chicken from pot, drain, and allow to cool. Debone and cut into bite size pieces. Set aside. Mix next 8 ingredients in a small bowl. Pour over chicken and marinate in refrigerator for several hours. Toss marinated chicken with one can bean sprouts. Serve over Chinese noodles. Garnish with fresh parsley.

Yield: 4 servings

CHINESE NOODLES

1 cup flour
1 tablespoon water

1 egg

Mix ingredients in a food processor until dough forms a ball and spins around in the bowl. More flour may be added if needed. Pat dough with cornstarch and store in a plastic bag at room temperature for 1 hour. Cut dough into thirds and make manageable sizes to work with pasta machine. Using cornstarch instead of flour, work dough through machine to number two or number three setting. Cut noodles. Dry noodles about 1 hour or longer. Cook in boiling water for 2 to 3 minutes. Drain and rinse thoroughly in hot water.

Yield: 4 servings

LIL'S CHICKEN VAL VERDE

⅓ cup onion, chopped
1 2½-ounce jar sliced
   mushrooms
3 tablespoons butter
1 5-ounce package green
   noodles
Chicken stock
2 10-ounce packages
   frozen chopped spinach,
   thawed and drained
5 cups white meat chicken,
   cooked and cut in bite-size
   pieces
1 10¾-ounce can cream of
   mushroom soup

1 cup mayonnaise
Juice of 2 lemons
1 cup milk
1 6-ounce can water
   chestnuts
1 2-ounce jar pimentos,
   chopped
1 tablespoon salt or to taste
Buttery flavored cracker
   crumbs
3 tablespoons butter, melted
½ cup Parmesan cheese,
   grated

Preheat oven to 350°. Saute onion and mushrooms in 3 tablespoons of butter. Cook noodles according to package directions, using chicken stock for liquid and drain. Mix spinach, chicken, sauteed onion, mushrooms, and noodles together in a large bowl. Add soup, mayonnaise, lemon juice, milk, water chestnuts, pimentos and salt. Pour into a 3-quart casserole dish. Top with cracker crumbs. Drizzle with 3 tablespoons butter and sprinkle with Parmesan. Bake for 45 minutes.

Yield: approximately 12 servings

TEXAS TERIYAKI, TOO

A good sauce to stir-fry pork, chicken, or vegetables.

¼ cup soy sauce
¼ cup oil
2 tablespoons wine vinegar

3 tablespoons honey
1½ teaspoons ginger
1½ teaspoons garlic powder

Mix all ingredients with a wire whisk. To serve, brush sauce on chicken breasts and grill outdoors.

Yield: 1 cup

MARINADE FOR CHICKEN BREASTS

A *tasty low calorie entree.*

6 tablespoons soy sauce
6 tablespoons Italian salad
  dressing
4 teaspoons sesame seeds
4 teaspoons lemon juice

¼ teaspoon ground ginger
¼ teaspoon garlic powder
4 chicken breasts, skinned
  and boned

Mix all ingredients except chicken in a container with a lid. Shake vigorously. Pour over chicken and let stand for 2 hours. Drain chicken and grill over moderate heat until done. Serve on cooked noodles or slice for chicken fajitas.

Yield: 4 servings

CHICKEN TETRAZZINI

½ cup green bell pepper,
  chopped
1 cup onion, chopped
¼ stick butter
1 8-ounce package spaghetti,
  cooked and drained
¼ cup pimentos, chopped
¼ teaspoon salt
¼ teaspoon celery salt
2 10¾-ounce cans cream of
  mushroom soup

3 cups Cheddar cheese,
  shredded
1 cup chicken broth
½ pound fresh mushrooms,
  sliced
4 cups chicken, cooked and
  diced
Paprika

Preheat oven to 350°. Saute green pepper and onion in butter. Combine all ingredients except paprika and pour into large greased casserole dish. Sprinkle with paprika. Cover and bake for approximately 1 hour.

Yield: 8 servings

CHICKEN MARINARA FETTUCCINE

You can layer the sauce over the noodles in a casserole and top with Parmesan and Cheddar cheese if you prefer.

4 whole chicken breasts,
  boned and cubed
3 tablespoons olive oil
1 large onion, chopped
4 cloves garlic, pressed
½ pound fresh mushrooms,
  sliced
2 ribs celery, sliced
1 carrot, scraped and grated
1 14½-ounce can Italian
  tomato sauce
2 14½-ounce cans Italian
  style stewed tomatoes,
  undrained

1 green bell pepper, chopped
½ cup Burgundy wine
1 teaspoon salt
½ teaspoon pepper
½ teaspoon oregano
1 tablespoon Worcestershire
  sauce
1 package fettuccine, cooked
  according to package
  directions
Parmesan cheese, freshly
  grated

Saute chicken in olive oil in a large heavy skillet. Add onion and garlic. Brown lightly. Add mushrooms, celery, and carrot and continue to saute. Add tomato sauce, tomatoes, pepper, wine, and seasonings. Simmer for 1 hour. Serve over fettuccine with Parmesan cheese sprinkled on top.

Yield: approximately 6 servings

ELEGANT CHICKEN LIVERS

6 strips bacon, cooked and
  crumbled reserving
  drippings
6 green onions, chopped
1 2½-ounce can mushroom
  pieces, drained

1 pound chicken livers
1 beef bouillon cube
½ cup water
½ cup white wine

Saute onions and mushrooms in bacon drippings for 1 minute until onions are tender. Add livers and saute 5 minutes more. Add bacon and remaining ingredients, heat through. Serve over hot cooked rice.

Yield: 4 servings

DOVES WITH ARTICHOKE HEARTS

10-12 doves
Flour
½ stick butter, melted
½ pound fresh mushrooms, sliced
1 20-ounce can artichoke hearts, drained
1 tablespoon Worcestershire sauce

1-2 drops Tabasco sauce
¼ cup dry sherry
Salt and pepper to taste
3-4 cups Cream Sauce (recipe follows)
½ cup Parmesan cheese, grated
Paprika

Preheat oven to 350°. Butter 3-quart baking dish. Dust doves with flour and saute in butter in a large skillet until brown. Remove from pan and add mushrooms; saute about 5 minutes. Arrange artichokes in bottom of baking dish. Add doves and sprinkle with mushrooms. Mix Worcestershire, Tabasco, sherry, salt and pepper with Cream Sauce and pour over doves. Sprinkle top with Parmesan cheese and paprika. Bake for 45 minutes to 1 hour.

Yield: 4 servings

CREAM SAUCE

1 tablespoon butter
1 tablespoon flour
¼ teaspoon salt

1 cup milk or part milk and Half and Half

Melt butter in heavy saucepan on low heat. Add flour and salt and whisk until bubbly. Slowly add milk and stir constantly. Cook until thick and smooth consistency is reached.

Yield: 1 cup

DELIGHTFUL DOVES

Flour
Seasoned salt to taste
16-20 doves
10 strips of bacon
¼ cup Worcestershire sauce

1 cup red wine or beef
  consomme
1½ cups sliced mushrooms
2 tablespoons butter
Juice of ½ lemon

Mix flour and seasoned salt. Roll doves in flour. Cook bacon, remove, and reserve drippings. Brown doves in drippings. Turn doves breast down and add Worcestershire sauce and wine or consomme. Cover and cook over low heat for 20 minutes. Turn doves breast up and cook, covered, for an additional 20 minutes. Cook mushrooms in butter and lemon and add to the doves for the last 10 minutes of cooking. Serve doves over cooked rice and sprinkle with crumbled bacon.

Yield: approximately 6 servings

DUCKS TENDERLOIN

This can be an expensive dish to prepare when you add in the price of the lease, hunting dogs, and guns!

1 medium onion, minced
½ cup red wine
10 black peppercorns
1 bay leaf
½ teaspoon thyme
1 clove garlic, minced

2 tablespoons butter
1 teaspoon flour
2 large or 3 small ducks
Seasoned salt and pepper to
  taste
1 tablespoon butter

Cook onions in red wine with next 4 ingredients over low heat until mixture is reduced by half, about 20 minutes. Add butter and flour. Stir until thickened. Press through a strainer and discard remainings. Set wine sauce aside.

Preheat oven to 475°. Season ducks with salt and pepper. Place ducks in large roasting pan and cook 15 minutes per pound. Slice duck meat and save juices. Add juice to heated wine sauce, stirring slowly. Heat slowly adding salt and pepper to taste. Remove from heat and stir in 1 tablespoon butter. Serve duck sliced with sauce over top.

Yield: ½ pound per person

DUCK WITH GREEN PEPPERCORN SAUCE

4 whole wild duck breasts,
  boned and skinned
1½ teaspoons salt
½ teaspoon white pepper
2 tablespoons flour
3 tablespoons butter, melted
6 shallots or green onions,
  chopped

2-3 tablespoons green
  peppercorns, canned in
  water, drained and mashed
2 tablespoons cognac
½ cup chicken stock
1½ cups heavy cream
2 tablespoons fresh parsley,
  chopped

Preheat oven to 180°. Remove tendon from duck breasts and pound breasts flat. Season with 1 teaspoon salt and pepper. Dredge with flour and shake off excess. Saute breasts in butter in a large skillet over medium heat for about 3 minutes per side. Remove breasts and keep warm in oven. Saute shallots in pan with drippings, about 30 seconds. Add peppercorns, cognac, chicken stock, and remaining salt. Bring to boil. Add cream; bring to second boil. Add parsley. Slice meat diagonally and cover with sauce. Serve with cooked wild rice.

Yield: approximately 8 servings

CORNISH HENS A LA ORANGE

8 Cornish hens
4 medium onions, chopped
1½ sticks butter

½ cup chicken stock
1 cup orange marmalade
Salt and pepper to taste

Preheat oven to 325°. Wash hens and pat dry. Stuff each hen with chopped onion. Place hens in a large shallow roasting pan. Combine butter, chicken stock, and orange marmalade, in a small saucepan. Cook over medium heat, stirring with a wooden spoon, until mixture is well blended. Pour evenly over hens and bake for 1½ hours, basting often. Add more chicken stock if necessary. Serve with sauce from roasting pan.

Yield: 8 servings

OYSTERS ON THE WING

The oysters add a great flavor to this dish. Wonderful with Orange Rice.

¼ cup flour
Salt and pepper to taste
Seasoned salt to taste
8 quail, washed and dried
  well
¼ cup vegetable oil
½ stick butter
¾ cup onion, chopped
1 cup chicken broth

¾ cup dry white wine
1 teaspoon Worcestershire
  sauce
¾ cup fresh mushrooms,
  sliced
2 tablespoons fresh parsley,
  chopped
1 cup Half and Half
1 pint oysters

Preheat oven to 350°. Mix flour and seasoning together in a paper bag. Drop birds into bag, one at a time, and shake, coating well. Heat oil and butter in a large skillet. Brown birds on both sides. Remove to baking dish. Lightly saute onion in remaining oil and butter. Add chicken broth, wine and Worcestershire sauce. Simmer 2 to 3 minutes. Pour over birds in casserole. Cover with foil and bake for 1 hour and 15 minutes, basting occasionally. Add remaining ingredients. Bake an additional 15 minutes.

Yield: approximately 6 servings

LAMB KABOBS

This recipe is good also prepared with a roast.

2 pounds boneless leg of
  lamb, cubed
3 firm tomatoes, cored and
  quartered
12 small whole onions,
  peeled and parboiled 10
  minutes

2 green bell peppers, seeded
  and cut into 1-inch wide
  strips
12 whole fresh mushrooms

Marinade:
1 cup olive oil
1 clove garlic, mashed
⅓ cup lemon juice

1 teaspoon oregano
2 teaspoons salt
¼ teaspoon pepper

Sauce:
½ stick butter
1 bunch scallions, sliced
¼ cup flour

1½ cups beef broth
½ cup dry red wine
Salt and pepper to taste

Place first five ingredients into a shallow glass dish. Combine marinade ingredients and mix until smooth. Pour marinade evenly over lamb and vegetables. Allow to stand at room temperature for 1 hour, or refrigerate overnight.

Separate meat and vegetables onto different skewers. Place skewers on grill at moderate heat and cook until desired doneness about 15 minutes. Baste with marinade. May be cooked under oven broiler.

To prepare sauce: Heat butter and saute scallions for 1 minute. Stir in flour, beef broth and wine gradually over low heat until sauce bubbles and thickens. Season to taste with salt and pepper. Serve kabobs over a bed of rice and spoon sauce over top.

Yield: approximately 6 servings

BROILED BUTTERFLIED LEG OF LAMB

Remove from the oven before igniting, or you might burn down the house!

1 5-6 pound leg of lamb, boned and butterflied	¼ cup rosemary, crushed
2 cloves garlic, minced	1 cup gin, Bourbon, or consomme
1 tablespoon salt	2 tablespoons butter

Preheat broiler. Place rack 8-10 inches from the heat. Remove the thin skin that covers the fat of the lamb leg, or have your butcher butterfly it. Rub lamb with garlic, salt, and rosemary. Allow to stand at room temperature for at least 1 hour. Place fat side up in a buttered pan. Broil for 15 minutes. Remove from oven and pour ½ cup of gin over lamb and ignite. Allow alcohol to burn off, turn, and return to broiler for an additional 15 minutes. Remove from broiler and repeat with remaining ½ cup of gin. Add butter. Turn off broiler and return to oven to keep warm. Slice thinly and use juices as a sauce. Place rack lower in the oven and increase broiling time if you prefer your meat medium to well done.

Yield: approximately 8 servings

MOIST AND TENDER PORK CHOPS WITH RICE

For an easy meal-just add a salad!

4 thick pork loin chops	1 cup uncooked rice
Salt and pepper to taste	2 10½-ounce cans beef consomme
Flour	Water if needed
1 tablespoon vegetable oil	
1 medium onion, sliced	
1 large red or green bell pepper, sliced	

Preheat oven to 375°. Season pork chops with salt and pepper; dredge in flour. Heat oil in a heavy skillet; brown pork chops on both sides. Pour uncooked rice in a shallow baking dish and add 1 can consomme. Place pork chops on rice and top with a slice of onion and pepper on each. Cover and bake for 1 to 1¼ hours. Halfway through cooking, add more consomme or water as needed to complete the cooking of the rice.

Yield: 4 servings

SOUR CREAM PORK CHOPS

Serve with buttered noodles.

¾-1 cup flour
2 teaspoons pepper
½ teaspoon garlic powder
3-4 tablespoons paprika
Oil
6 thick-cut boneless pork
  chops

1 large onion, sliced into 6
  slices
1 10½-ounce can beef
  bouillon
1 16-ounce carton sour
  cream

Preheat oven to 375°. Combine first four ingredients in a plastic bag. Pour a small amount of oil in a skillet and heat. Dredge pork chops in flour; brown in oil 5 minutes on each side. Top each chop with onion slice. Remove pork chops and onions to a 9x13 inch baking dish. Add 2 to 3 tablespoons of remaining flour to pan drippings and cook for 2 to 3 minutes, stirring to blend well. Add bouillon and stir until smooth and thickened. Stir in sour cream and pour over pork chops. Bake covered 1 to 1¼ hours until chops are done.

Yield: 6 servings

STUFFED PORK TENDERLOIN

¼ pound ground pork
¼ cup onion, chopped
1 10¾-ounce can cream of
  mushroom soup
3 slices rye bread, crumbled

1 egg, slightly beaten
¼ teaspoon nutmeg
1 pork tenderloin
4-6 slices bacon
Salt and pepper to taste

Preheat oven to 350°. Brown pork with onion and drain. Stir in ½ can of soup, breadcrumbs, egg, and nutmeg. Cut tenderloin in half lengthwise. Fill with stuffing mixture and fasten with string. Wrap bacon around pork and bake uncovered in oven for 40 to 45 minutes per pound or until meat thermometer reaches 170°. Top with remaining soup and broil just long enough to heat well.

Yield: 4 servings

GRILLED MARINATED LOIN OF PORK

The fire is extremely important in preparing this recipe.

1 5-7 pound pork loin,
 boned, rolled and tied

Brine:

1½ cups sugar
1½ cups coarse salt
1½-2 quarts warm water,
 more if needed
3-4 cloves garlic, roughly
 chopped with skins

¼ cup gin
3-4 fresh thyme sprigs or 1
 teaspoon dried thyme

Marinade:

⅔ cup olive oil
3 cloves garlic, peeled and
 chopped
1 tablespoon fresh thyme
 leaves or ½ teaspoon dried
 thyme

2 teaspoons fresh rosemary
 leaves or ½ teaspoon dried
 rosemary

Mix brine ingredients together in a large pot to hold roast. Stir until sugar dissolves over low heat. Allow to cool. Place pork in the brine. Add cold water if necessary to cover the meat. Weight pork with a heavy plate to keep it under the surface. Cover and allow pork to cure in the brine refrigerated for two days.

A few hours before grilling, remove meat from the brine and wipe it thoroughly with paper towels. Allow the meat to come to room temperature. Prepare the grill and let fire burn to the low stage. There should be no visible flames, and the coals will sizzle only slightly and emit a small lick of flame when the marinade drips on them. Oil the grill and position it 5 to 6 inches from the coals.

Mix the marinade ingredients in a small bowl. Brush the pork with this mixture. Place pork on the grill and cook over low fire, occasionally turning and basting with the marinade. Cooking time will vary. Cook approximately 40 minutes. For a smaller roast, cook for 30 minutes. Allow meat to rest 10 minutes before carving.

Yield: approximately 12 servings

ORIENTAL STYLE SWEET AND SOUR PORK

Try this with chicken!

1 pound lean pork, cut in
  bite-size pieces
¼ teaspoon salt
3 tablespoons soy sauce
¼ teaspoon sesame oil,
  optional
1 tablespoon vegetable oil
4 teaspoons cornstarch
¼ cup brown sugar

¾ cup liquid, (syrup from
  pineapple with water
  added)
1 cup pineapple tidbits,
  drained and reserve juice
¼ cup vinegar
1 teaspoon catsup
2 tablespoons soy sauce
1 small green bell pepper,
  cut in bite-size pieces

Combine pork with next 3 ingredients and marinate in refrigerator 30 minutes. Remove from marinade and saute pork in vegetable oil about 10 minutes until all pink is gone. In a jar combine cornstarch, brown sugar, liquid, vinegar, catsup, and 2 tablespoons soy sauce. Shake with lid on jar until all ingredients are blended. Pour over pork in skillet, stirring until mixture is thick and clear. Stir in pineapple and pepper. Simmer an additional 5 minutes. Serve over Oriental Style Fried Rice.

Yield: 4 servings

ORIENTAL STYLE FRIED RICE

A good recipe for leftover rice!

½ cup onion, chopped
3 tablespoons butter
1 egg, slightly beaten

4 cups cooked rice
¼ cup water
2 tablespoons soy sauce

Saute onion in butter in a large skillet. Add egg and scramble. Add rice and saute, stirring over low to medium heat until rice is slightly browned. Stir water and soy sauce into rice. Heat and serve.

Yield: 4 servings

SWEET AND SOUR MUSTARD-GLAZED SPARERIBS

A wonderful dinner when the cook is tired of the kitchen or great for a casual supper when you entertain. The glaze is also good on chicken.

4 teaspoons fresh rosemary,
   minced
4 cloves garlic, minced

Sweet and Sour Glaze:
⅔ cup dark brown sugar,
   firmly packed
½ cup Dijon mustard

2 6-pound racks pork
   spareribs
Salt and pepper to taste

6 tablespoons cider vinegar
2 tablespoons molasses
1 tablespoon dry mustard

Preheat oven to 350°. Rub rosemary and garlic into both sides of the ribs. Sprinkle with salt and pepper. Arrange meaty side down on baking sheet. Bake 1 hour, turning once. (Can be made 1 day ahead. Allow to cool completely, cover with plastic and refrigerate.) Baking for one hour will reduce grilling time and melt away excess fat.

To prepare glaze, combine all ingredients in a heavy saucepan. Bring to simmer, stirring. Allow to cool.

Prepare barbecue grill. Place ribs on grill, meaty side up. Spread top with one third of the glaze. Cook until bottom side is crisp, approximately 5 minutes. Turn, spread with remaining glaze, and cook an additional 5 minutes. Transfer to platter and cut into individual ribs.

Yield: 4 servings

JAMBALAYA

A simple version for a complicated dish.

¼ pound sliced bacon, cut to 1 inch pieces
½ cup onion, chopped
2 medium green bell peppers, cut in 1 inch strips
1 cup uncooked rice
1 teaspoon minced garlic
1 16-ounce can whole tomatoes, drained and chopped

½ teaspoon thyme
1 teaspoon salt
Pepper to taste
1 tablespoon fresh parsley, chopped
1½ to 2 cups chicken stock
½ pound cooked smoked ham, cut in 2x½ inch strips
1 pound raw shrimp, peeled

Preheat oven to 350°. Fry bacon until brown in a heavy skillet. Remove, drain and reserve drippings. Saute onions in fat for 8-10 minutes. Add green peppers and cook about 3-5 minutes. Add rice and stir until grains are opaque. Add garlic, tomatoes, bacon, thyme, salt, pepper, and parsley. Pour in 1½ cups stock and boil. Add ham and stir. Add shrimp and push beneath rice. Cook in oven until rice is tender, approximately 30 minutes. Add the remaining stock if necessary.

Yield: approximately 6 servings

HAM RAISIN SAUCE

A Good Housekeeping prize winner from the 1930's. Serve with sliced ham.

1 medium white onion, chopped
½ cup cider vinegar
¾ cup brown sugar
1 cup seeded raisins
1 large tart firm apple, unpeeled and chopped

½ teaspoon each salt, cinnamon, cloves, and allspice
1 tablespoon Worcestershire sauce

Mix all ingredients together in a large saucepan. Cook for fifteen minutes, stirring constantly. Re-heat before serving.

Yield: 1¾ cups

HAM LOAF AND HORSERADISH SAUCE

Uncooked ham loaves freeze beautifully!

Ham Loaf:

2 pounds lean ham, ground
1½ pounds lean pork, ground
1 cup milk
1 cup dry breadcrumbs

¼ cup onion, chopped
4 eggs, well beaten
1½ teaspoons salt
2 tablespoons parsley, chopped

Glaze:

¾ cup brown sugar
¼ cup water

¼ cup vinegar
2 teaspoons dry mustard

Sauce:

¼ cup horseradish
1½ tablespoons vinegar
1 tablespoon dry mustard
4 drops Worcestershire sauce

⅛ teaspoon cayenne pepper
⅛ teaspoon paprika
½ cup whipping cream, whipped

Ham Loaf: Combine all ingredients and mix well. Pack into two 9x5 inch loaf pans. Score top of loaf with knife blade. Bake for 30 minutes in preheated 350° oven.

Glaze: Mix ingredients together for glaze in a saucepan. Bring to boil and cook for 1 minute. Spread glaze on loaves and bake for 1 hour.

Sauce: Combine horseradish, vinegar, mustard, Worcestershire, cayenne, and paprika together in a mixing bowl. Fold mixture into whipping cream blending well. Spoon sauce over each slice of ham loaf.

Yield: approximately 12 servings

CHEESY BROILED FISH

2 pounds flounder or 6 fillets
  orange roughy
2 tablespoons lemon juice
Salt and pepper to taste
½ cup Parmesan cheese,
  grated

½ stick butter, softened
3 tablespoons mayonnaise
3 green onions, chopped
¼ teaspoon salt
Garnish: sliced lemons and
  parsley sprigs

Place fish on a greased broiler pan. Brush with lemon juice; salt and pepper to taste. Combine next 5 ingredients and set aside. Broil fillets 4-6 minutes. Remove and spread with cheese mixture. Broil 30 seconds more until lightly browned and bubbly. Garnish.

Yield: 6 servings

FLOUNDER FLORENTINE

¼ cup onion, chopped
⅛ teaspoon rosemary
2 tablespoons butter, melted
1 10-ounce package frozen
  spinach, cooked and
  drained
½ cup cooked rice
¼ cup toasted almonds,
  chopped

1 tablespoon lemon juice
6 fillets flounder or turbot,
  1½ pounds
1 10¾-ounce can cream of
  mushroom soup
⅓ cup water
Paprika

Preheat oven to 350°. Cook onion with rosemary in butter in a saucepan until tender. Add spinach, rice, almonds, and lemon juice. Heat and stir occasionally. Place ¼ cup mixture on each fillet. Roll and secure with a toothpick. Arrange in a 10x6 inch baking dish. Bake for 20 minutes. Blend soup and water and pour over fish, stirring around sides. Bake an additional 15 to 20 minutes until done. Stir sauce before serving. Sprinkle with paprika.

Yield: 6 servings

PORT MANSFIELD
STUFFED FLOUNDER OR DEVILED CRAB

Spread on English muffins with grated cheese and broil as an appetizer.

½ cup onion, minced
¼ cup celery, minced
¼ cup green bell peppers,
  minced
1 clove garlic, minced or
  garlic juice
1 tablespoon parsley,
  chopped
1 stick butter
2 cups soft breadcrumbs
½ cup heavy cream

2 eggs, beaten
1 tablespoon wine vinegar
1 teaspoon Worcestershire
  sauce
1 teaspoon thyme
Few drops Tabasco sauce
1 teaspoon salt
1 pound lump crab meat
4 small flounder fillets,
  optional
12 crab shells, optional

Preheat oven to 450°. Saute onion, celery, green pepper, garlic and parsley in 6 tablespoons butter until tender. Cool mixture and combine with 1 cup breadcrumbs, cream, eggs, vinegar, Worcestershire, thyme, Tabasco, and salt. Add crab meat and toss lightly to mix. Stuff flounder or fill crab shells or six individual ramekins.

Melt remaining 2 tablespoons butter and toss with remaining 1 cup breadcrumbs. Use this as a topping. Place flounder, ramekins, or stuffed crabshells in baking dish with ¼ inch water in bottom. Bake ramekins or crab in oven for 10 minutes or until golden brown. Bake flounder in oven for 30 minutes basting often with liquid.

Yield: 4 servings flounder or 6 servings crab

FISH EN PAPILLOTE

A great company dish. Sauce and poaching can be done ahead of time.

6 fish fillets (Pompano, Flounder, Orange Roughy, or Monkfish)
3 cups water
Juice of 1½ lemons
3 bay leaves
⅛ teaspoon thyme
½ tablespoon salt
¾ teaspoon white pepper

3 tablespoons butter
4 tablespoons flour
1 6-ounce can mushrooms, chopped
3 dozen shrimp, cooked, peeled and chopped
6 green onions, chopped
3 cloves garlic, chopped
6 tablespoons white wine

Preheat oven to 400°. Poach fillets for 5 minutes in a skillet with water, lemon juice, bay leaves, thyme, salt, and pepper. Remove fillets carefully with slotted spoon and set aside. Strain and reserve fish stock. Melt butter in saucepan. Stir in flour; slowly add fish stock. Stir until sauce thickens. Add mushrooms, shrimp, green onion, and garlic. Bring to a boil. Reduce heat and cook for 5 minutes. Add wine and turn off heat.

Cut six pieces of parchment paper or foil into 11x14 inch heart shapes. Place fillets on right side of heart shape. Top with one sixth of the sauce. Fold left side over filling. Crimp edges together tightly to form a well sealed package. Bake on a cookie sheet for 20 minutes. Slit around crimped edge but serve closed in the package.

Yield: 6 servings

SHARRON'S SALMON CROQUETTES

You can usually find these ingredients in your pantry.

1 15½-ounce can pink salmon with liquid, deboned
2 eggs
1 cup crackers, (whole wheat, butter flavored, or saltines)
½ cup onions, chopped
¼ cup fresh parsley, chopped
1 tablespoon sage
½ teaspoon thyme
Corn oil for frying

Pour salmon with liquid into a medium bowl. Add eggs and mix with a fork. Crush crackers with fork. Mixture should be moist, but not soupy. Add onion, parsley, sage, and thyme; mix well with fork. Pat into 3 inch patties and fry in hot oil until crispy. Drain well on paper towels.

Yield: 8 servings

TROUT MEUNIERE

This is a favorite recipe of a fisherman's family. It is easy to make, and the taste is exceptional.

6 trout or fresh-water bass fillets
2 cups fine saltine cracker crumbs
½ stick butter
1 4-ounce package slivered almonds
Juice of 1 lemon
½-1 cup dry white wine
2 sprigs fresh parsley, minced

Roll each fillet in crumbs and brown gently on each side in 2 tablespoons melted butter. Do not overcook. Five minutes on each side is the maximum. Carefully remove from skillet. Add 2 tablespoons butter and brown almonds. Return fish to skillet and add lemon juice, wine, and minced parsley. Simmer for 2 to 3 minutes. Garnish with lemon twist and a parsley sprig.

Yield: 6 servings

CHARLES' FAMOUS STUFFED CRAB

1 medium potato, peeled
3 tablespoons butter
1 bunch green onions, finely
chopped
1 cup celery, chopped
2 tablespoons parsley,
chopped
1 large green bell pepper,
finely chopped
2 hard boiled eggs, chopped
1 tablespoon Worcestershire
sauce

¼ teaspoon Tabasco
¼ teaspoon each salt and
pepper
1 teaspoon prepared mustard
1 teaspoon lemon juice
½ stick butter
¼ cup flour
½ cup milk
1 pound crab meat
1 cup buttered breadcrumbs

Preheat oven to 350°. Boil potato in saucepan until tender. Remove from pan and cream with 1 tablespoon butter. Set aside until ready to use. Saute onions in 2 tablespoons butter until transparent but not browned. Add celery, parsley, and bell pepper and saute until tender. Remove from heat and fold into creamed potatoes and hard boiled eggs. Add seasonings and set aside.

Melt remaining ½ stick butter in a small saucepan and add flour. Stir constantly until flour and butter are blended and mixture is slightly cooked but not browned. Slowly add milk and stir until sauce has thickened. Remove from heat and fold in crabmeat. Mix crabmeat mixture and vegetables. Season to taste and divide mixture into 12 buttered crab shells or ramekins. Top with buttered breadcrumbs and bake for 30 to 40 minutes.

Yield: 12 servings

SHRIMP BATTER

This makes a wonderfully crisp crust.

1 cup flour	36 saltine crackers
1 cup milk	1 pound shrimp, peeled and
2 eggs	deveined
1½ teaspoons garlic salt	Oil

Beat first four ingredients together in a mixing bowl. Crush crackers with fingers only. Dip shrimp in batter and roll and pat in cracker crumbs. Fry in hot oil for approximately 5 minutes.

Yield: 1 pound

SHRIMP TEMPURA

This batter is so light it will melt in your mouth. Serve with soy sauce and lemon. Dip vegetables in Tempura batter and fry until golden brown.

24 large raw shrimp, peeled and deveined, leaving tails intact	1 cup flour
	1½ teaspoons seasoned salt
	½ teaspoon Accent
2 egg yolks	1¼ teaspoons salt
1 cup cold water	Cooking oil

Split shrimp down back, cutting almost through. Open to butterfly shape. Rinse and dry well.

Beat yolks well. Gradually stir in water. Beat with fork, slowly adding flour and rest of ingredients, except oil. Batter will be lumpy. Heat 2 inches oil to 375°. Dip shrimp in batter and deep fry until golden brown.

Yield: 4 servings

SHRIMP AVERY ISLAND

This is a very elegant dish. It's a good idea to double the sauce recipe.

Shrimp:
1 pound shrimp, peeled and deveined
2-3 eggs, slightly beaten
¼ teaspoon salt

1-2 cups saltine crackers, mashed to meal
2 sticks butter

Sauce:
1 cup green onions, finely chopped
1 large clove garlic, mashed or chopped, or 2-3 small cloves
2 tablespoons butter
1 10½-ounce can beef consomme

2 tablespoons steak sauce (Heinz 57)
1½ teaspoons prepared mustard
½ teaspoon salt
½ teaspoon Tabasco
2 tablespoons fresh lemon juice

Roll shrimp in mixture of egg and salt, then in cracker crumbs. Brown shrimp in melted butter over medium heat for 6 to 9 minutes. Remove shrimp and keep warm while preparing sauce.

To prepare sauce: Saute onion and garlic in butter over medium heat until tender. Add remaining ingredients except lemon juice. Bring to a boil and simmer 15 minutes or until volume is reduced to one-half. Add lemon juice just before serving. Arrange shrimp on large bed of rice and pour sauce over all.

Yield: 4 servings

CHEESY AND SPICY SHRIMP

This makes a delicious and elegant first course. Serve in individual ramekins. Top with breadcrumbs and broil.

1 pound shrimp or crab
½ pound fresh mushrooms, sliced
½ stick butter
1 6-ounce roll jalapeno cheese

1 10¾-ounce can cream of mushroom soup
1 2-ounce jar pimentos, chopped
Salt and pepper to taste

Cook shrimp in boiling water with a dash of salt and pepper for 3 to 4 minutes. Peel and devein shrimp. Saute mushrooms in butter in a small skillet. Set aside. Melt cheese over low heat in a double boiler or heavy saucepan. Add soup, mushrooms, pimento, seasonings and shrimp. Heat until very hot. Serve over cooked rice or noodles.

Yield: 4 servings

SHRIMP NEWBURG OR SEAFOOD CREPES

This sauce is delicious in crepes. Substitute ½ pound of crabmeat for ½ pound shrimp. Place about one tablespoon sauce inside crepes. Roll up and place in greased casserole. Sprinkle with 1 cup bread-crumbs and dot with ½ stick butter. Bake at 375° for 40 minutes.

2½-3 pounds shrimp
Lemon slices
Onion slices
½ teaspoon red pepper
1 stick butter
7 tablespoons flour
1½ cups milk
1½ cups Half and Half
2 teaspoons Worcestershire sauce

½ teaspoon dry mustard
1 teaspoon each salt, white pepper and paprika
¼ teaspoon garlic powder
1 whole pimento pepper, shredded
1 3-ounce slice Gruyere cheese

Boil shrimp in water with lemon, onion and red pepper. Peel and de-vein. Rinse shrimp and set aside to use in sauce.

Sauce: Melt butter in a large saucepan, add flour gradually. Add milk and Half and Half and allow sauce to thicken. Add seasonings and all remaining ingredients except shrimp. Add shrimp about 10-15 minutes before serving. Serve over cooked rice.

Yield: approximately 8 servings

SHRIMP CURRY IN A HURRY

1 10¾-ounce can cream of celery or cream of mushroom soup

1 10¾-ounce can cream of shrimp soup

1 4½-ounce jar mushrooms, sliced and drained

½ teaspoon Tabasco sauce

1 10-ounce package frozen green peas, run under cold water and drained

1 teaspoon curry powder

1½ pounds fresh shrimp, or 24-ounce frozen package shrimp; cooked, peeled, and chopped in bite-size pieces

1 8-ounce carton sour cream

2 cups long grain rice, cooked according to package directions

1 3-ounce can chow mein noodles

4 hard boiled eggs, chopped

Chutney, chopped peanuts, coconut, optional

Combine soups, mushrooms, Tabasco, peas, curry powder, and shrimp in a large heavy 3-quart saucepan and heat over low heat for 15 minutes. Add sour cream and heat over low heat; do not boil. Top with noodles and eggs, and optional toppings.

Yield: 6 servings

WILD RICE AND SHRIMP CASSEROLE

2 6½-ounce packages wild rice

⅔ pound Velveeta cheese, cubed

1 24-ounce package frozen shrimp, thawed

2 10¾-ounce cans cream of celery soup

1 4-ounce jar pimento strips

Parsley flakes

Preheat oven to 350°. Butter a 4-quart casserole. Cook rice according to package directions and drain if needed. Layer rice, cheese, shrimp, soup, and pimento, in casserole. Sprinkle parsley over top. Bake for 45 minutes until bubbly.

Yield: 8 servings

CAJUN SEAFOOD CASSEROLE

1 8-ounce package cream cheese
1 ½ sticks butter
1 large onion, chopped
1 small green bell pepper, seeded and chopped
2 ribs celery, chopped
1 pound shrimp, shelled and deveined
1 10¾-ounce can cream of mushroom soup
1 pint crab meat, fresh or canned

1 4-ounce can sliced mushrooms, drained
1 tablespoon garlic powder
½ teaspoon Tabasco sauce
½ teaspoon cayenne pepper
2 10-ounce packages frozen chopped broccoli
1 cup sharp Cheddar cheese, shredded
Breadcrumbs for topping

Melt cream cheese and 1 stick butter in double boiler over boiling water. Saute onion, bell pepper, and celery in ½ stick butter. Add shrimp to vegetables and stir until tender. Add cream cheese mixture, mushroom soup, crab, mushrooms, and spices to shrimp mixture.

Cook broccoli according to package directions and drain well. Line large buttered casserole dish with broccoli. Pour shrimp mixture over broccoli. Top with cheese and breadcrumbs. Bake at 350° until bubbly, about 30 minutes.

Yield: 10 servings

SHRIMP CREOLE

Prepare the sauce a day ahead of time for best flavor. Serve over rice with green salad and hot bread for rave reviews.

1½ cups green onion, sliced
⅓ cup celery, chopped
¾ cup onion, chopped
½ green bell pepper, chopped
4 teaspoons garlic, minced
3 tablespoons parsley, minced
⅔ cup oil
½ cup flour
1 16-ounce can whole tomatoes
1 8-ounce can tomato sauce

1 tablespoon chives
⅓ cup white wine
4 bay leaves
2 teaspoons salt
½ teaspoon pepper
¼ teaspoon cayenne pepper
¼ teaspoon chili powder
¼ teaspoon each mace, basil, thyme, and allspice
Juice of lemon
2 cups water
2 pounds shrimp, peeled and deveined
Rice

Combine first six ingredients. Blend oil and flour in a large pot over low heat to make a roux. Cook until smooth. Remove from heat. Add vegetables. Return to heat and brown gently. Add remaining ingredients except shrimp and rice. Simmer uncovered over low heat for 45 minutes. (Refrigerate if prepared ahead of time). Before serving, add shrimp to tomato sauce mixture and bring to a boil for a minute or two. Reduce heat to low, cover, and cook 20 minutes. Remove from heat and let stand 10 minutes. Serve over cooked rice.

Yield: approximately 10 servings

CREOLE REMOULADE SAUCE

2 cloves garlic
½ cup fresh parsley
2 ribs celery
1 cup mayonnaise
¼ cup olive oil
3 tablespoons Zatarain's creole mustard
1 tablespoon red wine garlic vinegar

1 teaspoon paprika
1 teaspoon seasoned salt
1 teaspoon Worcestershire sauce
1 teaspoon Louisiana hot sauce
¼ heaping cup chili sauce

Place all ingredients in a food processor or blender and process until smooth. Refrigerate overnight.

Yield: 2 cups

SUPER SHRIMP COCKTAIL SAUCE

¾ cup catsup
¾ cup chili sauce
1 tablespoon mayonnaise
1 teaspoon Tabasco
1 tablespoon Worcestershire
  sauce
¼ teaspoon salt

1 large green bell pepper,
  finely chopped
1 cup celery, finely chopped
12 pickled onions, finely
  chopped
½ cup parsley, chopped
1 tablespoon horseradish

Mix all ingredients together in a mixing bowl. Refrigerate covered. Add catsup to thin, if needed.

Yield: 2 cups

TARTAR SAUCE

1 cup mayonnaise
2 tablespoons sweet pickles,
  chopped
1 tablespoon onion, grated
1 tablespoon parsley,
  chopped

1 tablespoon capers
1 tablespoon lime or lemon
  juice
¼ teaspoon garlic salt

Combine all ingredients together in a mixing bowl until smooth. Chill before serving.

Yield: 1½ cups

CLAM SAUCE SUPREME

4 tablespoons olive oil
4 tablespoons butter
2-3 shallots, chopped
1 clove garlic, finely chopped
2 tablespoons cognac
½ cup clam juice

1 cup minced clams
½ cup fresh parsley, finely
  chopped
½ pound spaghetti, cooked
  and drained
Parmesan cheese, grated

Heat oil and butter in a large skillet. Saute shallots and garlic over low heat. Add cognac and clam juice and simmer for 5 minutes. Stir in clams and parsley and bring mixture to a boil, stirring occasionally. Pour sauce over cooked spaghetti and sprinkle with cheese.

Yield: 4 servings

THREE CHEESE SPAGHETTI

You may want to add less green chilies.

3 tablespoons butter
1 tablespoon flour
1 cup milk
2 ounces Gouda cheese,
  shredded
2 ounces Cheddar cheese,
  shredded
1 2½-ounce can sliced
  mushrooms, drained

1 4-ounce can diced green
  chilies
1 tablespoon dried parsley
  flakes
¼ teaspoon salt
1 7-ounce package spaghetti
½ cup Parmesan cheese,
  grated

Melt 1 tablespoon butter in a heavy saucepan over medium heat. Add flour, stirring until smooth. Continue stirring and cook one minute. Gradually add milk. Cover and cook over medium heat, stirring occasionally until thick and bubbly. Stir in cheeses, mushrooms, chilies, parsley, and salt. Cook spaghetti according to package directions and drain. Combine with 2 tablespoons butter, parsley and Parmesan cheese. Stir well. Pour cheese sauce over spaghetti and stir.

Yield: 6 servings

TANGY CHEESE MANICOTTI

Tomato sauce:
¼ cup olive oil
1 large onion, finely
  chopped
2 cloves garlic, finely
  chopped
3 14½-ounce cans tomatoes,
  drained and finely
  chopped

1½ 6-ounce cans tomato
  paste
1 cup water
½ cup red wine
⅜ teaspoon salt
⅜ teaspoon sugar
1 tablespoon dried, crushed
  basil

Filling:
1 pound ricotta cheese
½ pound mozzarella cheese,
  shredded
2 ounces Parmesan cheese,
  freshly grated
2 eggs, beaten
3 tablespoons parsley,
  chopped

¾ teaspoon salt
Freshly ground pepper to
  taste
1 8-ounce package manicotti
  noodles

Tomato Sauce: Heat oil in a medium-size skillet. Cook onion and garlic until lightly browned. Add remaining sauce ingredients. Bring to a boil and simmer approximately 1 hour, stirring occasionally.

Filling: Combine all filling ingredients in a mixing bowl and blend well. Preheat oven to 350° and grease a 9x13 inch baking dish.

To Assemble: Cook manicotti noodles according to package directions. Drain and rinse. Stuff manicotti with cheese mixture. Place stuffed noodles in a single layer in a baking pan. Cover with tomato sauce. Bake approximately 30 minutes until hot and bubbly.

Yield: 8 servings

BEEF MANICOTTI MAGNIFICO

8 ounces manicotti shells, 14
shells or seashell type
1 pound Italian sweet
sausage links, mild or hot
1 pound ground beef
1 medium onion, chopped
2 16-ounce cans tomato puree
1 6-ounce can tomato paste
1¾ teaspoons basil

1½ teaspoons salt
1 teaspoon sugar
½ teaspoon pepper
1 cup water
2 pounds ricotta cheese
8 ounces mozzarella cheese,
shredded
2 tablespoons fresh parsley,
chopped
Grated Parmesan cheese

Preheat oven to 375°. Grease 9x13 inch baking dish. Cook manicotti according to package directions and drain well. Allow to cool in water. Cook sausage in ¼ cup water in a covered pan for 5 minutes. Uncover, drain, and brown. Brown ground beef and onion in a large skillet over medium-high heat. Stir in tomato puree, tomato paste, 1 teaspoon basil, 1 teaspoon salt, sugar, pepper, and 1 cup water. Simmer 45 minutes. Cut sausage into bite size pieces and add to beef mixture. Cook for 15 minutes.

Combine ricotta and mozzarella cheese, ¾ teaspoon basil, ½ teaspoon salt, and parsley. Stuff shells with cheese mixture. Spoon one half meat sauce into the baking dish and arrange stuffed shells on top in the dish. Spoon remaining sauce over top of shells. Sprinkle with Parmesan cheese. Bake for 30 minutes.

Yield: approximately 8 servings

JON MOZETTA

½ 8-ounce package egg
  noodles, cooked and
  drained
1 pound ground round
1 medium onion, chopped
2 tablespoons bacon grease
1 28-ounce can tomatoes,
  drained and chopped

½ pound sharp Cheddar
  cheese, shredded
Salt and pepper to taste
Dash Worcestershire sauce
Dash Tabasco
1 tablespoon sugar

Preheat oven to 350°. Butter 1½-quart casserole. Saute meat and onions in bacon grease until meat is brown and onions are transparent. Mix in tomatoes, one half of the cheese, and remaining ingredients. Spoon into casserole and top with remaining cheese. Bake for 1 hour.

Yield: 8 servings

CHICKEN LASAGNE

8 ounces lasagne noodles,
  cooked, drained and
  rinsed with cold water
1 10¾-ounce can cream of
  chicken soup
⅔ cup evaporated milk
½ teaspoon salt
8 ounces cream cheese,
  softened

1 12-ounce carton cream
  style cottage cheese
½ cup pimento stuffed
  olives, sliced
½ cup green onions,
  chopped
4-5 cups chicken, cooked
  and diced
8 ounces mozzarella cheese,
  shredded

Preheat oven to 375°. Butter 9x13 inch baking dish. Mix together soup, milk, and salt in a saucepan and heat just until boiling, stirring occasionally. Beat together cream cheese and cottage cheese, and add olives and onions.

Place ½ of the noodles in the baking dish and spread with ½ of the cheese, ½ of the chicken, and ½ of the soup. Repeat layers. Bake for 20 minutes. Top with mozzarella and bake for an additional 10 minutes. Allow to stand for 10 minutes before cutting into squares to serve.

Yield: approximately 8 servings

PIZZA

Takes a little time, but oh...so worth it. Wonderful crust. Freeze one of the pizzas (unbaked) for later use, if desired.

Dough:

1 package active dry yeast	1 teaspoon salt
1 cup warm water	2 tablespoons vegetable oil
1 teaspoon sugar	2½ cups flour

Sauce:

1 15-ounce can tomato sauce	Garlic salt to taste
1 large onion, chopped	Pepper to taste
⅛ teaspoon garlic powder	

Topping:

¾ pound fresh mushrooms, sliced and sauteed in 2 tablespoons butter	2 tablespoons dried oregano
	1 pound Monterey Jack cheese, shredded
1 3½-ounce package sliced pepperoni	Jalapeno slices, to taste
1 pound hot bulk sausage, cooked and well drained	

Dough: Dissolve yeast in the warm water with the sugar. Stir in remaining dough ingredients; beat vigorously. Allow dough to rest, covered, while preparing sauce.

Sauce: Combine tomato sauce, onion, and garlic powder. Season to taste with garlic salt and pepper.

Preheat oven to 425°. Lightly grease two 12x16 inch cookie sheets. Divide dough into two equal parts. With floured fingers, pat out each piece of dough to cover cookie sheet, leaving outer edge slightly thicker. Spread half of the sauce on each portion. Bake for 5 minutes. Remove from oven. Add toppings as desired. Return to oven and bake for 20 to 25 minutes.

Yield: 2 pizzas

PASTICCIO DI RISO

The extra time it takes to prepare this attractive and flavorful dish makes it very worthwhile.

Rice Mixture:
3½ cups chicken broth
¾ cup tomato sauce
2 cups uncooked rice
2 tablespoons butter

4 eggs, slightly beaten
1 cup Parmesan cheese, grated

Ricotta Cheese Mixture:
1 pound ricotta cheese
8 ounces mozzarella cheese, diced
2 teaspoons mint flakes, crumbled

½ teaspoon salt
¼ teaspoon pepper

Meatballs:
2 tablespoons minced onion
½ teaspoon minced garlic
¼ cup water
1 pound lean ground beef
1 egg, slightly beaten
½ cup soft bread crumbs

¼ cup Parmesan cheese, grated
1 tablespoon parsley flakes
½ teaspoon salt
⅛ teaspoon ground black pepper
1 tablespoon oil

Tomato Sauce:
2 tablespoons oil
⅓ cup onion flakes
1½ teaspoons minced garlic
1 28-ounce can tomatoes
1 6-ounce can tomato paste
½ cup water
1 teaspoon salt
1 bay leaf

1 tablespoon basil, crumbled
½ teaspoon sugar
¼ teaspoon pepper
2 tablespoons parsley flakes
2 cups chicken, cooked and diced

(continued)

Rice mixture: Bring broth and tomato sauce to boil in a medium saucepan. Stir in rice, cover, and reduce heat. Cook for 20 minutes. Remove from heat. Stir in butter; add eggs and Parmesan cheese. Cool slightly and set aside. Combine ricotta cheese mixture in a bowl and mix well.

Meatball mixture: Mix all meatball ingredients except oil together in a large mixing bowl. Shape meat mixture into about 24 balls. Heat oil in a large skillet and add meatballs; brown well on all sides, approximately 5 minutes. Set aside.

Tomato Sauce Mixture: Heat oil in a large saucepan and saute onion and garlic for 5 minutes. Stir in tomatoes, tomato paste, ½ cup water, salt, bay leaf, basil, sugar, and pepper. Bring to boil. Reduce heat, cover, and simmer 30 minutes. Set aside 1 cup sauce. Stir in parsley flakes in remainder of sauce. Add browned meatballs to sauce. Cover and simmer 30 minutes.

To Assemble: Preheat oven to 350°. Grease 10-inch spring-form pan. Place one third of the rice mixture in the pan. Spread one half of the ricotta cheese mixture over the rice mixture. In layers arrange half of the meatballs in tomato sauce and 1 cup chicken. Repeat. Top with rice layer and add reserved tomato sauce. Bake uncovered for 35 to 40 minutes. Remove from oven and allow to stand 20 minutes before removing the sides from the spring form pan. Slice into wedges and serve with additional sauce.

Yield: 8 servings

AUNT JANE'S CHICKEN SPAGHETTI

This is a rich and creamy chicken spaghetti. A big hit with men and children.

½ cup oil or 1 stick
  margarine
1 cup celery, chopped
1 cup green bell pepper,
  chopped
½ cup onion, chopped
1 10¾-ounce can cream of
  mushroom soup
1 10¾-ounce can cream of
  chicken soup

1 4-ounce jar sliced
  pimentos
1 2½-3 pound chicken;
  cooked, deboned, and cut
  into bite-size pieces
2 8-ounce boxes redi-cut
  spaghetti, cooked and
  drained
1 cup Cheddar cheese,
  shredded
Paprika

Preheat oven to 350°. Grease 4-quart baking dish. Saute celery, pepper, and onion, in oil in a large skillet. Add soups, pimento, and chicken; heat thoroughly. Combine spaghetti, cheese, and chicken. Pour into baking dish. Top with paprika. Bake for 30 minutes.

Variation: Add 1 cup chopped green olives, 8 ounces of sliced water chestnuts, and 4 ounces of sliced mushrooms.

Yield: approximately 6 servings

TURKEY SPAGHETTI

This spaghetti is an old family recipe that has been enjoyed by friends and family for years. Freeze excess in small packages.

1 12 to 14-pound turkey, cooked and boned, reserving stock
2 cups celery, sliced
2 cups onion, chopped
½ stick butter
1 2-pound can tomatoes
2 bay leaves
Salt and pepper to taste

2-3 2-ounce cans sliced ripe olives
1 16-ounce can mushroom pieces, with liquid
2 pounds spaghetti
Turkey stock
1 bay leaf
2 pounds Cheddar cheese, shredded
Tomato juice as needed

Cut turkey meat into bit-size pieces and refrigerate. Saute celery and onion in butter in a medium pan. Add tomatoes, bay leaves, salt, pepper, olives, and mushrooms with juice. Simmer for 2 hours. Cook spaghetti in turkey stock with bay leaf. Combine turkey and sauce. Simmer until heated thoroughly. Add cheese and spaghetti and mix well. Add tomato juice if needed for moisture.

Yield: 10 quarts

PASTA WITH SCALLOPS

Seafood and pasta lovers will enjoy this combination.

1 bunch green onions, chopped
1 clove garlic, minced
2-3 tablespoons olive oil
1 package bay scallops
2 tablespoons oyster sauce

1 teaspoon oregano
1 tablespoon fresh parsley, finely chopped
1 pound pasta (your choice)
Parsley sprigs for garnish

Saute onions and garlic in olive oil in a medium skillet over medium-high heat until onions are tender. Add scallops and continue to saute for 2 to 3 minutes. Add oyster sauce and spices. Simmer for 15 minutes. Cook pasta according to package directions, drain, and rinse with hot water. Toss scallop mixture with pasta and place on a large serving platter. Garnish with sprigs of fresh parsley. Serve immediately.

Yield: 4 servings

TRULY ITALIAN SPAGHETTI SAUCE

1½ pounds ground meat,
  browned and drained
1½ cups water
2 6-ounce cans tomato
  paste
2 8-ounce cans tomato sauce
1 cup Romano cheese,
  grated

1 teaspoon oregano
2 teaspoons basil
1 bay leaf
3 cloves garlic, minced
1 tablespoon sugar
1½ teaspoons salt
¼ teaspoon pepper
1 large onion, chopped

Place all ingredients in a large pot and simmer uncovered for about 3 hours.

Yield: 3-4 servings

Can add sausage
mushrooms
& gr pepper

ONE FOR ALL SAUCE

This makes a good sauce for all Italian dishes.

3 pounds ground meat
1 cup onion, chopped
1 cup celery, chopped
1 cup green bell pepper,
  chopped
2 14½-ounce cans tomatoes,
  chopped
3 6-ounce cans tomato paste
3 8-ounce cans tomato sauce
2 cups water
3 cloves garlic, minced
1½ tablespoons chili
  powder

1½ teaspoons salt
½ teaspoon pepper
2 teaspoons oregano
2 tablespoons parsley,
  chopped
1-2 tablespoons brown sugar
Juice of 1 lemon
3 tablespoons Parmesan
  cheese, grated
1½ cups fresh mushrooms,
  sliced or 1 6-ounce canned

Brown meat in a large pot over medium-high heat. Add onions, celery, bell pepper, and garlic to meat. Drain off grease. Add remaining ingredients and simmer for 1 to 2 hours. Serve over spaghetti noodles or layer in lasagne.

Yield: 6 servings

Desserts

Thank you for your financial support
of the following Junior League of Waco project:

GATE
Gain Awareness Through Education
(developed by the Junior League of Atlanta, Georgia)

The instruction of 4th grade students,
by Junior League volunteers, on the effects of drug and
alcohol on the young, overcoming peer pressure and
saying "no" to drugs.

BEST EVER CHEESE CAKE

A real "New York Cheese cake", wonderful and elegant. People beg for this recipe.

Crust:

1 cup flour, sifted
¼ cup sugar
1 teaspoon grated lemon
   peel

1 stick butter
1 egg yolk, slightly beaten
¼ teaspoon vanilla

Cheese filling:

5 8-ounce packages cream
   cheese, softened
¾ teaspoon grated lemon
   peel
¼ teaspoon vanilla
1¾ cups sugar

3 tablespoons flour
¼ teaspoon salt
5 eggs
2 egg yolks
¼ cup heavy cream

Preheat oven to 400°. Combine flour, sugar, and lemon peel. Cut in butter until mixture is crumbly. Add egg yolk and vanilla; blend well. Pat ⅓ dough on the bottom of a 9-inch spring form pan with sides removed. Bake about 6 minutes. Allow to cool. Butter sides of pan and attach to bottom. Pat remaining dough evenly and thinly up sides to a height of two inches.

Preheat oven to 500°. Combine cream cheese, lemon peel, vanilla, sugar, flour, and salt together in a large mixing bowl. Add eggs and egg yolks one at a time, beating well after each addition. Gently stir in cream. Turn into crust-lined pan and bake for 6 to 8 minutes or until top of crust is golden. Reduce heat to 200° and bake for one hour. Remove from oven and cool in pan for 3 hours. Remove sides from pan.

Yield: 12 servings

CHOCOLATE AMARETTO CHEESE CAKE

Crust:

1 cup almonds, finely
  chopped

2 tablespoons sugar
3 tablespoons butter, melted

Filling:

5 ounces milk chocolate
  chips
5 ounces semi-sweet
  chocolate chips
2 tablespoons butter
⅓ cup amaretto liqueur

2 8-ounce packages cream
  cheese, softened
⅓ cup sugar
2 eggs
1 cup sour cream, at room
  temperature

Preheat oven to 350°. Combine crust ingredients in a mixing bowl, mixing well. Press into bottom of a 9-inch spring form pan. Bake for 15 to 20 minutes or until lightly browned. Reduce heat to 325°.

Melt chocolate chips and butter with amaretto in a double boiler, stirring until smooth. Beat cream cheese and sugar together. Add eggs and sour cream, mixing well. Pour in chocolate mixture and blend together. Pour into prepared crust and bake for 45 minutes. Cool to room temperature and remove sides of pan. Refrigerate before serving.

Yield: 8 servings

DIDDY'S POUND CAKE

2 sticks butter or margarine,
  softened
2 cups sugar
5 eggs

2 cups flour, sifted
1 teaspoon vanilla
1 teaspoon almond extract

Preheat oven to 325°. Grease a bundt or tube pan. Cream butter and sugar together in a mixing bowl. Add eggs and beat until fluffy. Add flour slowly. Stir in extracts. Spoon into pan. Bake for 1 hour until top is barely browned and cracked.

Yield: 12 servings

FRESH APPLE CAKE

This cake gets better with age.

2 eggs, beaten
2 cups sugar
4 cups apples, chopped
1 cup vegetable oil
2 teaspoons vanilla

1 cup pecans or walnuts,
    chopped
2½ cups flour
1 teaspoon baking soda
1 teaspoon salt
1 teaspoon cinnamon

Brown sugar glaze:
1 cup brown sugar
½ stick butter

¼ cup milk

Mocha glaze:
1 cup confectioners sugar

3 tablespoons strong coffee

Preheat oven to 350°. Grease and flour a bundt pan. Mix first six ingredients together in a mixing bowl and set aside. Sift flour, soda, salt, and cinnamon together. Combine with apples. Allow to stand 20 to 30 minutes before cooking. Pour into pan and bake for 1 hour. Remove from oven and cool for 10 minutes and turn onto serving platter. Glaze as desired. Poke holes in top of the cake with a fork so glaze will soak into cake.

Brown sugar glaze: Mix ingredients together in a saucepan and boil slightly until thick. Pour over warm cake.

Mocha glaze: Blend sugar and coffee together until smooth. Pour over hot cake.

Yield: 12 servings

APRICOT DAQUOISE

¾ cup whole almonds,
  blanched
4 egg whites
1 cup sugar
Pinch of cream of tartar
¾ cup dried apricots
Strip of lemon rind
½ cup sugar
¾ cup water
Juice of ½ lemon

1 cup whipping cream,
  whipped until it holds soft
  peaks
Sugar to taste, optional
2 tablespoons confectioners
  sugar
½ cup whipping cream,
  whipped stiffly
1 1-ounce square semi-sweet
  chocolate, grated

Preheat oven to 275°. Line 2 baking sheets with silicone paper or foil and mark an 8 inch circle on each. To blanche, pour boiling water over almonds and allow them to soak for 10 minutes. Drain and grind in a blender.

Beat egg whites until they hold a stiff peak and add 1 tablespoon sugar and cream of tartar and continue beating for 1 minute or until glossy. Fold in remaining sugar and ground almonds. Divide mixture between the 2 circles, spreading carefully into marked circles. Bake 1 hour. To test if meringues are done, lift a corner of the paper and if it peels away easily, the meringues are baked. Set aside to cool.

Soak apricots according to package directions. Simmer gently in saucepan with strip of lemon rind. When tender, remove lemon rind, puree apricots in blender, and allow to cool. Heat sugar with water in saucepan until sugar is dissolved. Add lemon juice and boil for 3 minutes to make a lemon syrup. Stir ¼ to ⅓ of the apricot puree into the whipped cream and add sugar to taste. Spread the apricot and whipped cream mixture evenly over one meringue and top with remaining meringue. Sprinkle the top with confectioners sugar. Fill stiffly whipped cream into a pastry bag and decorate the top. Top with grated chocolate. Dilute remaining apricot puree with lemon syrup and serve the sauce separately.

Yield: approximately 8 servings

BANANA NUT CAKE

Freeze the cake layers and ice them later. A great dessert for weekend company. Also good with Cream Cheese Icing.

1⅓ cups sugar
2 cups flour
1 teaspoon baking powder
1 teaspoon baking soda
⅓ cup vegetable oil
2 eggs, separated

1 cup bananas, very ripe and
  mashed
⅔ cup milk
2 teaspoons vanilla
¾ cup pecans, chopped

Banana icing:
1 stick butter or margarine,
  softened
1 pound confectioners sugar
2 ripe bananas, mashed

1 cup pecans, chopped
Dash of salt
½ teaspoon lemon juice
Pecan halves for garnish

Preheat oven to 350°. Grease and flour two 9-inch cake pans. Mix dry ingredients in a large mixing bowl. Add oil, egg yolks, bananas, and half of the milk. Beat until smooth. Add remaining milk and 1 teapoon of vanilla. Stir in nuts. Pour into cake pans and bake for 15 to 20 minutes or until golden brown. Ice with Banana Icing and refrigerate.

Banana Icing: Cream butter and sugar together in a bowl. Add remaining ingredients and blend until smooth. Spread over cooled cakes. Garnish with pecan halves.

Yield: 12 servings

CREAM CHEESE ICING

1 8-ounce package cream
  cheese, softened
1 stick butter or margarine,
  softened

1 16-ounce confectioners
  sugar
1 teaspoon vanilla
1 cup pecans, chopped
  (optional)

Cream cheese and butter together in a mixing bowl. Add sugar slowly and mix in vanilla; stir until smooth and creamy. Add nuts if desired.

Yield: icing for 1 cake

CHOCOLATE BANANA CAKE

3 cups sugar
4 eggs
¾ cup buttermilk
4 medium bananas, mashed
1 cup shortening
2 teaspoons baking soda

3 cups flour
3 teaspoons cocoa
1 teaspoon vanilla
1 cup pecans, chopped
Cream Cheese Icing

Preheat oven to 325°. Flour four 9-inch cake pans. Cream sugar and eggs. Add buttermilk, bananas, and shortening. Mix dry ingredients and slowly add to sugar. Stir in vanilla and pecans. Pour into cake pans and bake for 35 to 40 minutes. Cool on wire racks before icing. Ice with Cream Cheese Icing.

Yield: 12 servings

CARROT CAKE

Even non-sweet eaters love this cake.

1 cup flour
2 cups sugar
2 teaspoons cinnamon
½ teaspoon salt
2 teaspoons baking soda
1 teaspoon baking powder

1½ cups corn oil
4 eggs
1 teaspoon vanilla
3 cups carrots, grated
Cream Cheese Icing

Preheat oven to 350°. Grease and flour three 9-inch cake pans. Mix dry ingredients together in a mixing bowl. Add oil, eggs, and vanilla and blend well. Blend in carrots. Pour into cake pans and bake for 30 minutes. Allow layers to cool on wire racks before icing. Ice with Cream Cheese Icing.

Yield: 12 servings

BAKED CHERRY TORTE

Torte:

1 egg, beaten
1¼ cups sugar
2 cups canned cherries, well
   drained, reserving juice
1 cup flour
¼ teaspoon salt

½ teaspoon baking soda
1 teaspoon cinnamon
1 tablespoon butter, melted
1 teaspoon almond extract
½ cup pecans, chopped

Sauce:

1 cup reserved cherry juice,
   adding water to make a
   cup
¼ cup sugar
1 tablespoon cornstarch
⅛ teaspoon salt

1 tablespoon butter
2 drops almond extract
½ cup whipping cream,
   whipped, adding sugar to
   sweeten

Preheat oven to 350°. Grease a 9-inch square cake pan. Gradually add sugar to beaten egg and continue beating until sugar is dissolved. Carefully fold in cherries. Sift dry ingredients together and fold into cherry mixture. Add melted butter and almond extract. Turn batter into cake pan. Sprinkle chopped nuts over top of batter. Bake for 45 minutes. Allow to cool.

For sauce, combine dry ingredients together with several tablespoons of cold juice. Heat remaining juice in saucepan. Add cornstarch mixture to the hot juice and cook until thick and no starch taste remains. Taste for sweetness and add more sugar if needed. Add butter and almond extract. Allow to cool. Top torte with cherry sauce and whipped cream.

Yield: 6 servings

QUEEN VICTORIA CHOCOLATE TORTE WITH CHOCOLATE GLAZE

Cake:
Parchment paper
4 1-ounce squares
  semi-sweet chocolate
1 stick unsalted butter,
  softened
⅔ cup sugar
3 eggs

1 cup almonds with skin on,
  finely ground
Rind of 1 large orange,
  grated
¼ cup breadcrumbs, very
  fine

Glaze:
2 1-ounce squares
  unsweetened chocolate
2 1-ounce squares
  semi-sweet chocolate

½ stick butter, softened and
  cut up
2 teaspoons honey

Preheat oven to 375°. Butter sides of an 8-inch round pan and line with parchment.

Melt chocolate in top of double boiler. Add butter and blend. Gradually beat in sugar, beating constantly. Add eggs one at a time beating well after each addition. Batter will look curdled but don't be alarmed. Stir in melted chocolate, ground nuts, orange rind, and breadcrumbs blending thoroughly. Pour into prepared pan and bake for 25 minutes. Remove from oven and cool for 30 minutes on cake rack. Turn out, discard parchment. Cool. Center of cake will not seem thoroughly done, because of the soft texture.

Glaze: Combine chocolates together with butter and honey in the top of a double boiler. Melt over hot water. Remove from heat and beat until cold but pourable. Pour over cake, allowing to dribble down sides.

Yield: approximately 8 servings

CHOCOLATE CREAM CAKE

Make the cake and frosting at the same time.

1 stick butter, softened
2 sticks margarine, softened
1 8-ounce package cream cheese, softened
1 3-ounce package cream cheese, softened
1 4-ounce package German sweet chocolate
¼ cup water

2 pounds confectioners sugar, sifted
¾ cup shortening
3 eggs
¼ teaspoon salt
1 teaspoon baking soda
2¼ cups flour
1 cup buttermilk
2 teaspoons vanilla

Preheat oven to 350°. Grease and flour four 8-inch cake pans or three 9 inch pans. Cream butter, margarine, and cream cheese together in a large mixing bowl until fluffy. Melt chocolate with water in the top of a double boiler. Add confectioners sugar and chocolate alternately to batter. Divide batter in half. Reserve one half to frost cake. To remaining half, add shortening, creaming well. Add eggs one at a time beating well after each addition. Sift together dry ingredients and add to batter alternating with buttermilk. Add 1 teaspoon vanilla and blend well. Pour into cake pans. Bake for 35 to 40 minutes. Allow to cool on wire racks.

Add 1 teaspoon vanilla to reserved batter, blend well, and frost. If frosting is too creamy, add more confectioners sugar.

Yield: 12 servings

CHOCOLATE RUM RAISIN CAKE

1 18½-ounce package
   chocolate pudding cake
   mix
4 eggs
½ cup oil
¼ cup rum
Water

1 cup pecans or walnuts,
   chopped
1 cup raisins
1 6-ounce package
   semi-sweet chocolate
   pieces

Glaze:
1 stick butter
1 cup sugar
¼ cup water

2 ounces rum or more to
   taste

Preheat oven to 350°. Grease a bundt pan. To cake mix add eggs and oil. Pour ¼ cup rum into measuring cup and add enough water to equal ⅓ cup. Add to batter and mix well, using an electric mixer for 2 minutes on high. Stir in nuts, raisins, and chocolate pieces. Pour batter into bundt pan. Bake according to package directions. Remove from oven and allow to stand until cake loosens from edges of pan. Combine glaze ingredients together in a saucepan and bring to a boil. Pour over hot cake, allowing it to run down sides and soak into cake. Turn cake out into serving plate when glaze is absorbed into cake.

Yield: approximately 18 servings

HERSHEY CAKE

To vary the icing, melt white chocolate and pour over the cake. Decorate with fresh strawberries. This makes a beautiful and elegant cake.

2 sticks butter, softened
2 cups sugar
4 eggs
2½ cups flour
¼ teaspoon baking soda
½ teaspoon salt

1 cup buttermilk
8 1.65-ounce size plain Hershey bars, melted
1 15-ounce can Hershey syrup
2 teaspoons vanilla

Chocolate glaze:
1 8-ounce bar German sweet chocolate
1 tablespoon butter
¼ cup water

1 heaping cup confectioners sugar
Dash salt
½ teaspoon vanilla

Preheat oven to 350°. Grease and flour a tube pan. Cream together butter, sugar, and eggs in a large mixing bowl until fluffy. Add flour, soda, salt and blend well. Mix in buttermilk. Add melted Hershey bars and syrup. Continue mixing and add vanilla. Pour into tube pan and bake for 1 hour and 20 minutes. Remove from oven, allow to cool and glaze or leave plain.

To prepare glaze: Melt chocolate, butter, and water together in a saucepan over low heat. Add sugar, salt, and vanilla and mix well. Consistency should be thin enough to pour over cake. Glaze when cake is cool.

Yield: approximately 12 servings

TURTLE CAKE

For a different filling, use 1 jar marshmallow cream spread over hot cake and add 1 cup chopped pecans to the batter.

Cake:
1 box German chocolate cake mix
1 stick butter or margarine, softened

1½ cups water
½ cup oil
½ can sweetened condensed milk

Filling:
1 pound bag caramels
½ can sweetened condensed milk

½-1 cup pecans, chopped

Frosting:
1 stick butter
3 tablespoons cocoa
6 tablespoons evaporated milk

1 box confectioners sugar
1 teaspoon vanilla

Preheat oven to 350°. Grease and flour a 9x13 inch baking dish. Combine cake mix, butter, water, oil, and milk in a mixing bowl. Pour ½ of the batter into the baking dish. Bake for 20 to 25 minutes.

Melt caramels and blend with milk in a saucepan. Spread evenly over baked cake layer. Sprinkle generously with chopped pecans. Cover with remaining batter and bake an additional 20 to 25 minutes. Melt butter, cocoa, and milk in saucepan. Add sugar and vanilla to mixture and blend well. Spread over cake.

Yield: approximately 24 servings

MILKY WAY CAKE

8 regular size Milky Way bars
2 sticks butter or margarine
2 cups sugar
2½ cups flour
½ teaspoon baking soda

¼ teaspoon salt
4 eggs
1 cup buttermilk
1 teaspoon vanilla
1 cup pecans, chopped

Preheat oven to 325°. Grease and flour a tube pan. Melt Milky Way bars with 1 stick butter in top of a double boiler. Cream together sugar and 1 stick butter. Sift together flour, soda, and salt. Add eggs to sugar and butter one at a time beating well after each addition. Add flour mixture alternately with buttermilk. Add vanilla, candy mixture, and pecans, mixing well. Pour into tube pan and bake approximately 1 hour and 30 minutes. Test for doneness at 1 hour and 15 minutes; cake is best when just barely done.

Yield: approximately 12 servings

VANILLA WAFER CAKE

2 sticks butter, softened
2 cups sugar
6 eggs
½ cup milk
½ cup flour
2 teaspoons baking powder

1 12-ounce box vanilla
   wafers, crushed
1 7-ounce package coconut
1 teaspoon vanilla
1 cup pecans, chopped
Confectioners sugar

Preheat oven to 350° Grease and flour a bundt pan. Cream butter and sugar together in a mixing bowl. Add eggs one at a time beating well after each addition. Add milk. Sift flour with baking powder and add to batter. Add vanilla wafers, coconut, vanilla, and pecans. Pour into pan and bake for 1 hour and 15 minutes. Allow to cool. Sprinkle with confectioners sugar.

Yield: 10 servings

SOUR CREAM POUND CAKE

Nice for strawberry shortcake. If you like coconut, substitute coconut extract for vanilla.

2 sticks butter, softened
3 cups sugar
6 egg yolks
3 cups flour, sifted
¼ teaspoon baking soda

1 cup sour cream
1 teaspoon almond extract
1 teaspoon vanilla extract
6 eggs whites, stiffly beaten

Preheat oven to 300°. Cream butter and sugar together in a mixing bowl. Add egg yolks one at a time beating well after each addition. Mix flour and soda together in a separate bowl. Add flour and sour cream alternately to batter. Add extracts and beat until smooth. Fold in egg whites. Pour into ungreased tube pan. Bake 1 hour and 30 minutes. This cake freezes well.

Yield: approximately 12 servings

MOTHER'S LEMON CAKE SAUCE

This is wonderful with pound cake or gingerbread. It also makes a delicious filling for lemon meringue pie.

Juice of 1½ medium to large
  lemons
Water
1 cup sugar
1½ heaping tablespoons
  flour

3 egg yolks
2 whole eggs
1½ tablespoons butter

In a 2 cup measuring cup mix the lemon juice and enough water to make 1½ cups of liquid. Place liquid in the top of a double boiler. Mix sugar and flour together and add to lemon juice. Beat egg yolks and whole eggs and add to the above. Place double boiler over high heat until water in bottom comes to a boil, then turn heat to simmer. Stir lemon sauce to keep from forming lumps and until it becomes thick. When liquid is thick, remove from heat and add butter, stirring until melted.

Yield: sauce for 1 cake

RUTH'S CANDIED FRUIT CAKE

2 cups flour
2 teaspoons baking powder
½ teaspoon salt
1 teaspoon cinnamon
1 teaspoon allspice
½ teaspoon nutmeg
½ teaspoon cloves
1 pound candied pineapple, coarsely cut

1 pound whole candied cherries
1¼ pounds pitted dates, coarsely cut
4 eggs
1 cup sugar
2 pounds pecan halves, 8 cups

Preheat oven to 275°. Grease and line with greased brown paper two 9-inch cake pans. Sift together first seven ingredients into a very large bowl. Add candied fruits and dates. Mix well with hands to coat each piece of fruit with flour mixture. Beat eggs until frothy. Gradually beat in sugar. Add to fruit and mix well with hands. Mix in pecan halves. Divide dough into pans and press down firmly with fingers to fill in empty spaces. Bake for approximately 1 hour and 30 minutes. Allow to stand in pans for 5 minutes, then turn out on racks to cool and remove paper.

Yield: 24 servings

ITALIAN CREAM CAKE

2 cups sugar
1 stick butter, softened
½ cup shortening
5 eggs, separated
2 cups flour
1 teaspoon baking soda

1 cup buttermilk
1 teaspoon vanilla
1 3½-ounce can coconut
1 cup pecans, chopped
Cream Cheese Icing

Preheat oven to 350°. Grease and flour three 9-inch cake pans. Cream sugar, butter, and shortening together in a mixing bowl. Add 5 egg yolks and beat well. Mix flour and soda. Add the flour mixture and buttermilk alternately to the batter. Add vanilla, coconut, and nuts (reserving some coconut and nuts for the icing). Whip the eggs whites on high speed until stiff. Fold eggs whites into the batter. Pour into pans and bake for 25 minutes. Allow to cool and ice with Cream Cheese Icing. Ice the layers and top; sprinkle with reserved coconut and pecans.

Yield: 12 servings

MIMI HALLER'S OATMEAL CAKE

1½ cups boiling water
1 cup minute oats
1 stick butter or margarine, softened
1 cup sugar
1 cup brown sugar, firmly packed

2 eggs
1 teaspoon vanilla
1½ cups flour
1 teaspoon baking soda
1 teaspoon cinnamon
½ teaspoon salt

Topping:
1 cup brown sugar
½ cup evaporated milk
½ stick butter or margarine

1 cup coconut
½ cup pecans, chopped

Preheat oven to 350°. Grease a 9x13 inch baking dish. Pour water over oats in a bowl and allow to stand for 20 minutes. Cream butter and sugars together in a mixing bowl. Add oatmeal, eggs, and vanilla, and beat well. Mix dry ingredients and add to the cake batter. Pour into baking dish and bake for 35 minutes. Allow to cool.

Topping: Blend ingredients together for topping and spread over cooled cake. Place under broiler until top is lightly browned, approximately 3 to 5 minutes.

Yield: 18 servings

PINEAPPLE CAKE

2 cups sugar
¾ cup vegetable oil
2 eggs
1 20-ounce can crushed pineapple, undrained

2 cups flour
1 teaspoon baking soda
1 teaspoon salt
Cream Cheese Icing

Preheat oven to 350°. Grease and flour a 9x13 inch baking dish. Cream sugar with oil and eggs. Add pineapple. Mix dry ingredients and blend into batter. Pour into baking dish. Bake for 30 to 35 minutes. Ice.

Yield: 18 servings

ORANGE GLAZED ZUCCHINI CAKE

Make a glaze with ¼ cup orange juice and 1 cup confectioners sugar. Pour over cake while still warm. Serve at your next coffee.

4 eggs
1½ cups oil
3 cups sugar
3 teaspoons grated orange
  rind
3 cups grated zucchini
3 cups flour

1 teaspoon baking powder
1½ teaspoons baking soda
3 teaspoons cinnamon
¼ teaspoon salt
½ cup walnuts or pecans,
  chopped

Preheat oven to 350°. Grease and flour a bundt pan. Blend together eggs, oil, sugar, and orange rind in a mixing bowl until creamy. Add zucchini and blend well. Sift together dry ingredients and mix with batter thoroughly. Add the nuts. Pour into pan. Bake for 1½ hours. Allow cake to cool for 15 to 20 minutes, then turn out of pan.

Yield: approximately 16 servings

CHOCOLATE ANGEL FROSTING

This frosting will ice one store bought or homemade angel food cake.

2 cups whipping cream
¾ cup sugar
½ cup cocoa

½ pound English toffee,
  broken into small chunks,
  or 12 Heath candy bars

Combine whipping cream, sugar, and cocoa in a large bowl and chill 1 hour. Beat until stiff. Add candy chunks to one-third of the frosting in a separate bowl, reserve some candy for top. Frost between layers with this mixture. Use remaining two-thirds frosting to cover cake. Lightly sprinkle top of cake with candy chunks.

Yield: icing for one cake

CUISINART PIE CRUST

1⅓ cups flour
1 stick cold unsalted butter,
  cut into 4 or 5 pieces

½ teaspoon salt
¼ cup ice water

Place flour, butter, and salt in a Cuisinart bowl fitted with a steel blade. Cut butter into flour until it looks like coarse meal. Add ice water slowly with machine running. Process until the dough forms a ball. Remove dough and roll out into pie crust.

Yield: 1 pie crust

FRENCH APPLE PIE

Absolutely scrumptious.

2 9-inch pie crusts
1 pound apples, peeled and
  sliced
2 tablespoons lemon juice
½ teaspoon nutmeg
½ teaspoon cinnamon
½ cup sugar

¼ cup seedless raisins
1 cup brown sugar
¼ stick butter
2 tablespoons flour
½ cup pecans, chopped
¼ cup milk

Hard sauce:
1 stick butter
1½ cups confectioners sugar

1 tablespoon boiling water
1 teaspoon brandy or rum

Preheat oven to 450°. Place one crust in a 9-inch pie pan. Pat into pan with dough hanging over sides. Place apples in pie shell and sprinkle with lemon juice, nutmeg, and cinnamon. Spread evenly with sugar and raisins. Mix brown sugar, flour, and butter in a mixing bowl, blending well. Spread over apples and sprinkle with pecans. Add most of the milk and cover with remaining pastry. Prick top of dough with a fork; brush remaining milk over pastry. Attach edge of pastry and flute with fingers. Bake for 10 minutes. Reduce heat to 350°, and bake for 30 minutes more.

Hard sauce: Cream butter until light and fluffy. Beat in sugar and add boiling water. Beat in brandy and serve over pie.

Yield: 8 slices

FRESH BLUEBERRY PIE

To serve top with vanilla ice cream while still warm.

2 9-inch pie crusts
2 pints fresh blueberries,
  washed and drained
1 tablespoon lemon juice
1 cup sugar
¼ cup flour
¼ teaspoon cinnamon

⅛ teaspoon nutmeg
⅛ teaspoon ground cloves
2 tablespoons butter or
  margarine
1 egg yolk
1 tablespoon water

Preheat oven to 400°. Place one pie crust in a 9-inch pie pan. Place blueberries in a large bowl and sprinkle with lemon juice. Combine sugar, flour, cinnamon, nutmeg, and cloves. Add to berries and toss lightly to combine. Turn into pie shell. Mound berries in the center and dot with butter. Place other crust on top of mixture and fold edges under bottom crust and seal. Make vents in top of pie crust for steam to escape. Beat egg yolk with water and brush on top of pie crust. Bake for 45 to 50 minutes. Cool on wire rack for approximately 1 hour.

Yield: 8 servings

ROSEMARY'S STRAWBERRY PIE

Serve in the summertime for a light and delicious dessert.

1 8-inch pie shell, cooked
  and cooled
½ cup sugar
1 envelope unflavored
  gelatin
½ cup cold water
1 10-ounce package of frozen
  sliced strawberries

Juice of ½ lemon
¼ teaspoon almond extract
1 cup whipping cream,
  whipped
6 to 8 fresh strawberries for
  garnish, optional

Stir together sugar and gelatin in a saucepan. Stir in water. Cook over low heat, stirring until just below boiling point. Remove from heat and add frozen strawberries, lemon juice, and almond extract. Stir, breaking up strawberries with a fork until they are thawed and mixture thickens. Fold in whipped cream. Pour into pie shell. Garnish and refrigerate.

Yield: 8 servings

SLICED LEMON PIE

Mama's Flaky Pie Crust
  recipe
1 stick butter, softened
1½ cups sugar
2½ tablespoons flour
¼ teaspoon salt
4 eggs

2 teaspoons grated lemon
  rind
2 lemons peeled, white
  membrane removed, and
  sliced in very thin rounds
2 teaspoons sugar

Preheat oven to 400°. Prepare 2 pie crusts and place one in pie pan. Blend butter, sugar, flour, and salt together in a large mixing bowl. Add eggs, reserving a small amount of white to brush on top of crust. Add lemon rind and mix well. Add lemon slices and stir gently. Pour mixture into pie shell. Add top crust and brush lightly with beaten egg whites. Sprinkle with sugar. Bake for 35 minutes.

Yield: 8 servings

FRUIT PIZZA

¾ 20-ounce roll refrigerated
  sugar cookie dough
1 8-ounce package cream
  cheese, softened
⅓ cup sugar
1 11-ounce can mandarin
  oranges, drained

1-1½ bananas, sliced
1 medium bunch grapes,
  halved
½ pint strawberries, sliced
1 kiwi fruit, peeled and
  sliced

Preheat oven to 350°. Pat cookie dough onto a 12 inch pizza pan to within 1 inch of the edge. Bake for 10 to 15 minutes or until golden brown. Allow to cool.

Combine cream cheese and sugar. Spread on cooled cookie crust. Arrange orange sections around perimeter, pointing to the center. Follow with banana slices, grapes, and strawberries; fill center of pizza with kiwi fruit.

Yield: 16 servings

BUTTERMILK PIE

Cuisinart Pie Crust
3 eggs
1¾ cups sugar

½ cup buttermilk
1 stick butter, melted
1 teaspoon vanilla

Preheat oven to 325°. Beat eggs and sugar together with a mixer until thick. Add buttermilk, butter, and vanilla and beat until well blended. Pour into unbaked pie shell. Bake for 40 minutes or until golden brown.

Yield: 8 servings

MRS. C'S COCONUT CREAM PIE

1 9-inch baked pie shell
1 cup sugar
Scant ¼ teaspoon salt
2 tablespoons flour
3 tablespoons cornstarch
2 cups milk

3 egg yolks
1 tablespoon butter
1 teaspoon vanilla
¼ teaspoon almond extract
1 4-ounce can coconut

Meringue:
3 egg whites
¼ teaspoon cream of tartar
6 tablespoons sugar

½ teaspoon vanilla
¼ teaspoon almond extract

Preheat oven to 325°. Mix sugar, salt, flour, and cornstarch together in a heavy saucepan. Gradually stir in milk. Cook, stirring constantly on medium heat, until mixture starts to boil and begins to thicken. Beat egg yolks and reserve whites for meringue. Add 3 or 4 tablespoons of hot filling to eggs mixing well. Pour egg mixture into saucepan with rest of filling and continue cooking until thickened, about 3 or 4 minutes. Remove from heat and add butter, vanilla, almond extract, and all but ¼ cup of coconut. Cool and pour into pie shell.

Beat egg whites with cream of tartar in a small mixing bowl until soft peaks form. Beat in 3 tablespoons sugar, then add the remainder of sugar. Add vanilla and almond extract and beat well. Spread on top of filling and seal edges well by making sure meringue is spread to edge of crust. Sprinkle remaining coconut on top of the meringue. Bake for 15 to 20 minutes or until golden brown.

Yield: 8 servings

GERMAN CHOCOLATE PIE

1 9-inch pie shell
1 4-ounce package German
  sweet chocolate
½ stick butter
1 13-ounce can evaporated
  milk
1½ cups sugar

3 tablespoons cornstarch
⅛ teaspoon salt
2 eggs
1 teaspoon vanilla
1⅓ cups coconut
½ cup pecans, chopped

Preheat oven to 375°. Melt chocolate with butter in heavy saucepan, stirring until well blended. Remove from heat and gradually add milk and set aside. Mix sugar, cornstarch, and salt together in a mixing bowl. Beat in eggs and vanilla. Blend in chocolate. Pour into pie shell. Combine coconut and pecans and sprinkle over filling. Bake for 40 to 50 minutes or until browned and puffed. Filling will be soft, but not set. Allow to cool at least 4 hours before cutting.

Yield: 8 servings

GRASSHOPPER PIE

A refreshing finale for an Italian dinner.

Crust:
1½ cups chocolate wafer
  crumbs

½ stick butter, melted

Filling:
25 large marshmallows
⅔ cup whipping cream
4-6 tablespoons creme de
  menthe

1 cup whipping cream,
  sweetened and whipped

Mix chocolate wafer crumbs together with butter and press into a 9-inch pie pan and chill. Melt marshmallows and ⅔ cup cream together in a saucepan. Allow to cool. Add creme de menthe and fold in whipped cream. Pour into chilled pie shell and freeze several hours or overnight before serving.

Yield: 8 servings

MARVELOUS MOUSSE PIE

Crust:

2 cups chocolate wafer
  crumbs

¾ stick butter, melted

Filling:

½ pound semisweet
  chocolate
1 egg
2 egg yolks

1 cup whipping cream
3 tablespoons confectioners
  sugar
2 egg whites

Topping:

2 cups whipped cream,
  sweetened and whipped

Combine crumbs and butter together and press in the bottom and sides of a spring form pan. Refrigerate.

Soften chocolate in the top of a double boiler over simmering water. Allow to cool to lukewarm. Add whole egg and mix well. Add egg yolks and mix until thoroughly blended. Whip cream with confectioners sugar until soft peaks form. Beat egg whites until stiff but not dry. Stir a small amount of the cream and egg whites into the chocolate mixture to lighten. Fold in remaining cream and whites until well blended. Turn into crust and chill overnight.

Loosen crust on all sides of pan using sharp knife and remove sides. Spread all but ½ cup whipped cream over top. Pipe remaining cream into rosettes in center of pie and around edges.

Yield: 10 servings

FRENCH CHOCOLATE DELIGHT

Prepare the crust and filling up to a week ahead of time. Ice on the day you serve.

Crust:
1 cup flour
1 stick unsalted butter, softened
½ cup pecans, coarsely chopped

½ cup dark brown sugar, firmly packed

Filling:
1 stick unsalted butter, softened
¾ cup sugar
2 large eggs

1 ounce unsweetened chocolate, melted and cooled

Cream topping:
1 cup whipping cream
2 heaping tablespoons confectioners sugar

2 teaspoons creme de cacao

Preheat oven to 350°. Combine flour, butter, pecans, and brown sugar together. Press into bottom of a 9-inch square pan and bake for 20 minutes. Allow crust to cool in the pan on a wire rack.

Cream butter in a mixing bowl with an electric mixer until smooth. Add sugar very slowly and beat until light and fluffy. Add eggs one at a time beating well after each addition. Add chocolate and beat for 3 minutes. Spread chocolate mixture on the crust. Cover loosely and chill for 2 hours.

In a chilled bowl, beat cream until it holds soft peaks. Gradually beat in sugar and creme de cacao until very stiff.

Remove chocolate cake from pan and cut in half, forming two 9x4½-inch rectangles. Place one half crust side down on a serving platter and spread with half of the whipped cream. Top with remaining half of cake. Fill a pastry bag fitted with a flute tip and pipe cream on top of cake, covering it completely and freeze. Allow cake to stand at room temperature one hour before serving. Slice into approximately ¾ inch slices.

Yield: 10 slices

BLACK BOTTOM PIE

This takes time to prepare, but it is worth it.

Crust:
12 large gingersnaps or 20
  small, crumbled

5 tablespoons butter or
  margarine, melted

Filling:
1 tablespoon gelatin
¼ cup cold water
2 cups milk
½ cup sugar
4 tablespoons cornstarch
4 egg yolks, slightly beaten
2 1-ounce squares chocolate

½ teaspoon vanilla
2½ tablespoons rum or ½
  teaspoon rum extract
4 egg whites
¼ teaspoon salt
¼ teaspoon cream of tartar
¼ cup sugar

Topping:
1 cup whipping cream
2 tablespoons confectioners
  sugar

½ ounce chocolate, shaved
  for garnish

Preheat oven to 350°. Combine gingersnaps and butter and press into a 9-inch pie pan. Bake for 10 minutes. Soak gelatin in cold water. Heat milk in a heavy saucepan to scalding. Combine sugar and cornstarch in a mixing bowl. Beat in egg yolks. Slowly stir in scalded milk. Place in a double boiler. Cook for 15 to 20 minutes, stirring occasionally, until custard heavily coats the spoon. Remove from heat.

Take out one cup of custard and place in a separate mixing bowl. To it, add chocolate and beat until chocolate is melted and well blended. Allow to cool. When cool, add vanilla and pour into pie crust.

Dissolve the soaked gelatin into remaining hot custard. Allow to cool, but do not let mixture stiffen. When cool, stir in rum flavoring. Beat 3 egg whites with salt and cream of tartar and beat 1 egg white with sugar until stiff. Fold egg whites into rum flavored custard mixture. Spoon over chocolate filling and chill until set.

Whip cream and confectioners sugar until stiff. Cover custard with whipped cream and sprinkle shaved chocolate over top. Refrigerate before serving.

Yield: 8 servings

MARY'S PEANUT BUTTER PIE

Crust:

1½-2 cups vanilla wafer
   crumbs

½ stick butter, melted

Filling:

⅓ cup peanut butter chips,
   melted
½ cup confectioners sugar
2 eggs
½ stick butter, softened
½ teaspoon vanilla
½ cup nuts, chopped

⅓ cup semisweet chocolate
   chips, melted
½ cup confectioners sugar
2 eggs
½ stick butter, softened
½ teaspoon vanilla

Topping:

1 cup whipping cream,
   whipped
2 tablespoons confectioners
   sugar

Grated chocolate for garnish

Combine vanilla wafer crumbs and butter; press into an 8-inch pie pan. Mix first five filling ingredients together with electric mixer, mixing well. Pour into pie shell. Cover with nuts and place in freezer. Mix last five filling ingredients together and pour over nut layer. Return to freezer and freeze pie.

Whip cream and confectioners sugar until stiff. Spread over frozen pie and garnish with grated chocolate. Allow to set at room temperature 10 minutes before serving.

Yield: 8 servings

FRUIT PASTRIES

Pastries can be prepared, placed on baking sheet, frozen and cooked the day of the party.

1 stick butter, softened
3 ounces cream cheese,
  softened

1 cup flour

Fillings:
Apricot jam
Strawberry jelly
Plum jelly

Confectioners sugar for
  garnish

Preheat oven to 400°. Grease baking sheet. Cream butter and cream cheese together and gradually add flour. Mix until smooth. Wrap dough in plastic wrap and chill for approximately 3 hours or overnight. Roll dough to ½ inch thickness on a floured surface. Cut into 2 inch squares. Place ½ teaspoon of your choice of jelly fillings on center of each square. Pull corners to the center. Place on baking sheet and bake for 12 to 15 minutes. Cool and sprinkle with confectioners sugar.

Yield: approximately 3 dozen

BANANAS FOSTER

Make sure liqueur and rum are very hot before adding in order to get a beautiful flame.

4 tablespoons dark brown
  sugar
2 tablespoons butter
2 bananas, sliced lengthwise
  and then halved
Dash cinnamon

1 ounce banana liqueur,
  heated
2 ounces white rum, 180
  proof
2 large scoops vanilla ice
  cream

Melt brown sugar and butter in a flat chafing dish. Add bananas and saute until tender. Sprinkle with cinnamon. Pour in liqueur and rum and flame. Baste with warm liquids until flame burns out. Serve at once over ice cream.

Yield: 2 servings

PECAN TARTS

You will need to prepare crust the day before serving.

Crust:

3 ounces cream cheese, softened

1 stick butter, softened
1 cup flour

Filling:

1 egg
¾ cup brown sugar
1 tablespoon butter or margarine, softened
1 teaspoon vanilla

Dash of salt
⅔ cup pecans, chopped
Pecan halves for garnish, optional

Mix cream cheese and butter together with flour in a small mixing bowl. Cover and refrigerate overnight. Divide dough into 24 small balls and place into miniature muffin tins. Using thumb, shape dough to fit tin. Mix filling ingredients together in a mixing bowl. Fill each tart shell approximately ¾ full. Top with peacn halves if desired. Bake for 25 minutes at 300°. Cool and remove from muffin tins.

Yield: 24 tarts

CHERRIES JUBILEE

The cognac must be very hot in order to flame.

1 20-ounce can bing cherries
2 tablespoons sugar

½ cup cognac, heated
1 quart vanilla ice cream

Heat cherries with juice and sugar in a chafing dish. Do not boil. When very hot, add almost all of cognac. Pour remaining cognac in a large silver spoon. Do not use stainless steel spoon. Ignite. Pour over cherries and let blaze. Pour flaming sauce over ice cream and serve immediately.

Yield: 6 servings.

CHERRY TARTS

Wonderful served warm with whipped cream or vanilla ice cream.

Crust:

1 3-ounce package cream
   cheese, softened

1 stick butter, softened
1 cup flour

Filling:

1 20-ounce can cherries
Dash of cinnamon
¾ cup sugar

¼ cup flour
3 teaspoons butter

Preheat oven to 375°. Grease muffin tins. Combine cream cheese, butter, and flour together and mix well. Chill 30 minutes. Divide dough into 12 balls. Pat to fit muffin tins.

Drain cherry juice into saucepan. Sift cinnamon, sugar, and flour together. Add to cherry juice and bring to a boil. Cook until thickened. Add cherries and butter, stirring well. Fill each muffin tin with cherry mixture. Bake for approximately 15 minutes or until golden brown.

Yield: 12 tarts

BAKED CUSTARD

3 eggs
¾ cup sugar
⅜ teaspoon salt

3 cups milk, scalded
¾ teaspoon vanilla

Preheat oven to 350°. Beat eggs, sugar, and salt together in a mixing bowl. Stir in milk and vanilla. Pour into 8 custard cups and place in a pan of hot water 1-inch deep. Sprinkle top with nutmeg. Bake for 45 to 50 minutes or until silver knife inserted one inch from edge comes out clean. Allow to cool. Refrigerate until ready to serve. Top with whipped cream.

Yield: 8 servings

BROWN'S HOLIDAY CHARLOTTE

You will need two bowls for this large recipe. After congealing in the refrigerator you may freeze it. Allow to thaw completely before serving.

3¾ tablespoons gelatin
¾ cup water
12 egg yolks
1¼ cups sugar
8 ounces Bourbon, or 1
    teaspoon almond or vanilla
    extract

3 pints whipping cream
12 egg whites
Nutmeg, chocolate curls, or
    fresh fruit for garnish

Soak gelatin in cold water and dissolve in a double boiler over hot water. Beat egg yolks in mixer until thick and lemon-colored. Gradually beat in sugar, then Bourbon. When well mixed and very thick, stir in gelatin. Allow to stand and thicken while you beat whipping cream and egg whites. Fold whipped cream into custard first and then follow with egg whites. Pour into serving bowl and refrigerate until set. Sprinkle each serving with your choice of garnish.

Yield: 12 servings.

BLOW YOUR DIET BREAD PUDDING

This old fashioned dessert is especially good topped with meringue. Also top with your choice of lemon sauce or custard sauce. It is so good it is sinful.

Pudding:
6 slices day old bread,
    buttered and cut into 1
    inch cubes
2 cups Pet milk
2 cups water

¾ cup raisins
6 egg yolks, beaten
10 tablespoons sugar
2 teaspoons vanilla

Meringue:
6 egg whites
¼ teaspoon cream of tartar

6 tablespoons sugar

(continued)

Lemon sauce:
1 cup sugar
4 teaspoons cornstarch
Dash of salt
Dash of nutmeg
2 cups water
4 egg yolks, beaten

½ stick butter, cut into small
   pieces
1 teaspoon grated lemon
   rind
4 tablespoons lemon juice

Custard sauce:
½ cup sugar
2 cups milk
2 eggs, beaten

1 teaspoon vanilla
1 teaspoon rum extract,
   optional

Preheat oven to 325°. Pudding: Arrange bread cubes in a deep baking dish. Mix milk, water, and raisins in a small saucepan. Scald milk and remove from heat. Combine egg yolks and sugar in a mixing bowl and slowly add scalded milk, stirring constantly. Add vanilla. Pour over bread cubes, tucking raisins around and beneath bread. Place baking dish in a shallow pan of water and bake for 50 to 60 minutes, or until custard is set. Remove from oven. Add meringue and serve with Lemon or Custard sauce.

Meringue: Beat egg whites with cream of tartar until soft peaks form. Gradually beat in sugar until egg whites form stiff peaks. Seal meringue over baked pudding and bake until meringue is nicely browned, about 15 minutes.

Lemon sauce: Mix sugar, cornstarch, salt, and nutmeg together in a saucepan. Gradually stir in water. Cook over low heat, stirring constantly, until thick and clear. Stir a small amount of hot sugar mixture into eggs and mix well. Stirring constantly, add eggs to sugar mixture and cook for 1 minute. Remove from heat and stir in butter, lemon rind, and lemon juice. Blend thoroughly. Serve over bread pudding.

Custard sauce: In the top of a 2-quart double boiler combine sugar and milk. Heat to almost boiling. Stir a small amount of hot milk into eggs. Stirring constantly, add eggs to milk in double boiler. Cook until mixture is thick and coats a spoon. Do not boil. Remove from heat and allow to cool. Add vanilla and rum extract. Serve over bread pudding.

Yield: 10 to 12 servings

BAKED LEMON CUSTARD

1 cup sugar	1 tablespoon grated lemon
¼ cup flour	rind
⅛ teaspoon salt	3 eggs, separated
2 tablespoons butter, melted	1½ cups milk
5 tablespoons lemon juice	

Preheat oven to 350°. Butter 8 custard cups. Blend sugar, flour, and salt together in a mixing bowl. Add butter, lemon juice, and rind, mixing well. Beat egg yolks. Add milk and egg yolks into mixture. Stiffly beat and fold in egg whites. Pour into custard cups and place in a pan of hot water. Bake 45 minutes.

Yield: approximately 8 servings

VANILLA RASPBERRY PARFAIT

Looks so pretty layered in a parfait glass. A wonderful light dessert after a heavy meal.

1 pint whipping cream	3½ cups milk
8 heaping tablespoons	3 tablespoons sugar
confectioners sugar	1 10-ounce box frozen
2 teaspoons vanilla extract	raspberries, thawed
1 teaspoon almond extract	
1 6-ounce package instant	
vanilla pudding mix	

Whip cream until amost stiff, then add confectioners sugar, 1 teaspoon vanilla, and almond extract. Continue whipping until cream forms soft peaks. Set aside.

Beat pudding, milk, sugar, and remaining vanilla, following package directions for pudding. Fold whipping cream into pudding. Refrigerate. Place thawed raspberries in a blender and puree. Optional: juice may or may not be strained. Serve raspberries on top of custard or layer in parfait glasses.

Yield: approximately 6 servings

VANILLA BAVARIAN CREAM

Use your imagination when preparing this dessert. Make chocolate and vanilla cream and alternate in layers when molding. There are many possibilities.

4 egg yolks
½ cup sugar
1 cup milk, scalded
1 envelope unflavored
   gelatin

¼ cup cold water
1 teaspoon vanilla
1 cup whipping cream,
   whipped

Liqueur Sauce:
1 scant cup strawberry or
   other flavored jam
1 tablespoon sugar

¼ cup water
Kirsch or other liqueur to
   taste

Beat egg yolks in top of double boiler. Beat in sugar. Add scalded milk gradually, stirring constantly. Place over simmering water. Cook, stirring constantly, until the mixture coats the back of a spoon (15 to 30 minutes).

Soften gelatin in water. Stir into custard. Strain with cheesecloth into a large bowl. Stir in vanilla. Return to double boiler. Cook, stirring occasionally, until custard begins to thicken. Remove from heat and cool slightly. Fold in whipped cream. Turn into a lightly oiled mold. Chill several hours or overnight. Serve Vanilla Bavarian Cream with choice of Liqueur Sauce.

To prepare Chocolate Bavarian Cream: Simply dissolve ¼ pound sweet chocolate in milk, and follow same procedure for Vanilla Bavarian Cream. The custard will look runnier than the vanilla, but it will mold just fine.

Sauce: Combine jam, sugar, and water in a saucepan. Boil slowly for 5 minutes. Skim off foam and push through a sieve. Add liqueur to taste. Serve at room temperature. Other combinations: peach jam and amaretto, raspberry jam and contreau, apricot jam and kirsch, orange jam and curaco, or currant jam and kirsch.

Yield: 6 servings

CHOCOLATE MOUSSE

2 envelopes unflavored
   gelatin
2 cups Half and Half
1 cup sugar, divided
¼ teaspoon salt
4 eggs, separated
1 12-ounce package
   semi-sweet chocolate
   pieces

2 cups whipping cream,
   whipped
1 cup confectioners sugar
1 teaspoon vanilla or 1
   teaspoon of the following:
   Kahlua, framboise, kirsch,
   or grand marnier

Sprinkle gelatin over Half and Half in a saucepan to soften. Add ½ cup sugar, salt, egg yolks, and mix well. Add chocolate chips and cook over low heat, stirring constantly, until chocolate is melted and gelatin is dissolved, about 10 minutes. Remove from heat and stir until smooth. Cool in refrigerator approximately 45 to 60 minutes.

Beat egg whites until stiff, adding ½ cup sugar, 1 tablespoon at a time. Whip cream until peaks, adding confectioners sugar and vanilla. Fold whipped cream and egg whites into chilled chocolate mixture. Pour into a 2-quart souffle dish with a 2-inch collar. Chill until firm.

Yield: 12 servings

PEARS IN WINE

6 pears; washed and peeled
   with stems attached
2 cups red wine
2 cups water
1 cup sugar
1 clove

1 cinnamon stick,
   approximately 1 inch piece
1 lemon, sliced
Whipped cream or toasted
   coconut for garnish

Combine pears with wine, water, sugar, clove, cinnamon, and lemon in a large glass or enameled sauepan. Cover and cook over low heat approximately 30 minutes or until tender. Remove pears to a serving dish. Reheat juice and boil uncovered to reduce liquid by one half. Pour over pears and chill. Serve with whipped cream or toasted coconut.

Yield: 6 servings

CHOCOLATE AND VANILLA BOMBE

Different shaped molds may be used for different occasions and holidays.

1½-2 quarts vanilla ice cream, slightly softened	6 eggs, separated
	3 teaspoons vanilla
1 12-ounce package semi-sweet chocolate chips	½ pint whipping cream
	Shaved chocolate for garnish

Place a 2½-quart mold into the freezer for 5 minutes to chill. Line bottom and sides of mold with about ½ ice cream. Return to freezer until firm.

Melt chocolate chips in top of double boiler or microwave. When melted, quickly stir in egg yolks and vanilla. Cool slightly. Beat egg whites stiffly and fold into chocolate. Whip the cream until thick and fold into the chocolate. Pour into ice cream-lined mold. Freeze until firm, about 4 hours. Cover top with other ½ ice cream. Freeze an additional hour. To unmold, dip in warm water for 30 seconds. Caution: if using a metal mold, the ice cream will melt quickly. Top with shaved chocolate. Serve immediately.

*Note: The chocolate filling makes a wonderful mousse when refrigerated and not frozen.

Yield: 12 servings

CALYPSO PIE

Pie:
18 Oreo cookie crumbs,
  about 2 cups
½ stick butter, softened

2 pints coffee ice cream,
  softened

Fudge sauce:
3 1-ounce squares
  unsweetened chocolate
½ stick butter
⅔ cup sugar
⅛ teaspoon salt

1 5¾-ounce can evaporated
  milk
1 teaspoon vanilla extract
½ teaspoon almond extract

Topping:
1 cup whipping cream
3 tablespoons confectioners
  sugar

1 cup nuts, coarsely chopped

Blend cookie crumbs and butter in a mixing bowl using a fork. Using the back of a spoon, press crumbs firmly and evenly into a 10-inch pie pan. Chill 2 hours. Spoon softened ice cream into chilled shell and spread evenly.

Melt chocolate and butter in top of a double boiler over simmering water. Remove from heat and stir in sugar and salt until blended. Gradually add evaporated milk, blending well. Cook over simmering water for approximately 4 minutes, stirring constantly. Remove from heat and add flavorings. Chill. Spread chilled fudge sauce over ice cream. Beat whipping cream with confectioners sugar until it peaks. Top pie with whipped cream and sprinkle with chopped nuts. Freeze until firm approximately 4 hours or overnight. Allow pie to soften a few minutes before serving.

Yield: 8 servings

ICE CREAM CAKE

Crust:
1 15-ounce package Oreo
 cookies
⅓ cup butter, melted

½ gallon vanilla ice cream,
 softened

Fudge sauce:
1 8-ounce package German
 sweet chocolate, melted
1 5¾-ounce can evaporated
 milk

½ stick butter
½-⅔ cup sugar
1 teaspoon vanilla
Chopped nuts, optional

Grind Oreo cookies in a blender. Grease bottom of a 9x13 inch pan. Combine cookie crumbs with butter until well blended and press into pan forming crust. Pour softened ice cream over crust and freeze until firm. Stir melted chocolate, milk, butter, and sugar together in a saucepan. Bring to a boil over medium high heat for 4 minutes. Allow to cool for 10 to 15 minutes. Add 1 teaspoon vanilla. Pour over ice cream and return to freezer and freeze. Garnish wtih chopped nuts.

Yield: 12 servings

CREME DE MENTHE PARFAITS

1 quart vanilla ice cream,
 softened
1 pint lime sherbet,
 softened
1 4½-ounce container frozen
 whipped topping, thawed

¼ cup green creme de
 menthe
1 half pint whipping cream
½ cup confectioners sugar
½ teaspoon vanilla

Combine ice cream, sherbet, whipped topping, and creme de menthe in a blender, until well mixed. Spoon into parfait glasses. Freeze 3 to 4 hours. Before serving, thaw slightly. While parfaits thaw, whip cream with confectioners sugar and vanilla. Top each parfait with a dollop of whipped cream and garnish with mint leaf or chocolate curls.

Yield: approximately 6 servings

HEAVENLY ICE CREAM TORTE

This recipe is easy to make for a smaller crowd using an 8-inch spring form pan and quarts of ice cream instead of gallons. The other ingredients seem fine for either size. An 8-inch pan will serve 8 to 10.

1 package Pepperidge Farm
  Bordeaux Cookies, finely
  ground
1 cup coconut

½ gallon coffee ice cream
½ gallon chocolate ice cream
1 6-ounce package English
  Toffee Brick o' Bits

Chocolate Lover's Sauce:
¾ cup confectioners sugar
½ cup Half and Half
2 4-ounce packages German
  sweet chocolate, slightly
  melted

3 1-ounce squares
  unsweetened chocolate,
  slightly melted
½ teaspoon vanilla

Combine cookie crumbs and coconut. Press one half mixture into bottom of a 10-inch spring form pan.

Chocolate sauce: Mix ½ cup sugar with cream in the top of a double boiler until sugar is dissolved. Add chocolate and stir. Cook over boiling water, stirring constantly, until smooth and thick. Remove from heat; gradually beat in remaining sugar and vanilla. Serve warm.

Layer ingredients into crust as follows: coffee ice cream, a thin layer of chocolate sauce, one half toffee bits, and remaining cookie mixture. Freeze approximately 1 hour to allow ice cream to harden. Remove from freezer and add chocolate ice cream, a thin layer of chocolate sauce, and remaining toffee bits. Freeze for 4 to 5 hours before serving. Allow torte to stand at room temperature for 10 minutes before serving. Remainder of chocolate sauce may be passed separately when serving.

Yield: 12-14 servings

ELEGANT ICE CREAM PARFAITS

½ gallon vanilla ice cream,
  softened
1 8-ounce can Hershey
  chocolate syrup

⅓ cup amaretto
⅓ cup dark creme de cacao

Mix all ingredients together in a freezer container. Place in freezer to harden. Spoon in parfait glasses and top with shaved chocolate and cinnamon.

Yield: 6 servings

STRAWBERRIES AND CREAM

½ gallon vanilla ice cream
2 ounces amaretto
2 ounces Kahlua or creme
  de cacao

2 ounces orange liqueur
2 teaspoons vanilla
1 quart strawberries, cleaned
  and hulled

Mix softened ice cream with liqueurs and vanilla. Place ice cream mixture in freezer overnight. Slice strawberries and place in the bottom of individual serving dishes. Spoon ice cream over strawberries and garnish with one whole strawberry.

Yield: 12 servings

RICH AND DELICIOUS ICE CREAM

Adaptable for peaches or strawberries.

1½ cups sugar
4 eggs
¼ teaspoon salt
1 12-ounce can evaporated
  milk
1 14-ounce can sweetened
  condensed milk

1 pint whipping cream,
  whipped with 4 heaping
  tablespoons confectioners
  sugar
1 quart Half and Half
1 tablespoon vanilla
Milk

Beat sugar, eggs, and salt together very well. Add milks, Half and Half, and vanilla. Fold in whipped cream. Pour into ice cream freezer container. Add milk as needed to fill container. Cover and freeze.

Yield: 1½ gallon

BETTY'S BANANA NUT ICE CREAM

7 eggs, separated
1½ cups sugar
1 pint whipping cream,
  whipped and sweetened
1 cup white Karo syrup
¼ teaspoon salt

1 tablespoon vanilla
3 bananas, peeled and
  mashed
1 cup pecans, chopped
Half and Half or milk

Beat egg yolks with ¾ cup sugar in a mixing bowl. Beat egg whites with ¾ cup sugar in a separate mixing bowl until soft peaks form. Beat egg mixtures together. Add Karo, salt, vanilla, bananas, and pecans. Fold in whipped cream. Place in ice cream freezer container. Fill container to top with Half and Half or milk. Cover and freeze.

Yield: 1½ gallon

CHOCOLATE MINT ICE CREAM

2 eggs
3 cups whipping cream
1 cup milk
½ cup sugar
¼ cup white Karo syrup
1 teaspoon vanilla
¼ teaspoon salt

⅓ cup green creme de
  menthe (non alcoholic)
Few drops green food
  coloring
2 1-ounce squares
  semi-sweet chocolate,
  shaved

Beat eggs until fluffy. Add whipping cream, milk, sugar, syrup, vanilla, and salt. Stir until sugar is dissolved. Add creme de menthe and food coloring. Pour into a 4-quart ice cream freezer container. Cover and freeze. Remove dasher and stir in chocolate. Cover and pack with ice and allow to sit for 3 hours.

Yield: 4 quarts

MILKY WAY ICE CREAM

6 cups milk
7 4-inch Milky Way
  candy bars

36 regular size
  marshmallows
1½ quarts heavy cream

Heat milk in a double boiler. Add candy bars and marshmallows and stir until melted. Remove from heat and let cool. Add cream and mix well. Pour into a 6-quart ice cream freezer container. Cover and freeze.

Yield: 6 quarts

CHOCOLATE COVERED CHERRY COOKIES

Definitely worth the time and trouble.

1½ cups flour
½ cup cocoa powder
¼ teaspoon baking powder
¼ teaspoon baking soda
1 stick butter, softened
1 cup sugar
1 egg

2 teaspoons vanilla
1 10-ounce jar maraschino
  cherries, about 48
1 6-ounce package chocolate
  chips
½ cup sweetened condensed
  milk

Preheat oven to 350°. Combine flour, cocoa, baking powder, and baking soda in a mixing bowl. Cream butter and sugar together until fluffy; add eggs and vanilla. Gradually add flour mixture and beat well. Shape dough into 1 inch balls and place on an ungreased cookie sheet; press down center with thumb. Drain cherries, reserving juice, and place one cherry in center of each cookie.

Mix together chocolate chips, milk, and 4 teaspoons cherry juice in a saucepan over medium heat until chocolate chips are melted. Drop 1 teaspoon icing on top of each cookie, spreading to cover cherry. Bake for 10 minutes.

Yield: 48 cookies

CHOCOLATE LOVERS' COOKIES

These are wonderful with ½ cup pecans added. Try substituting chocolate chips with peanut butter, butterscotch, mint, or white chocolate chips.

2½ sticks butter, softened	¾ cup cocoa
2 cups sugar	1 teaspoon baking soda
2 eggs	½ teaspoon salt
2 teaspoons vanilla	2 cups semi-sweet chocolate
2 cups flour	chips

Preheat oven to 350°. Cream butter and sugar in a large mixing bowl. Add eggs and vanilla, blending well. In a separate bowl, combine flour, cocoa, baking soda, and salt. Gradually blend into creamed mixture. Stir in chocolate chips. Drop by teaspoonfuls onto ungreased cookie sheet. Bake for 8-9 minutes. Do not overbake. Cookies will be soft; they will puff while cooking and flatten when cooled. Cool on cookie sheet until set, about 1 minute and remove to wire racks to cool completely. Sprinkle with confectioners sugar if desired.

Yield: 4 dozen

DATE FILLED SANDWICH COOKIES

1¾ cups flour	1 cup brown sugar
¼ teaspoon salt	¼ cup hot water
1 teaspoon baking soda	2 cups oatmeal
2 sticks butter, softened	

Date filling:

1¼ cups dates, pitted	½ cup brown sugar
½ cup hot water, more if needed	1 tablespoon lemon juice
	¼ cup nuts, finely chopped

Sift flour, salt, and baking soda together. Cream butter and brown sugar in a mixing bowl. Gradually add flour to butter and add water. Blend in oatmeal. Form dough into rolls about 1½ inches in diameter. Chill overnight. Slice cookie dough about ¼ inch thick and bake on cookie sheets in preheated 350° oven for 8 minutes. Cool.

Cook dates slowly in hot water with brown sugar in a saucepan until dates are soft. Beat mixture, add lemon juice and nuts, mixing well. Spread date filling between two cookies, making a sandwich.

Yield: 36 cookies

GEE-MA'S FRUITCAKE COOKIES

The longer these set, the better they get, so make a bunch.

1 stick butter or margarine, softened
1 cup brown sugar
4 eggs, slightly beaten
3 teaspoons baking soda
3 tablespoons buttermilk
3 cups flour, separate ½ cup
1 teaspoon cinnamon
1 teaspoon cloves

1 teaspoon allspice
4 ounces Bourbon
2 pounds pecan halves
1 pound candied cherries, halved
1 pound candied pineapple, cut in small pieces
½ pound white raisins

Preheat oven to 300°. Generously grease cookie sheet. Cream butter and sugar in a mixing bowl with an electric mixer. Add eggs. Dissolve baking soda in buttermilk. Combine flour and spices. Add alternately flour (½ cup at a time), buttermilk, and Bourbon to the butter mixture. Combine fruits in a large mixing bowl and dust with ½ cup of flour. Stir in nuts. Pour batter over fruit and nuts and mix well. Drop by teaspoonfuls onto a well greased cookie sheet. Bake for 15 to 20 minutes.

Yield: 12 dozen

GINGERSNAPS

¾ cup shortening
1 cup sugar
1 egg
¼ cup molasses
2 cups flour
1 teaspoon cinnamon

½ teaspoon ground ginger
Dash allspice
2 teaspoons baking soda
¼ teaspoon salt, optional
Sugar

Preheat oven to 350°. Grease a cookie sheet. Mix all ingredients in a large mixing bowl. Batter should be stiff enough not to stick to hands. Shape into small balls. Roll in sugar and place 2 inches apart on cookie sheet. Bake for 10 minutes.

Yield: approximately 3 dozen

LEMON WAFERS

2 sticks butter, melted
½ cup sugar
½ cup brown sugar
Juice of 2 lemons
½ teaspoon vanilla
½ teaspoon almond extract

2 tablespoons lemon juice
1 egg
2½ cups flour
½ teaspoon salt
½ teaspoon baking soda

Lemon icing, optional:
6 tablespoons butter or
  margarine, softened
1 16-ounce box
  confectioners sugar

Juice of one lemon
1 teaspoon lemon rind,
  grated

Preheat oven to 375°. Mix cookie ingredients together in a large mixing bowl. Shape into 1 inch balls; dough will be soft. Roll in sugar and place on an ungreased cookie sheet. Press ball lightly with bottom of a glass. Bake for 7 to 10 minutes.

Icing: Cream butter and confectioners sugar until light and fluffy. Add lemon juice and grated lemon rind. Ice wafers when cool.

Yield: 4 dozen

ROSE'S SAND TARTS

2 sticks butter, softened
5 tablespoons confectioners
  sugar
2 cups flour

2 cups pecans, chopped
½ tablespoon water
1 teaspoon vanilla
Confectioners sugar

Preheat oven to 350°. Grease a cookie sheet. Cream butter and sugar in a small mixing bowl. Add flour and pecans, mixing well. Blend in water and vanilla. Form into small crescent shapes. Place on cookie sheet and bake for 15 minutes or until lightly browned. Cool slightly on wire racks and roll in powdered sugar.

Yield: 5 dozen

COCONUT OATMEAL COOKIES

To give these cookies a different flavor add 2 cups corn flakes cereal and use butter-flavored shortening.

2 cups flour
1 cup sugar
1 teaspoon baking powder
1 teaspoon baking soda
½ teaspoon salt
1 cup brown sugar
1 cup shortening

2 eggs
1 teaspoon vanilla
1½ cups oats
1 cup pecans, chopped
1 cup coconut
Sugar

Raisin variation:
1 cup raisins
2 teaspoons cinnamon

1 teaspoon nutmeg

Preheat oven to 375°. Sift together first five ingredients in a mixing bowl. Add brown sugar, shortening, eggs, and vanilla. Beat well. Stir in oats, nuts, and coconut. Roll dough into small balls. Dip tops in sugar. Place on an ungreased cookie sheet and bake for 12 to 14 minutes.

Yield: 6 dozen

Variation: Omit coconut and add 1 cup raisins, cinnamon and nutmeg. Plump raisins by covering with boiling water for 30 minutes.

SHORTBREAD COOKIES

The top of a white crew sock makes a good jacket for your rolling pin when rolling out this dough.

2 sticks butter, softened
¾ cup sugar

2½ cups flour

Preheat oven to 300°. Cream butter and sugar in a large mixing bowl with an electric mixer. Add flour gradually until well mixed. Pat dough into a large ball and place in plastic wrap. Chill 30 minutes to an hour in refrigerator. Roll out ⅓ of dough, using cloth jacket on rolling pin. Roll dough to ¼ inch thickness. Cut cookies with a cookie cutter. Place cookies close together on a ungreased cookie sheet. Bake approximately 20 minutes. Cookies should be barely browned on bottom and white on top. Cool on wire racks.

Yield: 5 dozen

MOMMA'S CHEWY BROWN SUGAR COOKIES

½ cup shortening
1 stick butter, softened
1 16-ounce box brown sugar
2 eggs

½ teaspoon baking soda
2½ cups flour
¼ teaspoon salt
1 cup pecan halves

Preheat oven to 350°. Cream shortening and butter in a mixing bowl. Add sugar and eggs, mixing well. Add dry ingredients and mix until well blended. Drop by teaspoonfuls onto ungreased cookie sheet. Press pecan halves in center of each cookie. Bake for 10 to 12 minutes until cookies begin to brown lightly. Cool on baking sheet for 1 minute, then remove to waxed paper with pecan side down and cool. This will keep the cookies chewy.

Yield: 5 dozen

BLONDE BROWNIES

Try a variation of butterscotch or peanut butter chips.

⅔ cup oil
2 cups brown sugar, loosely
  packed
2 tablespoons hot water
2 teaspoons vanilla
2 eggs
2 cups flour, sifted

1 teaspoon baking powder
¼ teaspoon baking soda
1 scant teaspoon salt
1 cup pecans, chopped
1 6-ounce package chocolate
  chips

Preheat oven to 350°. Grease a 9x13 inch baking pan. Combine oil, brown sugar, water, and eggs in a mixing bowl. Sift together dry ingredients in a separate mixing bowl. Gradually add flour to egg mixture, blending well. Add pecans. Spread into baking pan. Sprinkle chocolate chips on top. Bake for 25 to 30 minutes, being careful not to overbake. Allow to cool in pan.

Yield: 35 brownies

CARMEN'S CREAM CHEESE BROWNIES

Chocolate mixture:

1 cup flour	6 tablespoons butter
1 teaspoon baking powder	4 eggs
½ teaspoon salt	1½ cups sugar
8 1-ounce squares	2 teaspoons vanilla
semi-sweet chocolate	1½ cups pecans, chopped

Cheese mixture:

1 8-ounce package cream	1 teaspoon vanilla
cheese, softened	½ cup sugar
½ stick butter, softened	2 eggs

Preheat oven to 350°. Butter a jelly roll pan. Sift together flour, baking powder, and salt. Set aside. Melt chocolate and butter together in a saucepan. Stir until smooth. Set aside to cool. In a large bowl beat eggs until foamy. Add sugar and vanilla and beat on high speed for 3 to 4 minutes. Turn to low speed and beat in chocolate mixture. Add flour and mix until well blended. Remove and set aside 1½ cups of the batter. To remaining batter add 1 cup nuts. Spread the chocolate mixture thinly and evenly into pan.

In a small bowl beat cream cheese and butter until soft and smooth. Add vanilla and sugar; beat well. Add eggs and beat until smooth. Spread cream cheese evenly over the chocolate batter layer. Place the reserved 1½ cups of the chocolate by heaping tablespoonfuls onto the cheese layer, letting the cheese mixture show through. With a small spatula or knife, cut through the chocolate mounds and the cheese layer, to marbleize in a zigzag pattern. Do not cut through to the bottom layer. Sprinkle with reserved nuts. Bake for 25-28 minutes. Cool completely and refrigerate for at least one hour before cutting.

Yield: 5 dozen

CHOCOLATE PEPPERMINT SQUARES

Attractive and delicious for a Christmas coffee.

First Layer:

2 1-ounce squares unsweetened chocolate

1 stick butter or margarine, softened

2 eggs, beaten

1 cup sugar

½ cup flour

1 cup nuts, chopped

Second Layer:

1½ cups confectioners sugar

3 tablespoons butter, softened to room temperature

1½ tablespoons milk

1 teaspoon peppermint flavoring

3-4 drops green food coloring

Third Layer:

1½ squares unsweetened chocolate

1½ tablespoons butter or margarine, softened

Preheat oven to 350°. Line an 8-inch square pan with butter coated foil, allowing extra length to extend over edges for easy removal.

First Layer: Melt chocolate and butter together over low heat in a saucepan; stir. Combine eggs and sugar and beat until sugar is dissolved. Stir in flour, chocolate, and nuts. Pour batter in pan and bake for 20 minutes or until toothpick inserted in the center comes out clean.

Second Layer: Beat sugar and butter together in a mixing bowl. Beat in milk and peppermint flavoring. Spread over cooled first layer. Allow to set before adding third layer.

Third Layer: Melt chocolate and butter together over low heat, blending well. Pour over second layer, tilting pan so that the mixture covers the second layer completely. Cool. Lift out by foil. Cut into squares.

Yield: 36 small squares

FIRST-RATE FUDGE

This should be made only in cool, dry weather.

2¼ cups sugar
½ stick butter or margarine
16 large marshmallows
¼ teaspoon salt
1 cup evaporated milk

1 teaspoon vanilla
1 6-ounce package
    semi-sweet chocolate chips
1 cup pecans, chopped

Mix first five ingredients together in a heavy 3-quart saucepan. Stir over medium heat until mixture boils and is bubbly all over the top. Boil; stirring constantly over heat for 5 minutes. Remove from heat. Stir in vanilla and chocolate chips until melted. Stir in pecans. Spread fudge in an 8 or 9-inch buttered square pan. Cool on wire rack. Store in refrigerator. When fudge is cold, cover. Fudge is very creamy and must be stored in refrigerator.

Yield: approximately 24 pieces

ROSS' PEANUT BUTTER CUPS

Tastes just like the real thing!

2 sticks butter or margarine,
    melted
1 16-ounce box
    confectioners sugar, sifted
1 cup graham cracker
    crumbs, crushed

1 cup chunky peanut butter
1 12-ounce package
    semi-sweet chocolate chips

Mix butter with all other ingredients except chocolate chips and press into a 9x13 inch pan. Melt chocolate chips and spread over top. Cut into pieces before you refrigerate. This makes it easier to remove them from pan once they are cooled. Refrigerate 2 to 3 hours before serving.

Yield: approximately 4 dozen

STEAL HIS HEART TOFFEE

Do not double this recipe. If more are desired make separate batches.

2 sticks butter	3 tablespoons water
1⅓ cups sugar	1 cup almonds, slivered
1 tablespoon light Karo syrup	16 ounces milk chocolate, melted

Melt butter in a heavy saucepan. Stir in sugar, syrup, and water. Using candy thermometer, cook over medium high heat until candy reaches 300°. Be careful, the last 10 degrees go very quickly. Immediately add the almonds. Pour into a well-greased 11x16 inch cookie sheet, working quickly. Spread thin and set aside to cool. When cool, in 10 to 15 minutes, spread melted chocolate evenly over the top. Allow chocolate to harden, refrigerating if you are in a hurry. Flip candy out onto waxed paper and break into chunks. Store in an airtight container. Do not store with other types of candy as the toffee will absorb their moisture.

Yield: approximately 1 pound

CHOCOLATE KRISPIES

1 stick butter	1½ cups pecans, chopped
2 cups peanut butter	1 8-ounce Hershey bar
1 16-ounce box confectioners sugar	1 6-ounce package chocolate chips
3½ cups Rice Krispies cereal	½ bar paraffin

Melt butter in a saucepan. Add peanut butter, sugar, cereal, and pecans. Mix together and roll into balls.

Melt chocolate bar and chocolate chips in top of a double boiler with paraffin. Dip balls in chocolate. Set on waxed paper to cool. These may be frozen.

Yield: 4 dozen

Index ❤ ❤ ❤ ❤ ❤ ❤ ❤ ❤ ❤ ❤

317

COOKBOOK

Please send me _____ copies @ $14.95 each $_____

+ Postage and handling @ $2.50 each $_____

Texas residents add sales tax @ $1.20 each $_____

TOTAL PAYMENT ENCLOSED $_____

NAME _____

ADDRESS _____

CITY _____ STATE _____ ZIP _____

Please make checks payable to JLW Cookbook.

VISA ☐ MASTERCARD ☐ # _____ EXPIRATION _____

SIGNATURE _____

Moneys from the sale of this cookbook help fund programs for children, including drug awareness and abuse prevention.

JUNIOR LEAGUE OF WACO, INC.   Phone: 817-776-COOK
6801 Sanger, Suite 160B   24-Hour Answering
Waco, Texas 76710   Machine Available

COOKBOOK

Please send me _____ copies @ $14.95 each $_____

+ Postage and handling @ $2.50 each $_____

Texas residents add sales tax @ $1.20 each $_____

TOTAL PAYMENT ENCLOSED $_____

NAME _____

ADDRESS _____

CITY _____ STATE _____ ZIP _____

Please make checks payable to JLW Cookbook.

VISA ☐ MASTERCARD ☐ # _____ EXPIRATION _____

SIGNATURE _____

Moneys from the sale of this cookbook help fund programs for children, including drug awareness and abuse prevention.

JUNIOR LEAGUE OF WACO, INC.   Phone: 817-776-COOK
6801 Sanger, Suite 160B   24-Hour Answering
Waco, Texas 76710   Machine Available